Image Studies

Image Studies offers an engaging introduction to visual and image studies. In order to better understand images and visual culture the book bridges between theory and practice; asking the reader to think critically about images and image practices, but also *simultaneously* to engage with image-making processes. Looking across a range of domains and disciplines, we find the image is never a single, static thing. Rather, the image can be a concept, an object, a picture or medium – and all these things combined. At the heart of the book is the idea of an *ecology of images*, through which we can examine the full 'life' of an image – to understand how an image resonates within a complex set of contexts, processes and uses.

- Part 1 covers theoretical perspectives on the image, supplemented with practical entries on making, researching and writing with images.
- Part 2 explores specific image practices and domains, with chapters on drawing and painting, photography, visual culture, scientific imaging; and informational images.

A wide range of illustrations complement the text throughout and each chapter includes creative tasks, keywords (linked to an online resource), summaries and suggested further reading. In addition, each of the main chapters includes selected readings by notable authors across a range of subject areas, including: Art History, Business, Cognitive Science, Communication Studies, Infographics, Neuroscience, Photography, Physics, Science Studies, Social Semiotics, Statistics and Visual Culture. Companion website: www.imagestudies.net

Sunil Manghani is Reader in Critical and Cultural Theory at Winchester School of Art, University of Southampton, UK. He is author of *Image Critique* (2008) and co-editor of *Images: A Reader* (2006), an anthology of writings on the image from Plato to the present.

Image Studies

Theory and Practice

Sunil Manghani

LONDON AND NEW YORK

First published 2013
by Routledge
2 Park Square, Milton Park, Abingdon, Oxon OX14 4RN

Simultaneously published in the USA and Canada
by Routledge
711 Third Avenue, New York, NY 10017

Routledge is an imprint of the Taylor & Francis Group, an informa business

British Library Cataloguing in Publication Data
A catalogue record for this book is available from the British Library

Library of Congress Cataloging in Publication Data
Manghani, Sunil.
    Image studies: Theory and Practice/Sunil Manghani. — 1 [edition].
        pages cm
    Includes bibliographical references and index.
    1. Visual communication. 2. Visual sociology. 3. Popular culture.
    4. Image (Philosophy) I. Title.
    P93.5.M36 2012
    302.2'2–dc23   2012021773

ISBN: 978-0-415-57339-9 (hbk)
ISBN: 978-0-415-57340-5 (pbk)
ISBN: 978-0-203-13491-7 (ebk)

Typeset in FS Albert and Perpetua
by Keystroke, Station Road, Codsall, Wolverhampton
Printed in Great Britain by Ashford Colour Press Ltd

Contents

List of illustrations

The following were reproduced with kind permission. While every effort has been made to trace copyright holders and obtain permission, this has not been possible in all cases. Any omissions brought to our attention will be remedied in future editions.

Supplement I: Just what is it that makes images so different?

2   Understanding images

Supplement II: Image research

3   Image and text

Supplement III: Writing with images

4 Drawing and painting

5 Photography

8 Image and information

9 Afterword: Image studies in the making . . .

Acknowledgements

Readings

2 Understanding images

'On the Family of Images' from Mitchell, W.J.T. (1987) *Iconology: Image, Text, Ideology*. Chicago: Chicago University Press, pp.12–17.

3 Image and text

'Image as Likeness' from Mitchell, W.J.T. (1987) *Iconology: Image, Text, Ideology*. Chicago: Chicago University Press, pp.31–36.

4 Drawing and painting

'Taking a Line for a Walk' from Klee, Paul (1953 [1925]) *Pedagogical Sketchbook*, trans. by Sibyl Moholy-Nagy. London: Faber and Faber, pp.16–19.

5 Photography

'Photography and Arithmetic' © Sean Cubitt, 2012.

6 Visual culture

'Showing Seeing' from Mitchell, W.J.T. (2005) *What Do Pictures Want? The Lives and Loves of Images.* Chicago: University of Chicago Press, pp.336–356.

7 Scientific imaging

'How to Look at the Inside of Your Eye' from Elkins, James (2000) *How to Use Your Eyes.* New York: Routledge, pp.232–237.
'Magnetic Resonance Imaging' © Alain Pitiot, 2012.
'Ripples in an Electron Pond' © Philip Moriarty, 2012.

8 Image and information

'Images of Climate Change' © Darryn Anne DiFrancesco, 2012.
'Image Management' © Mimei Ito, 2012.
'Sketchnotes' © Craighton Berman, 2012.

Notes on contributors

Previously unpublished texts have been generously supplied by the following contributors:

Sean Cubitt, Professor of Film and Television at Goldsmiths, University of London; Professorial Fellow of the University of Melbourne and Honorary Professor of the University of Dundee.

Darryn Anne DiFrancesco, Research Assistant and PhD student in sociology at The University of British Columbia, Vancouver, Canada.

Mimei Ito, Independent scholar, living and working in Tokyo, Japan.

Philip Moriarty, Professor of Physics at University of Nottingham, UK.

Alain Pitiot, Lecturer in the School of Psychology at the University of Nottingham, UK.

How to use this book

This book provides an introduction to visual and image studies, with the aim to both understand and engage with images and image culture in a critical and yet also active and creative manner. The opening three chapters, which comprise Part 1 of the book, offer theoretical perspectives on the image, and are supplemented with practical entries on making, researching and writing with images. Part 2 provides accounts of specific image practices and cultures, with chapters covering drawing and painting; photography; visual culture; scientific imaging; and informational images.

The book very purposely does not set out to provide a single system or model of image analysis. Instead, by thinking about the image in terms of its broader 'ecology' (see Chapter 2), the book engages the reader in a rich and varied investigation of the subject. Each chapter includes key features:

- Selected readings – either extracts from key texts in the field, or entries written specially for the book by a range of authors.
- A wide range of illustrations.
- Keywords referring to the entries of an online glossary or 'intertext', which provide definitions, commentaries, illustrative materials and hyperlinks.
- Creative tasks with accompanying questions and commentary.
- Chapter summaries and suggested further reading.

FIGURE 0.1

Notebooks ©
Simonetta Capecchi.

Creative tasks

The book includes a series of tasks, which prompt the reader to engage with images in a more creative and practical fashion, each with a view to test, challenge, extend and/or embed the ideas covered in the relevant chapter. In order to get most out of the tasks, the reader is encouraged to collect responses together in a notebook or sketchbook. The point of each task is not to produce a final piece of work, but rather to experience and record a process of engagement, with the aim to foster an ongoing curiosity about images and image practices. Questions and commentaries accompanying the tasks help the reader to reflect on their engagement with images.

List of tasks

Companion website

Image Studies companion website: www.imagestudies.net

Throughout this book keywords (highlighted in bold orange text, e.g. **image studies**) indicate to the reader entries available via an online glossary or 'Intertext'. To access these materials visit the above web address and follow the link for Intertext. Entries provide dictionary-style definitions for a variety of terms, as well as more extended commentaries, illustrative materials and hyperlinks.

The companion website aims to be more than simply a static online resource and instead provides various resources benefiting from a range of media. In addition to the Intertext, elements include: (1) Study materials, lecture slides and suggested further reading; (2) Introductions, links and reviews of further key reading in the field; (3) Practical tasks, tutorials and examples of project work; and (4) Blog entries and the use of social media to encourage contributions, ideas and feedback from a wide community of students and scholars of image studies.

Readings

Selected readings are embedded in the chapters. These entries take the form either of extracts from key texts in the field, or entries written specially for the book by authors from a diverse set of subject areas. The readings offer authoritative accounts of key theoretical ideas and allow for a range of different perspectives. An important principle of this book is that there should be a plurality of voices if image studies is to genuinely look across image domains. Inevitably, the readings offered here do not go far enough, but at least signal the beginnings of a broader process. Below is a list of the title/author of each selected reading, and in parenthesis their associated subject disciplines (though in most cases the texts are by default cross-disciplinary).

List of readings

Further study

References to various sources are provided throughout this book, with a full bibliography given at the end. In addition, a short list of suggested 'Further Reading' is given at the close of each chapter. Readers are encouraged to consult these materials as a way to extend and deepen understanding of the key ideas and debates. One particular book worth noting is *Images: A Reader* (Manghani *et al.*, 2006). This edited volume makes for a useful companion to this book, with its selection of over 80 key entries taken from writings ranging across the domains of philosophy, art, literature, science, critical theory and cultural studies. Many of the original sources are cited in this book. Where these entries appear in the bibliography at the end of this book they have been highlighted in bold and include details of the relevant extract as it appears in *Images: A Reader*.

Introduction

We are surrounded by images. In our day-to-day living we come into contact with all manner of images from advertising, newspapers, the Internet, television, films and computer games. We leaf through junk mail, display birthday cards, ponder graphs and charts, deliberate over what to wear, and manipulate digital photographs. The public domain is framed by architectural design, interior décor, landscaping, sculptures, shop fronts, traffic signals, and a plethora of video screens and cameras. Whether in print or online, we pore over or just look fleetingly at all number of images in instructional booklets, entertainments, educational materials, brochures, magazines and catalogues. In addition, of course, there is a rich and long history of visual arts. But equally, we can think about images in less tangible ways. Our dreams are made up of pictures, corporations trade on the strength of elusive brand associations, we can be moved by literary images, political parties are said to win or lose elections on their ability to present a 'vision' of society, and science shows us colourful, in-depth exploration of realms well beyond that which we can see with the human eye. Images are everywhere and nowhere all at once.

Yet, for all the profusion of images, or maybe precisely because of their variety and ubiquity, we remain unable to say definitively what images are and what significance they hold. This book, in a similar vein to the edited volume, *Images: A Reader* (Manghani *et al.*, 2006), is a response to W. J. T. Mitchell's (1987, p. 155) remark that 'there is, at present, no real "field" in the humanities . . . no "iconology" that studies the problems of perceptual, conceptual, verbal and graphic images in a unified way'. *Images: A Reader* collects together a range of key, and diverse, critical writings on the image from Plato through to the present. In response, this book, *Image Studies*, provides chapter-length narratives to help navigate and synthesize these readings (and others besides). Throughout, the book offers a consideration of a variety of image forms and practices, it also prompts the reader to review key texts and engage in task-based activities. The aim is to present contemporary **Image Studies** as a clearly defined and practical subject area.

At the heart of the book are two deceptively simple questions: (1) What is an image? and (2) How do images differ to words? Alongside which, we can ask: What is it that images *do* and/or what is it we *do* with images? In line with Mitchell's three excellent books, *Iconology* (1987), *Picture Theory* (1994) and *What Do Pictures Want?* (2005) – elements of which will be discussed in more detail in Chapters 2 and 3 – we need to go beyond a **hermeneutics** of the image, to ask not simply what is *in* an image, but also more practically what we use images for, how we make or manipulate them and how their use informs our understanding of them and more generally of the world around us.

Of course, this book is full of words about images, which may seem a contradiction. But, words have long been a part of our understanding (and use) of images. At a basic level, graphic images are frequently captioned, whether in galleries, in books and in newspapers and magazines. This is referred to as anchorage, whereby a linguistic message is applied to the image, which is otherwise considered polysemous in its meaning. However, as will be considered in Chapter 3 on image and text, there is a deeper level to which words come to be considered a dominant force in our ways of making and transmitting meaning. Our endeavours to study all manner of subjects remain structured and disseminated by words. It is no surprise subject areas have their own *text*books from which we begin the learning process. This book is no different. It primarily uses words to establish a set of precepts and interests for image studies. Nevertheless, a challenge can be brought to the established dominance of the word. The point of which is not to attempt to overthrow the word, but nonetheless to examine how we come to understand things differently from our engagement with words and/or images. This can be understood as a matter of **epistemology**, to consider how differences arise through different ways of understanding and creating knowledge, whether through the use of words or images, or indeed their combination.

Images, then, present a fascinating and challenging field of interest. There can be no one single defining system of analysis. Instead an **interdisciplinary** approach is required, which will not always meet with satisfying conclusions, but rather will likely prompt further questions and doubts. It is not enough to simply consider in abstract terms what an image is, or what images do, how they are formed and what we use them for. There is a need to understand the various meanings of the term 'image' as used in different contexts, and to consider how these contexts differ or interrelate and what the significance is of their relationships. So, for example, how is it (and what does it signify) that we can move from considering a picture in a gallery in aesthetic, technical terms to then ponder a visual metaphor in a political speech? How do we understand (and experience) the difference between the pictures we dream and the magnetic resonance imaging scans readily available of the brain? Answering these kinds of questions requires an informed and critical approach to image culture, which includes an awareness of a wide range of images types, uses and contexts.

When we say the word 'image' we tend not to be explicit about what we mean by the term. We do not usually make a point of differentiating between different image types and experiences. It is similar, for example, to how the word 'media' is commonly used. Critics can be heard to say such things as 'the media were hostile to the government's proposals', or 'the media is heavily controlled by the state'. It is generally understood what we mean by such statements, but 'media' is a plural noun. There are all types of media, or mediums. When people speak about '*the* media' they are conflating all sorts of mass media forms, such as print, broadcast television, radio, cinema and the Internet. Yet, within each of these types, there are a wide range of different forms and ideologies at stake. At a basic level, it would seem useful to begin to make more analytical sense of the *variety* of image types and processes.

Equally, however, we might accept the fact when we use the word 'image' we may not always know what we mean, or, rather, we may be saying more or less than we first thought. The philosopher Ludwig Wittgenstein, one of the twentieth century's most influential thinkers (not least for his '**picture theory**' of language), considered it futile to definitively pin-down the term 'image'. A word in itself does not show us the essence of a thing, but rather 'the meaning of a word is its use in language' (Wittgenstein, 1958, §43). We generally know what words such as 'image' and 'media' mean when they crop up in everyday use without necessarily needing to explain their meaning in precise terms. There is no single definition or 'essential nature' of images, though different meanings and usage can overlap. For Wittgenstein, we make sense of a term such as 'image' by perceiving a complex network of relations between the different meanings. This book sets out to examine some of those networks, and more generally to aid a sense of critical awareness of the different occurrences and currencies of the image. Taking Wittgenstein's point of view, we cannot expect absolute clarity in terms of a philosophical concept of the image, nor consider a designated set of tools that can guide our research in advance, though we can take many cues from everyday language and by looking more clearly at what we think images are and what they do. Chapters 1–3 explore in more depth different ways of understanding the image, but suffice to say even from our everyday use of the word there is clearly *something* we designate as 'image', which differs from verbal language and which suggests a particular set of understandings, skills, experiences and significance.

An image-maker's approach

John Berger's *Ways of Seeing* (1972) begins with the enigmatic lines: 'Seeing comes before words. The child looks and recognises before it can speak.' The book was originally published in 1972 and was based on the highly acclaimed BBC television series of the same name. It is regarded as a seminal work, which prompted much interest amongst scholars and to this day remains a valuable and highly accessible introduction for students. One of the delights, both in print and on screen, is the immediacy of its argumentation, created through a lively use of both words and images. The television series begins with Berger situated in what looks like a traditional art gallery. He stands before a gilt-framed oil painting and, before uttering a word, proceeds to apply a penknife to the canvas to remove a fragment of the picture. He literally cuts out a piece of the picture to show us something about its nature and significance. Or, more specifically, about the significance of it as a reproduction. As we see and hear the knife rip through the canvas, Berger narrates as follows:

> '. . . I want to question some of the assumptions usually made about the tradition of European painting, that tradition that was born about 1400 and died about 1900. [. . . I]t isn't so much the paintings themselves that I want to consider, as the way we now see them: Now, in the second half of the twentieth century, because we see these paintings as nobody saw them before. If we discover why this is so, we shall also discover something about our selves and the situation in which we are living.'
>
> (John Berger, *Ways of Seeing*, Programme 1: Reproduction)

It was his hands-on, direct questioning of the image that set the tone and manner of a new critical approach. In *Ways of Seeing*, Berger utilizes various juxtapositions and manipulations of the image as a way to literally *show* and experiment with ideas about the visual world and our faculty of vision.

FIGURE 0.2 Classroom viewing of *Ways of Seeing* (BBC, 1972).

An image, according to Berger, 'is a sight which has been recreated or reproduced. It is an appearance, or a set of appearances, which has been detached from the place and time in which it first made its appearance and preserved – for a few moments or a few centuries' (1972, pp.9–10). It is a definition influenced by debates of photography and the means of image reproduction (see Chapters 5 and 6). A crucial theoretical influence, explicitly acknowledged by Berger, is the work of the German critic Walter Benjamin. In particular, it is his seminal essay written in 1936, **'The Work of Art in the Age of Mechanical Reproduction'** (Benjamin, 1992, pp.211–244), which prompts much of Berger's thinking and approach. Most importantly in the 'Artwork' essay, Benjamin highlights how the then new mass means of reproduction (i.e. advances in printing techniques and early developments in broadcast media) were leading to the destruction of what he termed the 'aura' of the artwork. Modern means of reproduction were undoing the authority of the 'original' artwork. It became possible, for example, to see Leonardo Da Vinci's 'Mona Lisa' (c.1503–1506) without even going to the gallery (see Chapter 6). In fact, all manner of things were becoming readily available as images, whether in magazines, on billboards, or in the cinema, which in turn fed a more widespread visual culture and collective memory. It is the legacy of this burgeoning visual culture that Berger considers we have all now inherited: 'For the first time ever, images of art have become ephemeral, ubiquitous, insubstantial, available, valueless, free. They surround us in the same way as a language surrounds us. They have entered the mainstream of life over which they no longer, in themselves, have power' (1972, p.32). There is something very exciting and potentially radical about this new 'language'. Yet, equally, it is suggestive of new dilemmas and dangers, not least (as were the concerns of Benjamin writing in the time of Nazism) the rise in the 'dark arts' of political propaganda and the new persuasive powers of advertisers and commercial corporations.

At the time of writing, in the 1970s, Berger's contention was that 'very few people are aware of what has happened because the means of reproduction are used nearly all the time to promote the illusion that nothing has changed except that the masses, thanks to reproductions, can now begin to appreciate art as the cultured minority once did' (1972, pp.32–33). Today, of course, we are embedded in a digital culture that has opened up access to powerful tools of reproduction (breaking down in places the barriers between professional and amateur producers). We might want to argue that Berger's concerns are no longer, or at least much less, relevant. Berger wrote at the time, '[i]f the new language of images were used differently', by which he means if the new means of reproduction were used for new, progressive purposes, 'it would, through its use, confer a new kind of power. Within it we could begin to define our experiences more precisely in areas where words are inadequate' (p.33). There are two key ideas at stake. Firstly the new language of images could arguably enable new, richer forms of expression, and secondly, that there lay in this new 'language of images' the potential for a democratization of meaning-making. In relation to which, a crucial element would be for images to show something about the context of their own making. In other words, suggestive of a new kind of **'visual literacy'**, we might arrive at a more reflexive understanding about the make-up of our social and cultural experiences.

In thinking about Berger's work today, the question remains open as to whether or not contemporary, digital culture does indeed fulfil such hopes or whether it only continues to replicate traditional power relations. There is no single answer, with positive and negative examples readily at hand. If we take just one example, the rise in digital photography, we can argue cases for and against. On the one hand, access to cameras has become ever more affordable (indeed they are all but ubiquitous with the inclusion on even the most basic of mobile phone handsets). This has led not only to a sharp rise in the number of photographs being taken but also, due to the synergy with online social networking, an explosion in the sharing of photographic images. We can now keep in touch with loved ones through the richness of pictures, share ideas about the world around us with great speed and across great distances. It has also given rise to the phenomenon of 'citizen journalism', which has enabled the traditional power-structures of the press to be circumvented, prompting in some cases swifter on-the-spot reporting and even reporting within zones that are otherwise officially regulated or censored. On the other hand, however, the over abundance of photographs and of course the ease with which images can now be digitally enhanced and manipulated has arguably lessened their impact. We can become blasé about photojournalistic images of death and suffering, and photographs of family and friends once neatly collected together as an album are now too voluminous and mundane. Often, it seems we are more intent on 'capturing' a picture of something or an event (typically with a mobile phone to relay to someone else far away) rather than spending the time looking and engaging with the thing or moment in and of itself (see Chapter 5).

As we'll go on to see, the implication here of images being 'things' in the world needs further consideration, and relates to a need to consider a broad range of image types (to include, for example, literary imagery and dreaming, etc). Nonetheless, Berger's work remains an important touchstone. He reminds us of the need to take images seriously, and particularly the potential we have to *use* images and their effects for critical and creative purposes. There are genuine and far-reaching political, social and cultural ramifications stemming not only from the use of images, but from our understanding of their use. For Jon Simons (2008, p.78), working specifically with political images, it is not simply that image studies need involve the reflexive consideration of the image, but that 'astute, fascinated scholars of the visual aspects of the world' need as much, if not more, to be 'astute citizens in that world'. In recounting a simple classroom exercise in which students are required to 'sell' a political message (using nothing more than an overhead transparency, the whiteboard, or brief oral presentation), he remarks upon the 'inventiveness of the students, who in minutes came up with some startling ideas'. This prompts him to ask more broadly:

> 'What could they achieve given more time and resources? What would they learn about political imagery if the rest of the module taught them some graphic design, including computer graphics; some copywriting; something about marketing; and some psychology? In other words, how much could students

learn about being engaged and critical citizens if they learned the skills needed to produce as well as "read" political imagery? [. . .] When we become literate in a language, we learn to write as well as read. Competence in political imagery would thus demand the ability to make as well as interpret political images, just as science students learn to make as well as interpret images that represent data.'

(Simons, 2008, p.86)

Simons' observations lead us to consider how we might break out of a dichotomy that persists between *thinking about* images on one side and their *making* on the other. The art historian and theorist, James Elkins, makes the argument that visual studies, as it currently stands, has proved to be too easy. He urges it to become 'more ambitious about its purview, more demanding in its analyses, and above all more difficult' (2003, p.vii). Importantly, he stresses the need to bridge between theory and practice:

'The making of images, whether it is copying paintings or simply learning the basics of digital video editing, needs to be practiced in the same seminar rooms where historical and interpretive work takes place. Only then will it become apparent just how difficult it is to knit the two kinds of experience together and how tremendously important it is to try; otherwise, entire image-making practices will remain partly or wholly inaccessible to historical understanding. And what is worse, visual theory will be able to consolidate the notion that study is sufficient to the understanding of images, and independent of actual making.'

(Elkins, 2003, pp.158–159)

Elkins draws upon a wealth of experience in teaching drawing and painting to graduate students who 'had not picked up a charcoal since elementary school'. An underlying interest is to 'critique certain assumptions that are made about differences between art history and studio practice'. What is revealing, he suggests, is 'a surprising new kind of visual competence', and the crucial fact that 'some of the insights that emerged are not replicable in classrooms where images are not produced' (2003, p.158).

It is crucial we maintain a critical, questioning approach to the image. We might even consider an image-based critique, or more simply an 'image critique' (see Manghani, 2008). The political theorist Susan Buck-Morss writes: 'We need to be able to read images emblematically and symptomatically, in terms of the most fundamental questions of social life. This means that critical theories are needed, theories that are themselves visual, that show rather than argue' (Buck-Morss, 1996, p.31). The journalist and professor of philosophy, Régis Debray, suggests 'if you want to make yourself known everywhere and establish dominion over the world, manufacture images instead of writing books. Of course postcards are not forbidden either; nor making films "based on the novel". But if everyone knows the name of the actor and directors, who cares about the screenwriters?' (Debray, 1996, p.155).

Sarcasm aside, there is a grain of truth in this observation, and as with Benjamin's account of the artwork in the age of mechanical reproduction, there are both dangers and opportunities at stake in a new 'language' of images. Berger urged, back in the 1970s, '[w]hat matters now is who uses that language for what purpose' (1972, p. 33). The same point remains true today.

This book, *Images Studies*, is inspired by the critical and creative work that John Berger and others have engaged in since the latter half of the last century. It is also prompted by what has been a recent energetic period of writing and thinking about images and visual culture. However, Elkins' remark on the relationship (and all too often separation) between theory and practice remains a live issue. Rather than enumerate yet another set of political critiques of the image and visual culture, the intention of this book – and more generally in marking out the field of 'image studies' – is to slow down our engagement with the image. Social, political critique is important, and numerous points of interest are raised in all the chapters here (particularly Chapters 3, 5, 6, 7 and 8). However it is vital we do not rush to overlay a critical analysis that has not first engaged with an exploration of images at a more fundamental level. In Chapter 7, for example, a problem is noted about how the sciences and the arts often possess an inadequate understanding of one another, which then undermines how we can come to understand images and practices within these domains. Unlike literary criticism, which can assume basic competence in reading and writing the text, image studies requires we re-equip ourselves in approaches to viewing and making the image. This book offers *ways of thinking about* and *ways of engaging with* images in a critical, reflexive fashion; to include not just the analysis and manipulation of images, but also their making too. Or at least (given this is only a book, as Debray would have us remember) to set in motion a train of thinking about what happens when we make, manipulate and respond to images in all their variety and complexity. In the end, the book can only hope to offer the beginnings of questions and observations about the image. If, however, it then prompts the reader to explore subject areas in more depth and experiment with images themselves, it will have done what it sets out to do.

Further reading

Berger, John (1972) *Ways of Seeing*. London: Penguin Books.

Debray, Régis (1996) *Media Manifestos: On the Technological Transmission of Cultural Forms*, trans. by Eric Rauth. London: Verso.

Elkins, James (2003) *Visual Studies: A Skeptical Introduction*. New York: Routledge.

Elkins, James (ed.) (2009) *Visual Literacy*. New York: Routledge.

Manghani, Sunil, Piper, Arthur and Simons, Jon (eds) (2006) *Images: A Reader*. London: Sage.

Mitchell, W.J.T. (1987) *Iconology: Image, Text, Ideology*. Chicago: University of Chicago Press.

Mitchell, W.J.T. (1994) *Picture Theory: Essays on Verbal and Visual Representation*. Chicago: University of Chicago Press.

Mitchell, W.J.T. (2005) *What Do Pictures Want? The Lives and Loves of Images*. Chicago: University of Chicago Press.

Stafford, Barbara Maria (1996) *Good Looking: Essays on the Virtue of Images*. Cambridge, Mass.: MIT Press.

Sturken, Marita and Cartwright, Lisa (2009) *Practices of Looking: An Introduction to Visual Culture*. Second Edition. Oxford: Oxford University Press.

Taylor, Mark C. and Saarinen, Esa (1994) *Imagologies: Media Philosophy*. London: Routledge.

PART 1
Defining images

The opening three chapters of this book examine a range of theoretical, philosophical and historical accounts of the image and image debates. A key approach to image analysis is provided through the consideration of an 'ecology of images' (in Chapter 2). A series of three 'supplements' also prompt creative and practical engagement with making, researching and writing with images.

1 Beyond semiotics

One of the most prevalent analytical approaches to the image has been the so-called 'science of signs', semiotics (also referred to as semiology). If this book can hope to provide anything new by way of approaches to the image, it is doubtless necessary to acknowledge the importance of semiotics, yet importantly to go beyond it, for reasons that will be explained.

In providing a method in the study of a wide array of cultural phenomena, including images, semiotics has been perhaps the most thoroughly discussed and theorized of approaches, so further cementing its perceived significance. It came to prominence – notably with the work of Roland Barthes, Umberto Eco, and a dedicated journal *Communications* – in the 1950s and 1960s, with its heyday in the 1970s and 1980s. It represented a whole new subject or area of interest, which – combining the concerns of anthropology, sociology, art history, literature, linguistics, philosophy, politics, history and psychology – quickly embedded itself as a scholarly pursuit and a force behind the establishment of new subject areas such as communications, media and cultural studies. Yet, by the turn of the millennium, semiotics had come under a sustained period of criticism and not least as a tool in the analysis of the image. It has long been criticized – though not always fairly – for being a-historical and overly formalist in purview (in that it provides a means to analyze everything and anything as a hermetic 'text'). More specifically, in relation to the image and visual culture, semiotics is criticized for being a linguistic-based theory. It is argued, then, the word (or verbal reasoning) comes to dominant the image; to colonize whatever is otherwise significant about that which is not articulated in linguistic terms. In other words, by explaining the image semiotically (which often involves complex language and neologisms), one effectively looks away from all that is specific to the *experience* of looking at an image.

Semiotics: a brief history

Semiotics offers a critical method of cultural and literary analysis, and has been applied to countless 'objects' of interest, from popular and classic literature to theatre, painting, television, film, advertising and fashion. Its initial development is attributed to the work of a Swiss linguist Ferdinand de Saussure (1857–1913). He is considered the founder of modern linguistics following his systematic view of how language works using a dualistic concept of the 'sign', which in turn gave rise to the prospect of a whole new 'science' or discipline to come: 'It is . . . possible to conceive of a science *which studies the role of signs as part of social life*. [. . .] We shall call it *semiology* (from the Greek *semeîon*, "sign"). It would investigate the nature of signs and the laws governing them' (Saussure 1983, pp.15–16).

NATURE OF THE LINGUISTIC SIGN

FERDINAND DE SAUSSURE

Ferdinand de Saussure's structuralist, dyadic model of semiotics focuses on the linguistic sign, which he argues does not correspond to its object or referent. Rather, there is an arbitrary relation between the signifier (meaning a sign that is the acoustic image of a sound) and the signified (meaning the concept corresponding to the signifier). The meaning of language comes from the differential relations between signs, or the place of a sign in a whole structure of interrelated signifying units.

Some people regard language, when reduced to its elements, as a naming-process only – a list of words, each corresponding to the thing that it names. [. . .] This conception is open to criticism at several points. It assumes that ready-made ideas exist before words [. . . and] it lets us assume that the linking of a name and a thing is a very simple operation. [. . .] The linguistic sign unites, not a thing and a name, but a concept and a sound-image. [. . .] The sound-image is sensory, and if I happen to call it 'material', it is only in that sense, and by way of opposing it to the other term of the association, the concept, which is generally more abstract. [. . .] I call the combination of a concept and a sound-image a *sign,* but in current usage the term generally designates only a sound-image. . . Ambiguity would disappear if the three notions involved here were designated by three names, each suggesting and opposing the others. I propose to retain the word *sign* to designate the whole and to replace *concept* and *sound-image* respectively by *signified* and *signifier*. [. . .] The bond between the signifier and the signified is arbitrary. Since I mean by sign the whole that results from the associating of the signifier with the signified, I can simply say: *the linguistic sign is arbitrary.* [. . . In] language there are only differences. Even more important: a difference generally implies positive terms between which the difference is set up; but in language there are only differences *without positive terms.* Whether we take the signified or the signifier, language has neither ideas nor sounds that existed before the linguistic system, but only conceptual and phonic differences that have issued from the system. The idea [signified] or phonic substance [signifier] that a sign contains is of less importance than the other signs that surround it. [. . .] But the statement that everything in language is negative is true only if the signified and signifier are considered separately; when we consider the sign in its totality, we have something that is positive in it own class. A linguistic system is a series of differences of sound combined with a series of differences of ideas; but the pairing of a certain number of acoustical signs with as many cuts made from the mass of thought engenders a system of values. . . (Saussure, 1983, pp.65–68, 120)

Another important founding figure in the development of semiotics is the American philosopher Charles Sanders Peirce (1839–1914), known for his complex (and at times quite opaque) contributions to debates on logic and pragmatism. Writing concurrently, but quite separately to Saussure, Peirce's semiotics expressly engages with visual as well as linguistic signs. His work has grown in importance with recent debates about the prospect of a visual semiotics, particularly as Peirce's formulation foregrounds a sense of process and the 'event' of signification as it relates to individual observers or readers. In both cases, what makes semiotics so powerful a tool of analysis is its definition of a constituent element: the **sign**. The art theorists Mieke Bal and Norman Bryson (1991, p.174) note: 'human culture is made up of signs, each of which stands for something other than itself, and the people inhabiting culture busy themselves making sense of signs'. From this perspective, one of the real strengths of semiotics (despite having been initially proposed within the terms of linguistics) has been its general applicability, particularly its usefulness in the analysis of popular culture, the media and visual culture; i.e. areas of cultural life that developed substantially in scope and importance at the time semiotics properly came to prominence, during the 1950s and 1960s.

There are debates over the relative merits of Sassurean and Peircean semiotics. Bal and Bryson, for example, along with fellow art historian, Margaret Iversen (1986), tend to favour the work of the latter, arguing that 'Peirce's richer typology of signs enables us to consider how different modes of signification work, while Saussure's model can only tell us how systems of arbitrary signs operate' (Iversen, 1986, p.85). Sturken and Cartwright (2009), in their book *Practices of Looking*, choose to concentrate on Saussure's model precisely because of its 'system of arbitrary signs', which they argue 'offers a clear and direct way to understand the relationship between visual representation and meaning' (Sturken and Cartwright, 2009, p.29).

SIGN, ICON AND INDEX
CHARLES SANDERS PEIRCE

Charles Peirce's semiotics, which expressly engages with visual as well as linguistic signs, involves a triadic model along with a series of layered taxonomies. Similar to Saussure's signifier and signified respectively, Peirce describes the interaction between a representamen (the form the sign takes) and an interpretant (the sense made of the sign), but also includes an object (to which the sign refers). Peirce argues all experience is mediated by signs. Overall, his notion of 'semiosis' – in contrast to Saussure's synchronic emphasis upon structure – describes a semiotic process. His much adopted classification of iconic, indexical and symbolic signs depends primarily upon the use of the sign, thereby emphasising the role of the 'reader' in semiotic analysis.

A sign, or *representamen,* is something which stands to somebody for something in some respect or capacity. It addresses somebody, that is, creates in the mind of that person an equivalent sign, or perhaps a more developed sign. That sign which it creates I call the *interpretant* of the first sign. The sign stands for something, its *object.* It stands for that object, not in all respects, but in reference to a sort of idea, which I have sometimes called the *ground* of the representamen. 'Idea' is here to be understood in a sort of Platonic sense, very familiar in everyday talk; I mean in that sense in which we say that one man catches another man's idea, in which we say that when a man recalls what he was thinking of at some previous time, he recalls the same idea, and in which when a man continues to think anything, say for a tenth of a second, in so far as the thought continues to agree with itself during that time, that is to have a *like* content, it is the same idea, and is not at each instant of the interval a new idea.

A sign is either an *icon,* an *index,* or a *symbol.* An *icon* is a sign which would possess the character which renders it significant, even though its object had no existence; such as a lead-pencil streak as representing a geometrical line. An *index* is a sign which would, at once, lose the character which makes it a sign if its object were removed, but would not lose that character if there were no interpretant. Such, for instance, is a piece of mould with a bullet-hole in it as sign of a shot; for without the shot there would have been no hole; but there is a hole there, whether anybody has the sense to attribute it to a shot or not. A symbol is a sign which would lose the character which renders it a sign if there were no interpretant. Such is any utterance of speech which signifies what it does only by virtue of its being understood to have that signification. (Peirce, 1932, pp.135, 143–144, 169–173)

Saussure presented a 'structuralist' account of language. The sign as a unit of meaning only makes sense in relation to a wider system or structure of meanings. A sign does not have any intrinsic, essential meaning; instead there is an arbitrary relation between the sign and the thing it represents. The fact that there are many languages in the world, each of which can have its own word for everything in the world, is one way of highlighting the arbitrary nature of the sign, in this case of words themselves:

> 'Language, according to Saussure, is like a game of chess. It depends on con-
> ventions and codes for its meanings. [. . . T]he relationship between a word
> . . . and things in the world is arbitrary and relative, not fixed. For example,
> the words *dog* in English, *chien* in French, and *hund* in German all refer to the
> same kind of animal; hence the relationship between the words and the animal
> itself is dictated by the conventions of language rather than some natural
> connection. It was central to Saussure's theory that meanings change according
> to context and to the rules of language.'
>
> (Sturken and Cartwright, 2009, p. 28)

The impact of Saussure's work goes very deep, influencing a whole intellectual movement referred to as structuralism, giving rise not only to semiotics, but also to semioticians, as those who practiced this 'art' of analysis and who, in turn, influenced a whole generation of post-war scholars, critics, writers and creative practitioners when thinking about the way we distinguish and manipulate the meaning of signs in the world. The French cultural critic, Roland Barthes, writing in the 1950s through to the late 1970s, is the best known of these semioticians. As we will see below, he not only helped give political depth to Saussure's speculative theory of semiotics, but also led the way in applying semiotics to all manner of cultural phenomena (including much visual phenomena) and in so doing can be credited, more than any other semiotician, with having given semiotics a wide and popular appeal.

It is important to state again, however, this book does *not* set out to provide a semiotics, nor even a 'new' semiotics, of the image. If anything it determinedly seeks not to do so. Nonetheless the spectre of semiotics remains (e.g. the idea of sub-semiotic marks is considered in Chapter 4, and the pertinence of Peirce's 'index' to photography is noted in Chapter 5). Saussurian semiotics (and structuralism more generally) relates directly to what the philosopher Richard Rorty (1979, p. 263) terms 'the linguistic turn', whereby – in the course of the twentieth century – all of social and cultural life came to be critically examined in terms of 'texts' and 'textuality'. Following which, in light of debates about contemporary image culture and theory (as will be discussed in Chapter 3), W. J. T. Mitchell (1994, p. 16) suggests there has been now a 'pictorial turn', marked by a 'postlinguistic, postsemiotic rediscovery of the picture'. It is a line of argument this book seeks to explore. Yet, what is meant by 'postsemiotic' remains an open question. Does it refer to a wholly new understanding *after* semiotics, so marking its severance? Or, might this suggest further development on from semiotics, perhaps even a *visual* semiotics of some kind (see Chapter 4). Either way, any attempt to elucidate our real experience of the world and our interactions within it remains deeply connected to questions of context and systems of meaning. Semiotics and the analysis of 'texts' more generally leads on to the notion of **discourse**, to define a more complex interplay of groups of statements and structures of meaning – of which images play an important role. Image studies marks a definite shift away from semiotics, though it remains sympathetic to the critical questions it raises and connects directly with discourse analysis; being similarly interested in why and how meanings are made and shared (NB. for more on visual culture and discourse analysis, see Rose, 2012, pp.189–226, 227–260). Overall, image studies can be understood to evoke a structural, comparative account of, and critical enquiry into, a heterogeneous set of contexts and systems of signification apropos the images and image-making.

Nonetheless, there is something enduring about semiotics, which we might usefully consider in two ways: as a *teacherly* and a *writerly* semiotics. The former is an analytical, though arguably formulaic approach to image analysis; the latter an important philosophical understanding of – and creative engagement with – our ability (and limitations) to make and share meaning. As a taught subject, semiotics retains currency in the classroom; it is a feature of most introductory theory classes in the arts and humanities, as it has been for the past quarter of a century. This is not wholly surprising. Semiotics (and the associated intellectual movement of structuralism) was once at the very heart of radical social and philosophical thought. In the thick of the May riots of 1968, the phrase 'structures don't take to the streets' allegedly appeared as graffiti; certainly the phrase was in circulation. Calvet (1994, p.166) provides an account of how academics set up 'action committees' or open seminars for students. Barthes, along with his friend and colleague Algirdas Greimas, formed 'an action committee on language . . . which involved endless discussions on the underlying ideologies of semiological theories'. It was not well-received by students, being considerd too academic and out of touch with the upheavals taking place on the streets. During one particular session, chaired by Greimas, a student, Catherine Backès-Clément, arrived late and announced: 'I've come from the general assembly of the philosophy department. We have just passed a motion which concludes "It is clear that structures don't take to the streets"' (cited in Calvet, 1994, p.166). The phrase generated energetic debate amongst the students. Barthes, who was not at the seminar, knew nothing of what was discussed. Yet, 'the following day a huge poster appeared in the corridor of the fourth section of the Hautes Études on the first floor of the Sorbonne which read: "Barthes says: Structures do not take to the streets. We say: Neither does Barthes"' (Calvet, 1994, p.166). It was a cutting remark of a younger generation standing against its professors, and in particular against structuralist semiotics. For all the ability to deconstruct and challenge the dominant order through a semiotic analysis of society, the challenge being made was that the academic elite was not willing to put into practice or at least stand up for the ideological challenge that semiotics appeared to herald. On the surface, then, this was a direct criticism of semiotics, but of course more significantly it reveals

FIGURE 1.1 French Connection window display, Leeds. *This is the Woman/This is the Man* campaign, 2010. The imagery is very simple and direct, but includes ironic captions about gender identity, objectification and voyeurism. Video advertisements from the campaign (which can be viewed on the Internet) develop the witty ideas even further.

just how embedded the ideas were in the culture at that time and how the 'hopes' of semiotics were considered worth fighting over.

Today, semiotics might be said to be taught out of a nostalgia for its politically charged past. But, whatever its history, semiotics remains eminently 'teachable'; both easily demonstrated by the expert and reasonably accessible to the novice for application. As Rose (2012, p.105) puts it in her book, *Visual Methodologies*, 'semiology offers a very full box of analytical tools for taking an image apart and tracing how it works in relation to broader systems of meaning', and there are countless other books, recently published, offering either directly or indirectly an introduction to semiotics. Arguably, however, semiotics would seem to be a victim of its own success; there is something altogether too simplistic in textbook accounts. Frequently, when students are tasked to provide a semiotic analysis of an image, what ends up being privileged is the need to understand semiotics (in all its jargon) rather than the image itself. Typically, advertising images are diligently explained as a system of meaning, but with little or no sense of the irony that the advertisers themselves engage with images in precisely the same way (if only to entertain and ultimately to seduce us into buying the products and 'buying into' associated brand meanings or identities). The problem can be explained further by looking at the work and influence of the best known of semioticians, Roland Barthes; and in particular his book *Mythologies*.

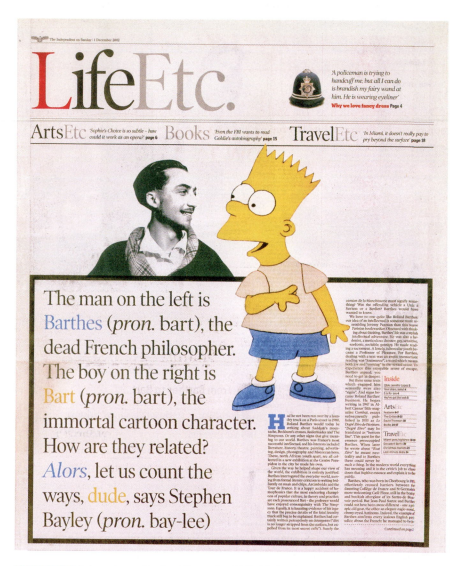

FIGURE 1.2 *Independent on Sunday*, 1 December 2002, *Life Etc.* Supplement, p.1. Review article of an exhibition about Roland Barthes, R/B, at the Centre Pompidou, Paris. An illustration of Bart Simpson, from the cartoon *The Simpsons*, is included to make note of the same pronunciation of 'Bart' and 'Barthes' and to remind the reader of Barthes' pioneering critique of popular culture.

From Barthes to Bart, and back again!

It is unusual, if not unique, for a theorist to be the subject of a major public exhibition, but in November 2002, the Centre Pompidou in Paris opened *R/B*, an exhibition of the life and works of Roland Barthes. A full-page review article, which appeared in *The Independent on Sunday*, playfully notes of a happy coincidence 'that the most endearing champions of popular culture, in theory and practice, are each pronounced "Bart" – the professor would have enjoyed consanguinity with *The Simpsons*' (Life Etc. Supplement, *The Independent on Sunday*, 11 December 2002). It is a humorous remark, but there is a serious point as to how Barthes' conceptual thinking impacted upon the very culture he examined. Certainly the cutting wit of a TV programme such as *The Simpsons* as well as the appetite of a sophisticated audience, able to read off its layered meanings, can easily be associated with Barthes' writings on popular culture.

Back in the late 1950s, a time when advertising was still developing as an 'industry', Barthes's work was quickly taken on board by image professionals (the producers of the mass culture that Barthes sought to critique). In particular, he caught the attention of Georges Péninou, the head of research at the Publicis advertising agency in Paris.

> 'Inspired by what he had read, Péninou began to attend Barthes' seminar at the École Pratique des Hautes Études in the early 1960s, enrolled for a doctorate on the semiology of advertising, invited Barthes to speak at the Publicis offices (where the science of signs was becoming common currency), and later gave the author a contract to analyse the semiology of the Renault company.'
>
> (Badmington in Barthes, 2009, p.xi)

As Calvet notes, the fact that Barthes had accepted the Renault contract, to apply his critical ideas to potentially improve car sales, 'might lead to the conclusion that he himself was fascinated by a world which elsewhere he criticized' (1994, p.143). There is an important principle at stake here when thinking about the scope and terms of image studies. There is as much a need for fascination and cross-fertilization of ideas and experiences, as there is a need for taking a critical stance. There is also something to be learnt from how ideas and processes are adapted and extended. Where Barthes, for example, examined a single advertising poster, the professional advertisers took it upon themselves to analyze 'two, three, four hundred posters in the same way, in order to criticize the work of the people who had thought them up, to detect errors in strategy' (Calvet, 1994, p.143). The scale of this activity reminds us again of Simons' comments (in the introduction to this book) on what would happen if we can give more time and resource to nurturing 'astute citizens' in the world.

It was Barthes' book *Mythologies*, originally published in French in 1957, which set in train both his own popularity and that of the semiotic 'method'; as picked up, for example, by media professionals. In the main, the book is a collection of short, unrelated essays, written over a period of two years, each a satirical commentary on 'myths' of French daily life. What Barthes meant by myth in this context was contemporary 'collective representations' or beliefs that make aspects of daily life appear as if 'natural' and not socially and historically determined. His starting point, as he describes in the preface to the book, 'was usually a feeling of impatience at the sight of the "naturalness" with which newspapers, art and common sense constantly dress up a reality which, even though it is the one we live in, is undoubtedly determined by history' (Barthes, 2009, p.xix). He wrote on a wide range of topics, capturing the spirit of an eclectic and burgeoning, post-war popular culture, including the world of wrestling, soap-powders and detergents, the face of Garbo, wine, the brain of Einstein, ornamental cookery and perhaps most famously of all the D.S. 19 Citroën car, which he described as 'obviously' having 'fallen from the sky inasmuch as it appears at first sight as a superlative *object*' (Barthes, 2009, p.101). His witty, at times biting accounts, written in journalistic fashion, were originally published on a monthly basis for the literary magazine *Les Lettres nouvelles*. However when collected together to form a book, a long concluding essay was added entitled 'Myth Today'. It is this piece, written in far more didactic, theoretical language, that is Barthes' semiotic legacy; in particular a small diagram used to explain what he refers to as a 'second-order semiological system'.

Building upon Saussure's account of the linguistic 'sign', which is explained in dyadic form made up of 'signifier' (e.g. the word that designates a thing) and

FIGURE 1.3

Classroom blackboard showing diagram adapted from Roland Barthes' 'second-order semiological system'.

'signified' (e.g. the concept of a particular thing or phenomenon), Barthes' contribution to the field of semiotics is to define 'myth' as a second-order system of signification. It works upon existing signs, or units of meaning, in order to construct new meanings. A typical example would be how 'rose' as a sign (being a word, the signifier, which we associate with a particular type of flower, its signified) is mythologized when we think about it as a sign of romance, or Englishness, or as a gothic symbol, etc.

> '. . . myth is a peculiar system, in that it is constructed from a semiological chain which existed before it: it *is a second-order semiological system*. That which is a sign (namely the associative total of a concept and an image) in the first system, becomes a mere signifier in the second. We must here recall that the materials of mythical speech (the language itself, photography, painting, posters, rituals, objects, etc.), however different to start, are reduced to a pure signifying function as soon as they are caught by myth. Myth sees in them only the same raw material; their unity is that they all come down to the status of a mere language. Whether it deals with alphabetical or pictorial writing, myth wants to see in them only a sum of signs, a global sign, the final term of a first semiological chain.'
>
> (Barthes, 2009, p.137)

What was so powerful about Barthes' work was not simply the potential for all kinds of signs to be drawn under the one lens of semiotics (though this was highly significant), including, as he lists here, things as disparate as photography, painting, rituals, etc.; but that also this eclectic, contemporary mix was reflective of the then new dynamic, malleable world of mass culture. Along with the actual growing ubiquity of plastic, which allowed for all kinds of new and unusual forms for products and objects, Barthes presented a way of theorizing the *plasticity* of all cultural codes. As a more recent reference, in the realm of digital culture, we might think of the film *The Matrix* (1999), which portrays a simulated reality or 'construct' of the world so elegantly 'coded' that it is more inhabitable than the reality behind it. Barthes would certainly have recognized in this how a constructed reality comes across as being natural. Indeed the Matrix is nothing less than a second-order system of signification.

Of course, with respect to the aims of this book to chart a field of image studies, there is a specific problem with Barthes' account of myth, which sees everything in the terms of 'the same raw material' and brings all 'down to the status of a mere language'. We can agree upon the elements of an alphabet and the grammar of a language, but to what extent can we agree upon the units of meaning in a painting? It does not necessarily make sense to say where one mark begins and another ends, nor is it easy to determine how such marks can be reiterated elsewhere. In this sense there is no 'language' of painting. Yet there remains *something* we regard as painting. We quickly appear to reach the limits of semiotics, certainly in terms of a simple method of analysis. While a formulaic approach gives the means to *read* the sign, we lose touch with a more complex and *productive* engagement with signs and those signs yet to be formed. (For more on the subject of mark-making, see Chapter 4.)

Importantly, however, we should not overlook Barthes' professed willingness, in *Mythologies* and elsewhere, to deal with both 'alphabetical or pictorial writing' (and more besides). In order to do so, we need to look beyond the schematic nature of Barthes diagram of a second-order system of signification and consider a more productive, or 'writerly' notion of semiotics (which will allow for images to behave as images, yet instil critical, reflective thinking). In a key passage in 'Myth Today', under the sub-heading 'Reading and Deciphering Myth', Barthes indentifies three different levels of understanding, that of the *producer* of myths (such as a journalist for example); the *mythologist* (such as the critic who undertakes an analysis of myth); and finally the *reader*, or consumer of myth. The first two types of focusing, he notes, 'are static, analytical; they destroy the myth, either by making its intention obvious, or by unmasking it: the former is cynical, the latter demystifying'. The third type, however, 'is dynamic, it consumes the myth according to the very ends built into its structure: the reader lives the myth as a story at once true and unreal' (Barthes, 2009, p.153).

The journalist and critic see straight through myth. The former in order to knowingly construct it, the latter in order to take it apart again. Yet, whilst these professionals are engaged in such duties, the division provides a false picture. If it were that simple there would be no mythologies, in effect there would be no culture. What is easily missed is how Barthes' diagram of the second-order semiological system is itself mythological. One of the examples he mentions when explaining the system is of a Latin grammar exercise typically given to school pupils, with a line that reads '*quia ego nominor leo*', meaning 'because my name is lion'. Semiotically, the pupil understands this as being simply a grammatical example and as having nothing to do with a real (or even fictional) lion. In other words, one does not expect to read a story about the lion, it is merely an element within the grammatical example, just as numbers might be used in a mathematical example. In a similar way Barthes' diagram of second-order signification speaks to us semiotically as just that: a schematic diagram to explain a certain set of principles. Yet, we can argue, a mythology sets in as a result of the repetition of this diagram in countless books (including this book) and as a focal point in numerous theoretical classes and as quoted in essay questions. What is this myth? Not least that the world around us can be cut up into constituent elements, of signifiers and signifieds. Yet, while a signified can have several signifiers (there are numerous words we use for the same thing, as any thesaurus will attest), it is only in abstract we can separate these elements. In *use* such separation would be meaningless, literally. We cannot point, knowingly, to a rose without some concept of what a rose is; conversely we cannot hold such a meaning without any means to refer to it. To quote Gertude Stein's most famous line of poetry: 'A rose is a rose is a rose. . .'. In this seemingly simple line, without suggesting meaning is fixed for time immemorial, Stein 'performs' the idea, or indeed the experience we have that things simply are as they are; that the name of a thing appears already to invoke the imagery and emotions associated with it.

For Barthes, 'it is the reader of myths himself who must reveal their essential function' (2009, p.153). We must train attention upon the 'reader' of myths, or rather the occasion upon which we 'consume' myth (as in that 'moment' captured by Stein's enigmatic line, when 'something' just is!). It is only the reader who enters into the moment in which myth assumes its full ambiguity – when it is neither too obviously constructed nor missed entirely, but at some level recognized. Barthes argues how the myth comes to naturalize what we see before us, to make a purposeful construction appear just as if it were always so. Crucially it does so without taking anything away from the elements on display: 'Myth hides nothing and flaunts nothing: it distorts; myth is neither a lie nor a confession: it is an inflexion' (Barthes, 2009, p.153). In understanding myth, then, as an inflexion, and as a facet of popular culture, we can see how Barthes would surely have appreciated *The Simpsons*. The television show provides a humorous, though satirical, semiotic approach to contemporary culture while staying entirely embedded in that same culture. In effect, *The Simpsons* is *of* a particular image culture (it stays 'consumed' within it), and as such provides a very fluid critique that bypasses the need of a schematic analytical approach.

The point of difference is between what has been described in this chapter as a *teacherly* semiotics (stemming from Barthes' diagrammatic account of a second-order system of signification) and this more *writerly* semiotics, that essentially defies pinning down as it is always in process. In his later work, writing about literature, Barthes explicitly articulates the idea of the 'writerly'. He establishes an 'opposition between irreversible and reversible textual elements [which] allows him to build up a theory concerning the *lisible* (readerly) text and *scriptable* (writerly) text' (Allen, 2003, p.88). The distinction allows one to differentiate between informational texts that offer the reader little 'productive' work and more complex texts which set the reader off in a more imaginative, productive sense – as if writing their own thought at the same time as reading. Barthes' identification of a *writerly experience* of texts leads to an important methodological principle of needing a more creative response. In one of his best-known articles, 'From Work to Text', he ends with the prophetic line: 'the Text is that *social* space which leaves no language safe, outside, and no subject of the speech-act in a situation of judge, master, analyst, confessor, decoder: the theory of the Text can coincide with a practice of writing' (Barthes, 1989, p.64). Image studies similarly seeks to consider a more expanded notion of the image, which in turns needs to coincide with a necessary *practice of the image*.

Operation Margarine!

In the same year as the article 'From Work to Text', Barthes (1977, pp.165–169) published 'Change the Object Itself: Mythology Today' in the French literary magazine *Esprit*, in April 1971. This short piece offers an explicit reflection on his book, *Mythologies*, from the 1950s. Aware of the success of semiotics, he describes how it has become something of a blunt instrument, having been subsumed within the very same popular culture it sought to critique. He makes a somewhat difficult argument that we need to 'switch from the demystification of myths to a radical critique and dismantling of the very notion of the sign itself' (Allen, 2003, p.65). Barthes states that the task of any foregoing semiotics is 'no longer simply to *upend* (or *right)* the mythical message, but rather to change the object itself, to produce a new object' (1977, p.169). He expresses the idea that we need to become more engaged in creating or writing cultural texts, not simply reading them. In accordance, then, with the notion of the *writerly*, he implies the need for a specific kind of writing: '. . . as a baroque and parodying rhetoric [to] encourage people not only to read in a deeply critical way but to "fissure the very representation of meaning"' (Stafford, 1998, p.164). The idea of needing to go beyond the mere 'reading', or interpretation of signs, but actually to 'write' (or at least being aware of what it means to produce) signs is an important underlying consideration for the field of image studies.

Mythologies is generally considered a part of Barthes' earlier 'structuralist' phase, offering little, if any, of the so-called *writerly* mode. This is certainly the case when emphasis is placed on the closing theoretical essay and in particular *that* diagram of the second-order system of signification. Yet, if we turn our attention to the short, journalistic articles that make up the bulk of the book, we see the *writerly* coming through, with the very 'logic' of myth brought into play in Barthes' own analyses (making the gap between Barthes and Bart not so distant!). As Allen (2003, p.37) describes: 'Taking very common images and ideas of modern cultural life, Barthes does not simply expose the mythology behind them, but perhaps more importantly exposes the fact that we were somehow aware of the mythological character of such images and ideas all along'. A good example is the article entitled 'Operation Margarine' (Barthes, 2009, pp.39–41). We might think from the title it offers an exposé of a certain myth attached to margarine; a product that became increasingly popular as the post-war market opened up with the end of rationing and developments in brand marketing. There is a myth attached to margarine, which Barthes derives from the publicity of *Astra* margarine, whereby prejudice against it (as being inferior to butter) stands in the way of progress and common sense, and will literally 'cost you dearly' (Barthes, 2009, p.40). However, this is not what the article seeks to unravel. Rather it assumes we all share in this knowledge, and as such can *use* the myth of margarine as an effective means to expose something of greater significance.

The article is actually concerned with how the 'Established Order' (those in power, etc.) can turn their weaknesses to advantage. He gives two specific examples, how the army and church both openly note their failings, yet in doing so herald their continued importance and virtue. 'It is a kind of homeopathy: one cures doubts about the Church or the Army by the very ills of the Church and the Army. One inoculates the public with a contingent evil to prevent or cure an essential one' (Barthes, 2009, p.40). The argument being made is that we put up with ongoing, seemingly temporary complaints (or 'contingent' wrong-doing), in order to uphold the idea of some greater good. It does not matter if the church or army has its failings; they are 'essentially' important institutions. Having made this case, Barthes ends the article with the allusion to margarine, which in all its banality would seem to have the effect of both inoculating us against Barthes' own critical argument, yet equally seeming to expose the fact, as Allen notes, 'that we were somehow aware of the mythological character of such images and ideas all along'. Thus Barthes writes: 'It is well worth the price of an immunization. What does it matter, *after all*, if margarine is just fat, when it goes further than butter, and costs less? What does it matter, *after all*, if Order is a little brutal or a little blind, when it allows us to live cheaply?' (2009, p.41).

In effect, Barthes manages to link – almost cognitively – the exposing of what he takes to be a deep-level flaw in society with the simple act of spreading margarine on one's toast at the breakfast table. He achieves a way of 'bringing home' to us an otherwise abstract, political problem. Thus, again, not so far removed from *The Simpsons*, Barthes takes up a metaphor, or an image from within our common, shared culture – in this case related to margarine – in order to 'entertain' certain critical concerns. This is by no means a simple image analysis, but is actually the *use* of an image itself for critical purpose. It is perhaps not such a surprise then, in his late period, Barthes (2000, p.475) claimed the semiologist needs to be 'an artist' playing with signs 'as with a conscious decoy, whose fascination he savours and wants to make others savour and understand'. The sign for this artist 'is always immediate, subject to the kind of evidence that leaps to the eyes, like a trigger of the imagination', which is why semiology in this case 'is not a hermeneutics: it paints more than it digs'.

In this vein, the purpose of image studies is not just to describe what is in the image and what it looks like, but to ask what the image does and indeed what *we* can do with images; to consider what effects can be achieved and how these vary according to different image types, practices and contexts. Of course, we are not necessarily aware just how often we are engaging with images – just as Barthes' reference to margarine shows, which is subtle and easy to pass over precisely because he uses it to get you thinking about something else. Image here becomes a medium. Image studies must equally train attention upon this phenomenon of the image as a 'carrier' of meaning – sometimes knowingly so, sometimes not. Thus, image studies needs to be concerned with the 'inflexion' of differing image types and processes and needs to be attuned to their effects not just at a descriptive level, but to be willing to explore at a creative, *writerly* or 'imagistic' level too. Only then can we begin to understand images in their own terms as images.

Summary

This chapter puts the case for *both* a critical and creative approach. It is not enough to simply analyze what we see in an image. We must also consider what images do and what we do with them; also how the process of imaging impacts on our ability to understand and relate to one another and the world in general. Described in terms of a *writerly* semiotics, it is an approach that can be understood to engage as much with the production of meaning as its interpretation. Nonetheless, in making images (or at least understanding how images are made, manipulated and disseminated) we must equally accept the need for critical and contextual understanding, which can include a structural, comparative approach to the image. Crucially, to repeat Elkins' observations noted in the introduction to this book, we need to find ways to knit together both critical and creative approaches to the image, and/or at least to understand just how and why this is so difficult to achieve.

Back in the 1970s, Barthes complained how contemporary education had tended to ignore rhetoric and 'the art of writing' in favour of an interest in reading and explication. 'Learning to read', he notes, 'has its positive side, but also a negative one, since the gap has been widened between the small number of people who write and the large number of people who read without transforming what they're reading into writing' (Barthes, 1985a, p.110). Something similar is at stake in approaches to the image. At the very least, we need to bridge the gap between those involved in making images and those who consume them. Following this chapter is the first in a series of three supplements, each of which aims to provide creative and/or practical consideration of what it means to engage in image studies. In the first supplement, a famous pop art image made by the artist Richard Hamilton provides the focal point to 'productively' elucidate a number of the themes raised in this chapter.

Further reading

Barthes, Roland (1977), 'Change the Object Itself: Mythology Today' in *Image Music Text*, trans. by Stephen Heath. London: Fontana, pp.165–169.

Barthes, Roland (2009) *Mythologies* (rev. edn, 2009), trans. by Annette Lavers. London: Vintage.

Chandler, Daniel (2007) *Semiotics: The Basics*. Second Edition. London: Routledge.

Elkins, James (ed.) (2009) *Visual Literacy*. New York: Routledge.

Rose, Gillian (2012) *Visual Methodologies: An Introduction to the Interpretation of Visual Materials*. Third Edition. London: Sage.

Sturken, Marita and Cartwright, Lisa (2009) *Practices of Looking: An Introduction to Visual Culture*. Second Edition. Oxford: Oxford University Press.

JUST WHAT IS IT THAT MAKES IMAGES SO DIFFERENT?

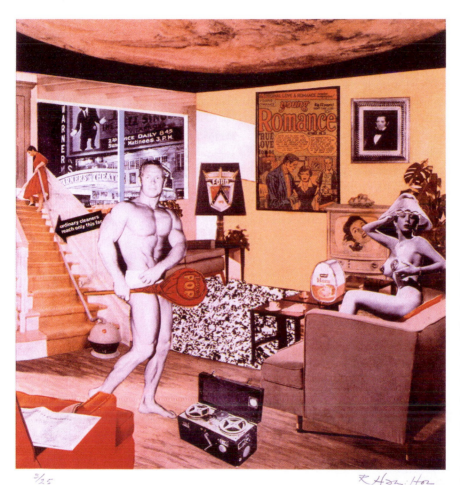

3/25

FIGURE 1.4
Reproduction of Richard Hamilton's *Just what is it that makes today's homes so different, so appealing?* (1956) [Richard Hamilton, *Just what was it that made yesterday's homes so different, so appealing?* (2004) Ink-jet print on paper, 420 × 297mm. © Tate, London 2012.]

One edition of Barthes' *Mythologies* (an English translation published by Paladin in 1973) chose for the cover image Richard Hamilton's iconic collage *Just what is it that makes today's homes so different, so appealing?* (1956). This artwork originates from the very same period in which Barthes was writing, and similarly offers a witty view upon the then emergent mass consumer culture. As the critic, Sarat Maharaj, explains:

'The scene reads as a vanitas, as essay on the styling of the five senses by consumer goods and gadgetry. What Hamilton is scanning is the "persuading image", the "look of things" how objects, bodies, the micro-texture of everyday life not only take on an irresistible erotic charge, but also serve as a system of signs, symbols and representations through which desires and needs come to be interpreted and voiced.'

(Maharaj, 1992, p.42)

Thus, like Barthes, if not more so, Hamilton engages *directly* with the materials of popular culture as a means of critical engagement. Furthermore, it is not just an engagement with tangible things, but also a system of signs. Hamilton grapples with form as much as content since it is largely 'the *way* in which an image is communicated through modern media that has made it compelling for Hamilton as the source of work' (Morphet, 1992, p.17, original emphasis). Almost all the images Hamilton brings together, and certainly each and every element in the collage piece shown here, derive from a prior process of mediation. There is a constant renewal and remaking of images, yet without disguising the original. Barthes' wish for the semiologist to be an artist, who, as noted in Chapter 1, plays with signs, 'whose fascination he savours and wants to make others savour and understand' (Barthes, 2000, p.475), appears to reach its apotheosis with Richard Hamilton.

Art historian and theorist, Hal Foster, suggests the approach taken in producing *Just what is it that makes today's homes so different, so appealing?* is 'neither satirical nor celebratory but at once analytical and playful'. Of course, as he goes on to note, this begs the question common to all pop art: 'critical or complicit?' – is this art simply in itself an outcrop of the mass consumer culture it draws its sources from, or does it in some way offer critical orientation? As Foster writes, 'the answer given by Hamilton, then and now, is *both* and intensely so' (Foster, 2010, p.146). We might think of Hamilton's collage in itself as a persuasive image such as we would suggest of an advertising image, but here the question remains: persuasive of what exactly? The fact it is difficult to answer is no doubt related to the picture's iconic status. The collage is made up of reproductions, which, when brought together, appear to 'comment' on their very reproducibility. Yet, all of which remains in the same 'language' of the individual images found from the pages of a popular magazine of the day.

The enduring charm of Hamilton's collage is evident with its continual reproduction (in all sorts of contexts) and a whole swathe of playful copies and pastiches, by amateurs and professionals alike. Figure 1.5, for example, shows how new digital technology – in this case the use of the graphics editing software, Photoshop – can quickly emulate and update the style and significance of Hamilton's work. Other more formal responses exist too. Vivek Vilasini, an Indian-born, multimedia artist and photographer, provides a direct reworking with a collage entitled *Between one Shore and several Others (Just what is it . . . after Richard Hamilton)* (2008). The work is a point for point reconstruction of Hamilton's original. It copies the exact

FIGURE 1.5 Photoshop montage (*after* Richard Hamilton). Courtesy of Lauren Pettitt, 2011. This digitally produced montage was made with explicit reference to Richard Hamilton's college of 1956. It echoes various elements, notably the re-mediation of cultural signifiers, including those framed through the windows and TV and computer screens. Like Hamilton's collage, the picture includes the image of both a man and woman. In this case, we might suggest the female figure is more salient and animated. Neither pay attention to the other, nor do they see what is shown on the TV screen or outside the windows. The creator of the picture notes the unique way in which working with images helps articulate ideas. 'It is easier to say what you mean with images', she suggests, 'as you select certain images which say certain things. When put altogether you get a feel for what is being said and see the significance of why certain images have been used.'

perspective of the room, complete with stairs leading up to the left, the image of the earth above, a muscle-man in the foreground, and a second figure upon a couch. The only difference is that all of the iconology is derived from Indian culture. So, for example, the figures in the picture adopt Indian dress, there is a Bollywood poster on the back wall, and the tape-recorder of Hamilton's original has been replaced with an Indian harmonium. Echoing the question 'critical or complicit?', Vilasini's deliberate re-staging of Hamilton's work can be viewed as a playful re-citing of an artwork within the context of contemporary India. 'By using image fragments from Indian popular culture, from news media, advertising, and Bollywood films [Vivek Vilasini] meshes Eastern and Western iconographies' (Hansen, n/d). Yet, look another way, and perhaps we start to ask questions about the long-standing dominance of a Western canon in fine art and of course more general political,

FIGURE 1.6
Richard Hamilton, *Just what is it that makes today's homes so different?* (1992) laser print, 176 × 267mm. © Tate, London 2012.

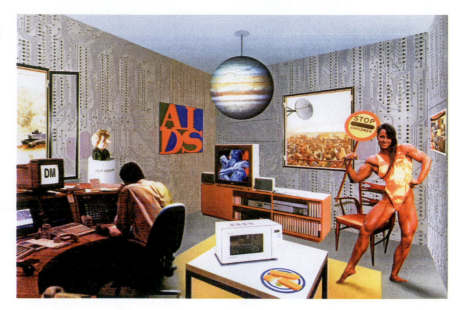

economic and social issues related to a global perspective of India. So, for example, it can be said 'the work explores how the vitality of modern Indian art is born out of economic and political change, media impacts, and by the rivalry between cultural traditions and globalisation' (Hansen, n/d).

Richard Hamilton was invited to update his image as part of a BBC television documentary in the early 1990s. Hamilton refers to the original collage as being 'tabular', since it began with a list, or table, of key words. He explains:

> 'As a preliminary I made a list. I simply took my pen and piece of paper and I said now what is significant in the life we now lead? And I said, well, what is important is that man and woman exist. So I started with man, woman, and then moved on to cinema, domestic appliances, cars, food. And then I found examples of each of these listings. In the case of the man, you can flick through a magazine and it is full of men, it's full of women, but each one you think, is this a symbol that represents man? And it wasn't until I hit on this muscle man, stripped off, I thought that is the symbolic man of our time.'
>
> (Hamilton, *QED: 'Art and Chips'* BBC, 1992)

The documentary observes Hamilton digitally acquiring and manipulating the various elements for his updated collage. Most prominently the male and female roles and their visual salience are transposed, but also new elements included: the AIDS painting by the Canadian artist's group General Idea, which parodies Robert Indiana's iconic 'Love' painting of the 1960s; the wallpaper of the interior is an image produced from scanning a circuit board, and frozen fish fingers, next to a microwave oven, are an update on the tin of ham found in the original. As Hamilton worked at his computer he remarked:

'The irritating thing is that it is taking far longer than using traditional methods and it's only because this particular electronic image processing machine allows the possibility of making all these refinements. You can't make these refinements with scissors and paste. But the fact that it is possible means that one is tempted to try and do it'.

(Hamilton, *QED: 'Art and Chips'* BBC, 1992)

There is surely more to the fact the new digital process allows all kinds of refinements and possibilities. Arguably, the original collage presents a 'way of seeing' that we have then sought to be able to replicate (and refine) by using computer technologies. In other words collage comes before the 'cut and paste' (and the scissor and pencil icons) of imaging software. This time around, then, the images Hamilton brings together are done so within a larger frame of reference, it is a parody or perhaps merely a pastiche as well as a technical re-staging of what has gone before (indeed, in the later collage, as part of its collection of contemporary icons and myths, we find the original artwork framed upon the right-hand wall).

Perhaps we might think the 'micro-texture of everyday life' and the 'irresistible erotic charge' that Maharaj suggests of the 1950s collage is less convincing in the later, digital re-incarnation. But, then, perhaps we have come to expect this type of image, or at least find it equivalent to the many competing images we come into contact with on a daily basis; whether in magazines, music videos, across the Internet, and even in corporate brochures. We might suggest Hamilton's original 1950s collage pre-empts his later digital attempt. As Richard Lanham (1993, p.40) suggests, the original piece suits today's 'digital rhetoric' and suggests that this piece of art, 'collaged up as it is with clip art and advertising icons', could just as well be titled: 'Just What Is it That Makes Today's Desktop so Different, So Appealing?'.

TASK

Just What Is It?

Using either scissors and glue or digital means (or a combination of both) create a collage of contemporary culture. Think about what keywords you might start with and what images initially come to mind. Richard Hamilton sourced all his images from magazines. Where are you likely to get your images from? Who is likely to see your finished work and what kind of reactions might you expect? Hamilton ran off 5000 copies of his digitally created collage on a standard colour laser printer. These were then given away to viewers of the BBC documentary. During the programme he remarks, 'I like this democratization of art, in that it's not just available to people who can walk into a gallery and buy something because they have the required amount of money for this rare item, . . . things should be that easy, but they should have the quality which gives them an authenticity'. Of course, it is not only new digital means that opened up art in this way. Pop art itself, and Hamilton's simple use of scissors, glue and commercial magazines, prompted a supposed 'democratization of art'. The availability of cameras on mobile phones, online image search engines and lower costs of art materials undoubtedly open up the means of participation. However, in making your own collage, consider what it actually feels like to be working with images. How much time does it involve? What frames of reference do you bring to the task? If, as Barthes had suggested, we are all now capable of decoding signs, does this also mean we have an *equivalent* ability to create or manipulate signs? How would you relate your answer to Hamilton's suggestive remark regarding the need to maintain 'quality' and 'authenticity'? In thinking about this last point, you might find it useful to read Chapter 1 of John Berger's *Ways of Seeing* (1972).

2 Understanding images

poly-sem-ous
↑ many ↑ semiotics

This chapter looks at ways in which we can account for images in all their complexity, range and difference. It attempts to ask more explicitly what we understand an image to be (which as we will find is no simple thing). This chapter, then, and the one that follows, provide conceptual, theoretical and historical consideration of the image. In this case, the focus is on understanding the image according to a wider *system*, *ecology* and *family* of images.

It is soon apparent that a single theoretical approach to the image is difficult to trace. 'One need only invoke the names of Walter Benjamin, Marshall McLuhan, Guy Debord, and Jean Baudrillard', Mitchell suggests, 'to get some sense of the totalizing theoretical ambitions of "image studies", iconologies, mediology, visual culture, New Art History, and so on' (2005, p.77). Needless to say, such 'ambitions' are not easy to pin down, indeed '[a] critique of the image, a "pictorial turn", has occurred across an array of disciplines . . . and it has brought with it new problems and paradigms' (Mitchell, 2005, p.77). We shall return to the significance of the phrase 'pictorial turn' in the next chapter, but it is worth noting the 'array of disciplines' Mitchell refers to are all placed within the arts and humanities, and can be understood as having an 'anthropological' approach to the image; being interested in how images are interpreted and consumed by people and how they come to be part of the 'structures' of human cultures and knowledge.

However, if we consider images in all their profusion, there is a need to move across many different subjects and subject boundaries. The art theorist and historian, James Elkins, has been particularly interested in this problem. In *Visual Practices Across the University* (2007), he stresses the value in going beyond the narrow interests of fine art and even beyond the interests of the field of visual studies, which he suggests has primarily been concerned with arts and mass media:

'It is widely acknowledged that ours is an increasingly visual society, and yet the field that wants to provide the theory of that visuality – visual studies, art history, philosophy, sociology – continue to take their examples from the tiny minority of images that figure as art.'

(Elkins, 2007, p.7)

As Elkins notes, many fields outside of the humanities such as biochemistry and astronomy are 'image-obsessed' and 'think and work *through* images' (Elkins, 2007, p.7). His book includes examples from a highly eclectic range of image-making practices, including no less 'the study of dolphins' fins, of porcelain teeth, of Cheddar cheese' (p.7). This book can hardly claim to encompass such a varied range of image-types and practices, but it does seek to adhere to the principle that we should be able to understand images in *all* their forms and effects. Generally, each chapter draws upon a mix of images and image-practices. Also, later chapters on science imaging and informational images offer an explicit account of practices outside of the humanities.

Given a professed interest in such a wide range of image-types, practices and cultures, it is difficult, or indeed misguided to present a single critical framework for understanding the image. The next three sections of this chapter present separate, but nonetheless compatible, 'image-systems'. These are by no means intended as rigid systems of analysis, but more playful, heuristic attempts to look again at images from a fresh critical and curious perspective. If there is really one principle to keep in mind it would be there is no such thing as *an* image (singular). As discussed in the next section, for example, even one, discrete visual image can be found suffused with a layer of pre- and after-images, whether resonating of literary imagery, or optical and perceptual effects. In fact, we can suppose there are whole 'ecologies' of images, or similarly, we can place images in a family tree. What these 'image-systems' reveal is not just how images do or do not relate to one another in formal terms, but that any understanding of images must consider the interrelation of various histories and structures of meaning.

Image-systems

We encountered the work of Roland Barthes in the previous chapter. As explained, he is perhaps best known as an architect of semiotics, the science of signs. However, also noted was his important contribution to the 'unravelling' of semiotics, with his late work described as being *writerly* and post-structural. One such example is his 'autobiography' *Roland Barthes* (1994), originally published in 1975. The book does provide some biographical details as one might expect, but Barthes does not present a conventional self-portrait at all. Instead, the book is about the construction and meta-analysis of his own 'image'. Adopting a theatrical metaphor, he writes of needing to 'stage an image-system':

'"To stage" means: to arrange the flats one in front of the other, to distribute the roles, to establish levels, and, at the limit: to make the footlights a kind of uncertain barrier. Hence it is important that the image-system be treated according to its degrees (the image-system is a matter of consistency, and consistency a matter of degrees), and there are, in the course of these fragments [as laid out in his book], several degrees of image-system. The difficulty, however, is that one cannot number these degrees, like the degrees of spirituous liquor or of a torture.'

(Barthes, 1994, p.105)

The phrase 'one cannot number these degrees' can be taken as a useful statement on image analysis. When we look at the image, we should resist applying any simple semiotic, or informational system of 'reading'. Unlike measurable units of alcohol, or film ratings to declare suitability for certain audiences, images are generally not understood by establishing clear points of measurement. Yet, there is something we can say about how and why they are 'staged' – that is, how they come to be arranged as they are, and what resonances of other images or experiences are associated with them; also to consider something about who they are meaningful and of use to; all of which reveals only an 'uncertain barrier' or complex set of connections.

FIGURE 2.1 'The History of Semiology', from the *International Herald Tribune*, October 12–13 (1974).

The History of Semiology

The cartoon in Figure 2.1 appears in the book *Roland Barthes*, and no doubt amused Barthes for its simple, yet insightful account of semiology. A reading of this picture might be quite straightforward, especially if we begin with the title, or caption, 'The History of Semiology'. We can read the picture from left to right as if a historical timeline; a view helped along by the apparent directionality of the caveman (and perhaps with resonance of the familiar illustration of the evolution of 'man', which typically shows from left to right the gradual emergence of a bipedal, upright-walking *homo sapien*). Firstly, we see the caveman register the sign that reads 'SIGN AHEAD'. After which we see a large depiction of a caveman on a stone unicycle. The fact that this picture has a border around it helps us to see it as a picture within the picture. Potentially, then, we read this as a picture set against the 'reality' of the 'real' caveman who happens to come upon the signpost alerting him to a representation of himself. In thinking back to the previous chapter, this portion of the cartoon depicts the early, structuralist phase of semiotics, which as a 'science of signs' maintained the distinction between an objective reality and its system of signification. We think of signs pointing to material things in the world and/or as used to offer a diagnostic account of the world. Here the caveman is given fore-warning of what lies ahead; despite in this case it being blatantly obvious, if only because, like a billboard, it is hard to miss!

The second portion of the cartoon appears to replicate the first. Our caveman again comes upon a sign, yet mysteriously it simply reads 'SIGN'. The seeming repetition is fitting, for this is again a depiction of the same thing – semiotics – only in its later form, post-semiotics. Now, instead of the sign referring to something separate, we acknowledge the sign itself as a *thing* in the world. A good example to help understand this shift is that of the brand commodity. When we buy a well-known brand, whether for example associated with a pair of trainers, an MP3 player or designer clothes, it is not always clear whether we are more satisfied by the object of our purchase, or the intangible brand associations that come with it. In effect, like the signpost reading 'SIGN' (which only points to itself), a brand appears to have no substantial reference in the world. A brand is a sign of itself, of its own making. Of course the high commodity value of brands reminds us these are hardly trivial phenomena. Indeed, we buy and sell signs. We contest and celebrate signs.

We can elaborate upon this reading of the cartoon with reference to the writing of sociologist and cultural theorist Jean Baudrillard, and in particular his well known work *Simulacra and Simulation* (1994), in which he refers to the 'hyperreal', to mean 'a real without origin or reality'. He begins with a reference to the Borges fable, 'in which the cartographers of the Empire draw up a map so detailed that it ends up covering the territory exactly' (p.1). The caveman peering at the sign that simply reads 'SIGN' is a good illustration of the idea of looking at an exact, or hyperreal cartography. The sign overlays the territory that it maps out, or points to. It *is* the map and territory at the same time. Even if you have not previously encountered the writings of Baudrillard, his book *Simulacra and Simulation* is perhaps familiar as it is directly cited in the popular film *The Matrix* (1999). The idea of simulation leads to questions about the representational *power* of images and the supposed falsehood of images. A topic we will turn attention to in Chapter 3.

Up to this point we have advanced a fairly obvious reading of the cartoon, which arguably overlooks its most salient feature: the *picture* of the caveman in the middle. How is it we skate past this portion of the cartoon? It is as if the caveman pedalling on his unicycle neatly whisks us along from one sign to the next precisely enacting the problem of semiotics (discussed in Chapter 1), with its propensity to only *read* the image. As Hans Belting puts it: 'Semiology . . . does not allow images to exist beyond the controllable territory of signs, signals, and communication' (2005, p.304). Something very different happens, however, if we divide the cartoon into *three* sections, not two. Instead of considering the sign which states 'SIGN AHEAD' as referring to the picture in the middle, so making the first portion of the cartoon take up two thirds of the overall layout, we can suggest it more accurately points to the final element in the picture, the sign which unequivocally declares itself as 'SIGN'. Understood this way, there is indeed *the* sign up ahead, now more faithfully reproduced at the start (on the left-hand side) of the cartoon. Of course, you may have seen this relationship between the signposts on first looking at the cartoon. However, perhaps one reason we do not necessarily linger too long in reading the cartoon in this way is that we are then left with an orphaned picture in the middle. If the picture is no longer the sign up ahead, it potentially loses its part in the overall narrative. If this is a picture and not a sign, the cartoon is suddenly less stable in how we respond to it (of course the art of cartoons, indeed comedy in general, frequently relies upon the instability and/or movement in one's reading).

Considered solely as a *picture* in the middle of the cartoon, we find a much richer set of possibilities. Where before we read off the joke about a sign up ahead (is it the picture in the middle, is it the second sign-post?), we perhaps raise a smile, but essentially we finish needing to look at the cartoon, just as we can finish reading a sentence before moving onto the next. A sign-post informs of something up ahead, just as a word or pictorial sign works to point to something, whether a concept or a thing. We use the word 'cat' to point towards an image of a cat, or indeed a real cat – 'Look over there . . .' we might say. As noted in Chapter 1, the philosopher and logician Charles Peirce describes a sign as an index where it has 'dynamical (including spatial) connection both with the individual object . . . and with the senses or memory of the person for whom it serves as a sign' (Peirce, 1932, p.170). For Peirce, the index is always in reference to something in the world. To put it simplistically, just as we use our index finger to point to something real, we share all sorts of sign systems (such as language) that point to *things*; that bring ideas together with some*thing* in the world. Yet, equally, the meanings we derive can be complex, subtle and contradictory. If we stop to look at the picture of the caveman in the middle of the cartoon *as a picture* we open up more possibilities. Does it fall out of the system of signification? Does it supplement further systems of meaning? Perhaps it is not a framed picture after all, but instead a window or mirror, which by coincidence happens to show a similar scene beyond. Instead of three representations of a single caveman, maybe there are three separate cavemen; in fact, maybe there is a race underway!

Thus, by looking at the cartoon from different perspectives – whether applying different conceptual understanding, or just looking at elements from a different viewpoint – we begin to see how the flats of the 'stage' can be arranged differently, leading to different effects and delineating boundaries both to the internal relationships within the image and our external engagement as a viewer. We can turn now to another example of a proposed 'image-system', which again is not meant to close down what an image is, but rather the opposite, to open up its varied possibilities.

An ecology of images

In her seminal book *On Photography* (1979), Susan Sontag closes with the evocative idea of an 'ecology of images':

> 'Images are more real than anyone could have supposed. And just because they are an unlimited resource, one that cannot be exhausted by consumerist waste,

there is all the more reason to apply the conservationist remedy. If there can be a better way for the real world to include the one of images, it will require an ecology not only of real things but of images as well.'

(Sontag, 1979, p.180)

Sontag's remark reflects upon the relationship between images and reality, which to this day is still frequently characterized in the terms of the Greek philosopher Plato, who advocated we 'loosen our dependence on images by evoking the standard of an image-free way of apprehending the real' (Sontag, 1979, p.153). The argument associated with Plato is that images are illusions; furthermore that the world revealed to us through our senses is only a poor copy of its true 'Forms', which can only be apprehended intellectually. We shall return to the significance of Plato's philosophical account of the image in Chapter 3, since it continues to resonate with contemporary debates on the image, particularly in relation to questions over their representational power, including, for example, Baudrillard's account of hyperreality as mentioned above.

For now, however, we can consider Sontag was interested, though ambivalent, about the way photography came to overturn much of the Platonic philosophy about images and reality. 'Cameras', she writes, 'are the antidote and the disease, a means of appropriating reality and a means of making it obsolete' (Sontag, 1979, p.179). This is a topic all of itself (see Chapter 5), but the key point is that a so-called 'ecology of images' urges us to take images seriously as *part of* reality.

'The powers of photography have in effect de-Platonized our understanding of reality, making it less and less plausible to reflect upon our experience according to the distinction between images and things, between copies and originals. It suited Plato's derogatory attitude towards images to liken them to shadows [. . . but] the force of photographic images comes from their being material realities in their own right, richly informative deposits left in the wake of whatever emitted them, potent means for turning the tables on reality – for turning *it* into a shadow. Images are more real than anyone could have supposed.'

(Sontag, 1979, pp.179–180)

Interestingly, when returning to the subject of photography some thirty years later, in her book *Regarding the Pain of Others* (2003), Sontag is highly sceptical of her own idea. Commenting on the ubiquity of war imagery, she declares: 'There isn't going to be an ecology of images. No Committee of Guardians is going to ration horror, to keep fresh its ability to shock. And the horrors themselves are not going to abate' (2003, p.108). In terms of a general 'ecology of images', we might suggest Sontag unnecessarily narrows down the concept. On the one hand, her lament for a 'Committee of Guardians' can equate with the point made in the introduction to this book that in being 'astute, fascinated scholars of the visual aspects of the world' we need equally to be 'astute citizens in that world' (Simons, 2008, p.78). In other words, there is a case for upholding certain political and ethical principles when dealing with images. However, the trouble with Sontag's 'Committee of Guardians' is that, firstly, it suggests those ordained to undertaken this task are some kind of elite group; and, secondly, provides no clear sense of how and on what basis the 'rationing' of images would take place. Perhaps, then, it is more fruitful to think of images in terms of the richer meaning of the word 'ecology'.

The term 'ecology', as a branch of science dealing with the relationship of living things to their environments, was coined by German zoologist Ernst Haeckel in the nineteenth century but has its roots in the long-standing tradition of natural history, dating from the work of the Greek philosopher Aristotle. The word 'ecology' has its root in the Greek *oikos*, meaning 'house, dwelling place, habitation' – the English prefix 'eco' also appears in 'economics', which of course can pertain to the running of a household as much as a national economy. Both terms 'ecology' and 'economics' resonate with each other, both concerned with models or systems of circulation and exchange. Aristotle studied the natural world as part of philosophy and as a pioneer of zoology is regarded as one of the first to apply an empirical and classificatory approach. It is important to note, however, with respect to modern ecology, Aristotle's teleological view of the world (of designed and invariable types) hardly paid attention to the full range of reciprocal and dynamic relationships of organisms and their environments. In other words, 'given his assumption of the eternal nature of species, Aristotle did not stress the adaptive character of fauna and flora, which is perhaps ecology's cornerstone' (Benson, 2000, p.59).

It is no doubt a precarious task to try to transpose ideas and terminology from a field of science such as ecology to that of image studies, not least because even within the field of ecology itself there have been numerous debates over its true focus and distinctiveness. Despite a classificatory and comparative mode of enquiry, for example, the roots of ecology are arguably as much 'buried deep within natural history, [within] the descriptive and often romantic tradition of studying the pro-ductions of nature' (Benson, 2000, p.59). However, as a metaphor for a desire to understand the interrelationships of things (the nature of change, adaptation and community), the classificatory, comparative and systems-based approach of ecology can be made pertinent to image studies, as it too seeks to locate how and why images operate in certain 'environments' or systems of meaning.

Typically, as a 'life science', ecology looks at key factors such as processes, community, distribution, abundance, energy, adaptation, and successions. These are all useful descriptors. So, how might they transpose upon an examination of images and the 'image-world' (to echo the title of a chapter from Sontag's *On Photography*). Putting aside the use of 'ecology' in political discourse (evoked, for example, in reference to being 'environmentally-friendly', etc.), ecology is essentially the study of the interrelationship of organisms and their environment. As Putman and Wratten (1984) note, '[t]he very word "environment" conjures up an impression of a struc-tural, physical "stage-set" upon which background biological processes are acted out' (p.15). There is an echo here of what Barthes described as our need to 'stage an image-system'. What we can borrow from ecology is a consideration of the funda-mental elements that any organism requires in order to exist in a given environment. We readily talk about images in isolation, the way they look, their 'power' and meanings. Yet, no one image can exist on its own. Images are 'environmental' in that they must always have some context and be delivered via a medium (their 'oxygen' as it were), whether it is paint, ink, chemicals, light rays or text upon a page.

First and foremost, ecologists are interested in the interrelationship between organisms and environment. Likewise, we can consider images in relation to their environments of production and reception. Of course an organism's environment also includes interaction with other organisms. Similarly, then, we can consider the interrelations of different images, image-types and image media. What we start to find are different *relations* of interactions, with a range of structures, hierarchies and/or differences on display. For ecologists there are three key 'units' of assessment: the organism, its community and the eco-system. 'No one organism lives in simple isolation, interacting, according to selfish physiological requirements . . . each organism is part of a complete *community* of creatures, each interacting with each other as well as with their abiotic environment [the wider eco-system], and each affecting each other's use of the resources that they share' (Putman and Wratten, 1984, p.43). There are differences of scale and complexity represented here. We can begin by imagining the single organism. But we know organisms always exist within a 'set of interacting organisms' (p.43), which we can broadly define as a community – though this does not mean necessarily a 'friendly' community. Animals and plants can rely on one another for habitat requirements, food and reproduction. Plants, for example, rely on insects for pollination or mammals and birds for the dispersal of seeds; yet they can also compete with one another for light and space. As we come to consider the overall, encompassing environment within which communities exist we begin to account for the full complexity of an eco-system as a 'self-contained ecological entity of both organisms and their complete biotic and abiotic environment . . . an independent self-contained and self-sufficient block' (Putman and Wratten, 1984, p.43).

Let us imagine something similar for the study of images. We can begin with the image itself, which like an organism is of course already complex, but what happens when we place it into a wider community of images? We can examine how images work with or against other images, and/or how they feed on other images. We can also consider the wider 'image-system' – all the contextual factors which allow images to exist in the first place. If we think back to the cartoon from *Roland Barthes* (Figure 2.1), we are aware that even though it is only black and white and comprised of fairly rough pen-strokes, the image is in fact highly complex. The image can be divided into different portions, though also we note the importance of repetition within the image. There are specific graphic conventions employed which we are familiar with. The use of shading underneath the caveman's unicycle (along with extraneous marks to the left of the wheel of the final image of the caveman, on the right-hand side of image) help denote movement. Yet, equally, the shading at the base of the sign-posts helps define the solid ground, in which the posts are fixed. The rectangular framing of the central portion of the image sets this image of a caveman apart from those on either side – suggesting a wholly different status in terms of representation.

However, the caveman cartoon is as much of interest for its interaction with a 'community' of images and meanings. The choice of a caveman nicely evokes ideas – images – of evolution, which then helps a play of associations with an *evolution* of semiotics (as suggested by the title, 'The History of Semiology'), and it is semiotics in particular that establishes a more complex 'community' of meanings in the cartoon. The use of text *as an image*, for the sign-post, is crucial to its humour, which you can only fully appreciate if you understand something about the meaning of the word 'sign' in the discourse of semiotics. These different elements, then, feed off one another to make the image meaningful (and in this case amusing). Crucially, the interaction of a community of images and references enables the cartoon to go beyond the basic status of its graphical, representational elements (i.e. the representation of a caveman on a unicycle).

Added to which, we can also consider the cartoon's wider image-system. What is it that allows the image to exist at all? On one level there is the concept and genre of the cartoon image, which can seem obvious enough, yet is only something we come to know and understand as we gain a certain competency with text and image. There are different kinds of cartoon drawings and used for different purposes. Where do we gain this understanding and what status is afforded a cartoon image? – it will differ according to different people, context and use. We might also examine more technical aspects, such as the significance of a signature – which in our example appears in the bottom-right of the image. Signatures represent ideas of authenticity, which we can relate to long-standing debates about the 'value' of art. The signature can be a mark of unique achievement and skill, which we attribute to an individual, but equally it can be a mark of exchangeable, repeatable economic value. Thus, whilst the 'History of Semiology' cartoon might not be of exceptional economic value, we can immediately place it within a marketplace of images. It was no doubt originally commissioned, and its ownership was transferred upon payment from that of an artist to a newspaper corporation. Today, were it to come up for auction, it would likely fetch more than other lesser-known images, and in part, this relates to its extended use. It originally appeared in the *International Herald Tribune*, in 1974, but arguably it is only because of its further circulation, in Roland Barthes' autobiography, that we still come across it and continue to value it. Newspapers are ephemeral, published one day and disappearing the next, with the exception of copies held by libraries. Today, with the Internet we archive and make accessible a great deal more than ever before. Nonetheless, in the case of newspapers, the Internet is heavily text-based. Even if it is possible to access the text of a newspaper article from the 1970s it is rare we see original print-layouts. However, if an image is repeated in a book it is likely to remain accessible for longer, though equally its status changes – it can, for example, be valued more than it was ever intended to be. In the case of the 'History of Semiology', the cartoon is immediately afforded further authority by virtue of a critic such as Barthes choosing to reproduce it; a process that further evolves – in one way or another – with its reproduction in this book.

Thus, so far, we can see in conjunction with images and an image-community there are various processes, structures and contexts that make up an 'image-system';

all of which need to be taken into account when trying to understand the nature, role and significance of any single image and the combination of images. Of course, trying to unpick the various interrelationships is no simple task and not least because we quickly recognize images and their meanings are never static. Evolution is a fundamental principle of ecology, and whilst we should not try to apply this too literally to images, it is important we consider how an ecology of images describes a dynamic set of relationships between images and the wider elements of an image-system. Darwin's concept of a 'polity of nature' or dynamic equilibrium marks a fundamental shift in the study of natural history away from a static or mechanistic understanding towards a relational, evolutionary one. Darwin was 'the first to stress forcefully that animals and plants were not perfectly adapted to their natural environments . . . When conditions changed, so the adaptive needs also changed' (Benson, 2000, p.60). It would be misleading to think about images in terms of the 'survival of the fittest'. However, there are narratives we tell about certain images or image-types which gain prominence. Some images gain greater popularity and interest than others. Some are important because they are unique, others because they are widely reproduced. Art images, for example, as unique items, tend to be highly valued and have whole discourses build around them. Yet, art images are not the most common images we come into contact with. In any given day we are far more likely to look at an instructional image (e.g. on the back of food packaging, or an emergency sign on a train) than we are to see a work of art. Yet, we tend to know a lot more about art images, how they were made, what they represent, their market value, even their attribution to a school of thinking.

Thus, in addition to understanding the complex make-up of images, their communities and the broad environment, or image-system, we can consider various attributes of their dissemination. We can borrow a set of keywords from ecology, to include: distribution, abundance, energy, adaptation and succession. Some of these words relate in quite straightforward ways to images. We can ask easily enough where and by whom images are distributed and in what kind of abundance. As mentioned, art images tend to be restricted in how they are distributed and in what quantities. It is rare now for an artwork *not* to be reproduced in some way (you can search on the Internet for almost all major artworks), but nonetheless, there remains a high degree of importance around an original artwork or set of prints. By contrast, marketing images are intended for wide distribution. The Coca-Cola logo, which essentially carries very little meaning in itself, gains its significance and prominence due to its multiplicity.

However, what about the words 'energy', 'adaptation' and 'succession'? In ecology, the sun is the ultimate source of energy and, in line with the principle that energy can neither be created nor destroyed, only transferred, ecologists are particularly interested in the rates and efficiency of energy conversion from one chain in the eco-system to another. The point of an 'ecology of images' is rather different, since, as Sontag points out, images 'are an unlimited resource, one that cannot be exhausted by consumerist waste'. Nonetheless, images can still be thought of in terms of energy and conversions, if only to ask what it is that leads to the

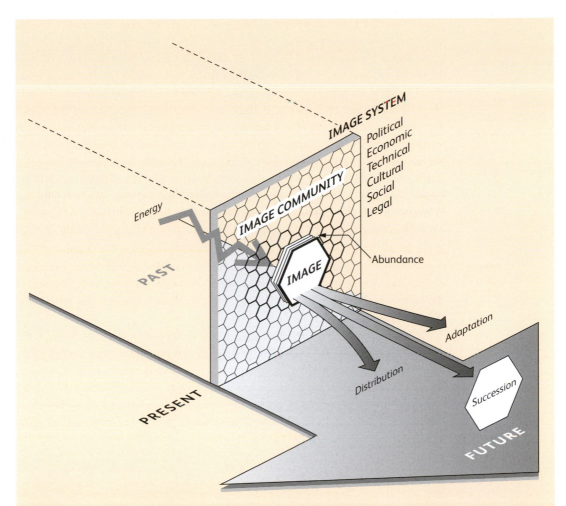

FIGURE 2.2 'An Ecology of Images'. This diagram summarizes the ideas behind an 'ecology of images'. Crucially, an image always exists in a set of contexts. An image is always part of an 'image community', which it works with or against. It is portrayed here with a honeycomb effect around the central image. Image community can be thought of as a genre and/or a modality of images. As such, there are formal, aesthetic properties and particular content and uses an image might share with other images, or indeed with which it is attempting to work against or appropriate. In addition, the image and its community will always be framed and mediated in specific ways. The square frame in the diagram denotes the presence of an 'image-system' which can range across and interconnect with political, economic, technical, cultural, social, and legal discourses and systems. In addition, language and the body provide ways in which we frame, communicate and comprehend the image (see final section of this chapter, 'A family of images'). Another crucial framing of the image is history. Past, present and future are plotted on the diagram to clearly evoke a sense of process and evolution of the image. The image itself will be formed of certain 'energies' or precedents and prior insights, which relate to the fact that an image-community and image systems are all historically determined. An image may well be found in great 'abundance' (as labelled on the diagram). A billboard image, for example, will clearly be in greater abundance than a child's drawing made at home one afternoon. Of course there are various potential futures of the image. The aforementioned child's drawing might end up the winning entry of a competition. As such it would likely receive greater distribution (through various means), leading to relative abundance. It may be re-worked for a final product, which we could understand as the succession of the image. Images can also be adapted. A good example of this would be how cartoonists appropriate images and manipulate them for satirical effect.

creation and longevity of an image. Images do not simply appear out of nowhere, they have gestation and context. In some cases, as with scientific imaging, we might argue abstract processes and technological developments lie at the heart of their creation (see Chapter 7). Whereas with graphics and consumer advertising many visual cultural influences (typically from the worlds of art and fashion) inform adopted styles and codes, even if these are not always apparent to the casual onlooker. Importantly, there is a history of all images, which we can examine in terms of their original sources, ongoing consumption, and associated adaptations. We can ask why an image comes into common currency: Is its consumption specific to a narrow band of 'consumers' or users (e.g. scientists, art historians), or is the image ubiquitous and widely adopted? If so, how? – through its repetition perhaps, or maybe due to adaptations? Cartoons are a good example of how images can be adapted and manipulated, lending them new currency. In some cases this can lead to the succession of an image, i.e. an image that takes prominence over another. This is particularly evident, for example, with the work of Public Relations companies which 'manage' the image of political leaders and celebrities, typically at times of difficulty when their image is perceived to be tarnished, perhaps due to specific events and associations.

Despite having traced the idea of an 'ecology of images' by looking closely at the study of ecology itself, it is important to stress the exercise is certainly *not* to impose scientific terms and concepts. The intention is purely to step back from the image, to think about its greater complexity and variety. The aim is to slow ourselves down before the image, to appreciate complexity; to seek to understand image histories, connections, cultures, and adaptations, as well as to ponder the future of any given image.

TASK

An Ecology of Images

In order to examine the different levels and layers to the production, meaning and consumption of an image consider the following:

(1) What are the dynamics and interrelationships between *image, image-community* and *image-system*?

(2) How would you describe an image in terms of its *distribution, abundance, energy, adaptation* and *succession*?

Re-read the preceding sections of this chapter to remind yourself of the key ideas. Having done so, use the above two questions to frame the analysis of one of the following images:

(a)   News media image (e.g. The Fall of the Berlin Wall)
(b)   Medical image (e.g. x-ray)
(c)   Art image (e.g. Van Gogh's 'Sunflowers')
(d)   Literary image (e.g. Alice in Wonderland)
(e)   Information image (e.g. The London Underground Map)

To complete the task: Take a large piece of paper and create a montage of visual elements to illustrate the image-community and image-system(s) you associate with the selected image. Alternatively, you can work digitally, cutting and pasting elements into a single document. The point of the exercise is not to create a neat diagram of relationships, but rather to open up as many different possible connections as you can reasonably consider. As you work, annotate your selections with notes about the different levels of interrelationships between *image, image-community* and *image-system*, as well as the various attributions of *distribution, abundance, energy, adaptation* and *succession*.

When you have completed the exercise, ask yourself the following questions:

■   How did you begin the process?
■   What were the most obvious associations?
■   Did you gain further ideas as you went along; if so, what prompted these ideas?
■   What did you find difficult about the process and how might you overcome these problems?
■   What further tools, information or understanding do you feel you need?

Attempts to construct an 'ecology of images' will likely lead in many different directions. Students who have completed the task found that they quickly began a process of brainstorming, leading to a range of associations. In addition, when proceeding to locate images they also soon discovered more images and connections than they had initially considered. It is very easy, for example, to type keyword entries into Internet search engines and to specifically designate a search for image media. Despite searching for a specific image or image-type, results typically reveal far more than you originally imagine. However, the Internet can be limited in how you explore images. We learn about images from other people, from visiting galleries, watching and listening to a range of media, consulting books and by looking around us all the time. It is important, then, to follow-up on a wide range of ideas, experiences and sources. This, for example, is how one student described the process of exploring x-rays:

'. . . I got more ideas as I went along, for example because the x-ray is a wave, I thought it would be relevant to include a table of all waves, such as Radio Waves and Gamma Rays and also to picture the person who discovered x-rays.

FIGURE 2.3

An Ecology of Images: X-ray. Courtesy of Alex Greenshaw and Laura Thompson.

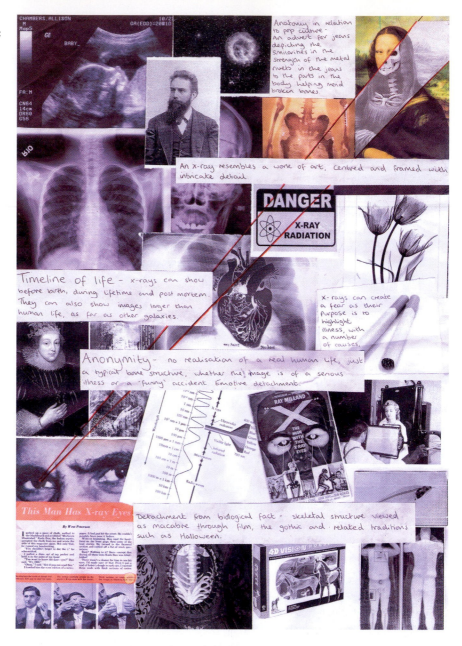

I also remembered how the news reported complaints about new x-ray scanners in airports and of an article I read about the discovery of a hidden painting that was painted over by the artist. Another thing I also decided to include was a gorgeous steam punk corset with an x-ray 'window' showing what your ribs might look like if you wear it too much. I thought it relevant, because it shows how something like a lung scan can be used in fashion. The Glass Catfish also reminds me of an x-ray because it is transparent; you can see its bones

. . . I also thought it relevant to include an image of cigarettes, because they can destroy your lungs if you smoke too much.'

(Alex Greenshaw, Media Graduate)

What is evident from this account is the wide range of sources and associations with a diverse set of image-types, all of which arise from a fairly idiosyncratic process. Looking at the montage produced (Figure 2.3), we find the x-ray located in a complex image-system. All sorts of images jostle with one another, suggesting perhaps specific image-communities; some of which overlap, some remain more hermetic. For example, we can see art images, popular culture references, science images and informational graphics. The design of the piece is also interesting, with graphical and text annotations which begin the process of delineating differences and connections. The next step – which might be undertaken in writing an essay, or completing a practical, creative assignment – would be to consider more carefully how the descriptors 'distribution', 'abundance', 'energy', 'adaptation' and 'succession' can help in thinking about the life-world of these images; how, for example, they come to exist, or are manipulated and positioned within an image-community and wider image-system. For those interested in looking at x-rays, one useful reference (which was given to students who produced this example) is an entry by James Elkins in his book *How to Use Your Eyes* (2000, pp. 34–47).

A very different example can be shown with a response to the image of the London Underground map. Two students working collaboratively produced a more linear account, picking out three thematic strands (Figure 2.4). The left-hand column of their work illustrates the specific historical event of the 7/7 bombing of the London Underground. The images chosen go beyond the transport system itself, with an editorial developing through the inclusion of an image of the American and British political leaders at the time and the iconic pulling down of a statue of Saddam Hussein in Firdos Square, Baghdad. The central column relates to the reform of the alcohol laws in the UK, which included a ban on the London Underground. A 'map' of cocktails is included with images relating to a final night of drinking on the Underground. In the right-hand column the iconic status of the Underground map is itself explored. Again, as an ecology of images, this example shows how a single image, in this case the map of the London Underground, can easily give rise to a range of images and sets of images. In this case, photojournalism and graphic design form two distinct image-communities, but which can be drawn into a wider image-system through their combination. The diagrammatic map of the London Underground dates back to an initial design by employee Harry Beck in 1931. It has since undergone various alterations, the history of which is fascinating with regards to ideas about adaptation and succession. However, of greater interest is the wider, iconic appeal of the map. There are plenty of diagrammatic maps of transportation systems from around the world, and yet the London Underground is arguably the most recognizable. It has transferred widely across different domains, coming to exist in great 'abundance', often through its parody and pastiche. Of the photojournalistic images shown, these again have been widely distributed, though generally

FIGURE 2.4

An Ecology of Images: London Underground Map. Courtesy of Simon Crowley and Matthew Selway.

This collection of images represents the immediate associations we made after initially seeing the image of the London tube map.

The first thread of image schema which we considered was to relate the initial image to a historical discourse, beginning with an event synonymous with the tube, the attacks of 7/7, we then sourced images which bore relation to the theme of the "war on terror".

Our second thought process related to the reform of drinking culture, of which the tube was an iconic institution, as a result of pub and club goers favouring the underground as a means of night time travel. When drinking on the tube became illegal, the pub and club goers threw an alcohol fuelled final farewell to one of London's favoured drinking venues.

This image showcases the way in which the iconography of the tube map not only can be related to drinking culture; but also has an impact on wider popular culture.

Here we can see examples of the way in which the imagery itself of the tube map becomes detached from its practical purpose and meaning, and becomes instead entrenched and assimilated into popular culture, which embraces the tube map only as a cultural icon and ubiquitous image, with little or no trace of the tube map's intended functionality.

Within this image we can see that the schema of navigation intended in the tube map has been applied to the vital organs of the body. Its displacing the initial schema into a new context.

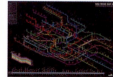

This final image maps out internet trends and popular websites, by implementing the tube map style and template. This exemplifies the way in which the tube map not only has a place in popular art, but also can still utilize the practical nature of the image's initial purpose.

without being adapted. Images such at the toppling of the statue of Saddam Hussein are particularly pertinent with regards to ideas about succession. Not only is it an image literally of succession, but equally *as an image* it can be said to have 'toppled' many other documentary images being gathered at the time, so becoming the more prominently reported image. By contrast, the images selected in the central column regarding the change in alcohol laws in the UK, whilst publicly disseminated at a specific point in time (and evidently still accessible via the Internet), are less well known. In terms of the various descriptors, of distribution, abundance, and adaptation, etc., they are of more limited scope and so can be understood to have been associated with the Underground map through a more specific connection, though this is not to lessen their value – they clearly demonstrate the richness of images and their interconnectivity.

If one were to consider the other suggested examples, whether the news media images of the fall of the Berlin Wall, Van Gogh's *Sunflowers*, or Alice in Wonderland, again, a whole swathe of connections and possibilities arise. Searching for Van Gogh's *Sunflowers*, for example, quickly reveals some thirteen different versions of this well known artwork; as well as the fact that for the Dutch sunflowers are a symbol of devotion and loyalty; and that Paul Gauguin painted a portrait of Van Gogh painting a picture of sunflowers. There is also a whole industry of souvenirs using the *Sunflowers* as a motif (Bohm-Duchen, 2001, pp.122–147). Similarly, consideration of the literary image of Alice in Wonderland will soon yield a wide range of associations and echoes. In visual terms, Lewis Carroll's own original drawings (held at the British Library) can be taken as the source 'energy' from which they spring, and which are then more famously adapted (through close correspondence with the author) by the illustrator John Tenniel (though of course we could equally explore from 'where' Carroll originally formed his ideas). Again, there is a whole 'industry' of images that stem from the initial literary text, which include numerous films, theatre productions, picture books and even sculptures. (We will return to *Alice* in Supplement III to consider specific relationships between word and image.)

Images of the fall of the Berlin Wall are seemingly very different to that of a painting or a literary source, and yet, as the book *Image Critique and the Fall of the Berlin Wall* (Manghani, 2008) demonstrates, there is a vast reservoir of associated images of all types; from cartoons to literature, from news footage to high art photography. This book-length study engages with a complex image-system as a way to consider how images themselves can be used to offer critical understanding of a political, news-media event. Similar studies could be made for a wider set of political, news media images. Hariman and Lucaites' *No Caption Needed* (2007) is a useful reference point. It looks at iconic photographs, such as those relating to the Great Depression, the Vietnam War, Iwo Jima and Tiananmen Square, revealing how key events circulate through public culture as images with various meanings and adaptations. Another good example is W. J. T. Mitchell's *Cloning Terror* (2011), which looks at specific images and the technologies of image-making in relation to the 'War on Terror'.

In order to write critically about images, or indeed to produce a creative image-based work, a full ecology of an image will need to be reigned in to some degree. However, students having completed the task have generally felt more confident to go on to create a more narrowly focused piece of work, finding they have more to say. It is typical in art-based studies, having been asked to write a critique of a painting, to find responses that over-emphasize the biography of the artist. This kind of information is extremely easy to obtain, but mostly takes us away from actually looking at the visual work. By contrast, locating a painting in a wider ecology of images is a deliberate attempt to make the image itself the focal point of an investigation. The point of the exercise – at least in the first instance – is not to cohere a single reading of the image, but to open up as many possibilities as one can, not all of which will interrelate. Following this, it is then possible to make choices about which elements to focus on to develop more detailed consideration of the values, associations and 'systems' of meaning we attribute to images.

A family of images

Barthes' staged 'image-system' and an 'ecology of images' are really only metaphors, or indeed pictures themselves, suggestive of how image studies can understand images in their variety, as complex and changing forms. They help us begin the process of placing the image at the centre of attention as we try to engage more carefully and critically, whether we are thinking or writing about images, or indeed making them. Nonetheless, adopting Mitchell's line of reasoning from his book *Iconology* (1987), we can identify two specific problems. Firstly, there is the wide variety of things we call images. 'We speak of pictures, statues, optical illusions, maps, diagrams, dreams, hallucinations, spectacles, projections, poems, patterns, memories, and even ideas as images' (p.9). All of these things, and more, can find their way into an ecology of images. How are we supposed to make sense of these differences? Does it even make sense to try? Mitchell goes on to say, 'the sheer diversity of this list would seem to make any systematic, unified understanding impossible' (p.9). The second, related problem is that 'the calling of all these things by the name of "image" does not necessarily mean that they all have something in common'. Mitchell suggests we can think of images as a 'far-flung family', which eschews a single, universal definition, and instead places *differences* between images at the very heart of one's analysis. He presents the following 'family tree' of images:

FIGURE 2.5

'The Family of Images', diagram from W.J.T. Mitchell's *Iconology: Image, Text, Ideology* (1987, p.10). Courtesy of the University of Chicago Press.

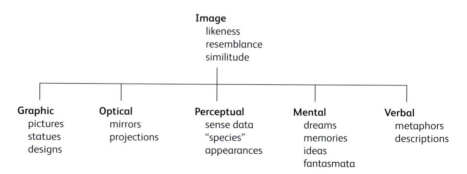

Each branch of the family tree identifies different types of imagery as defined by specific intellectual disciplines. Mitchell explains as follows:

'. . . mental imagery belongs to psychology and epistemology; optical imagery to physics; graphic, sculptural, and architectural imagery to the art historian;

verbal imagery to the literary critic; perceptual images occupy a kind of border region where physiologists, neurologists, psychologists, art historians, and students of optics find themselves collaborating with philosophers and literary critics. This is the region occupied by a number of strange creatures that haunt the border between physical and psychological accounts of imagery [. . . including] those "appearances" which (in common parlance) intrude between ourselves and reality, and which we so often refer to as "images" – from the image projected by a skilled actor, to those created for products and personages by experts in advertising and propaganda.'

(Mitchell, 1987, p.10)

All too often, a discipline will define and problematize the image in its own terms, without looking across to other disciplines and domains. Accounts of one type of image 'tend to relegate the others to the status of an unexamined "background" to the main subject' (Mitchell, 1987, pp.11–12). So, for example, whilst there is much interest in the intersection of art and science, not least with digital imaging now commonly applied in the experimental gathering and/or presentation of scientific data, there remains a great deal of mismatch in how these domains relate to and describe the image (see Chapter 7).

Interestingly, Mitchell's diagram does appear to have a root meaning of the image, identified as 'likeness', 'resemblance' and 'similitude'. In Chapter 3 we will explore what is meant by this, but essentially, rather than stabilize any definition of the image, Mitchell illustrates how a tension, particularly between text and image, underlines how we think and work with images. An initial response to Mitchell's diagram frequently leads to judgements over those members of the family of images we consider to be images in a literal sense, and those we feel suggest a more ambiguous, or even 'improper' definition of the image. In the following extract Mitchell explains the tendency to divide up commonplace definitions of the image between 'proper' images and their more 'suspect' counterparts. Nevertheless, he then goes on to show how this is a false contrast and reveals the image to be more complex, with both physical, material images and mental, intangible images bearing the same experience of being both 'there' and 'not there' at the same time.

THE FAMILY OF IMAGES

W.J.T. MITCHELL

(from *Iconology*, 1987, pp.12–17)

It is hard to resist the conclusion that the image 'proper' is the sort of thing we found on the left side of our tree-diagram, the graphic or optical representations we see displayed in an objective, publicly shareable space. We might want to argue about the status of certain special cases and ask whether abstract, nonrepresentational paintings, ornamental or structural designs, diagrams and graphs are properly understood as images. But whatever borderline cases we might wish to consider, it seems fair to say that we have a rough idea about what images are in the literal sense of the word, and along with this rough idea goes a sense that other uses of the word are figurative and improper.

The mental and verbal images on the right side of our diagram, for instance, would seem to be images only in some doubtful, metaphoric sense. People may report experiencing images in their heads while reading or dreaming, but we have only their word for this; there is no way (so the argument goes) to check up on this objectively. Even if we trust the reports of mental imagery, it seems clear that they must be different from real, material pictures. Mental images don't seem to be stable and permanent the way real images are, and they vary from one person to the next: if I say 'green', some listeners may see green in their mind's eye, but some may see a word, or nothing at all. Mental images don't seem to be exclusively visual the way real pictures are; they involve all the senses. Verbal imagery, moreover, can involve all the senses, or it may involve no sensory component at all, sometimes suggesting nothing more than a recurrent abstract idea like justice or grace or evil. [. . .]

[. . .] I will argue that all three of these commonplace contrasts between images 'proper' and their illegitimate offspring are suspect. That is, I hope to show that, contrary to common belief, images 'proper' are not stable, static, or

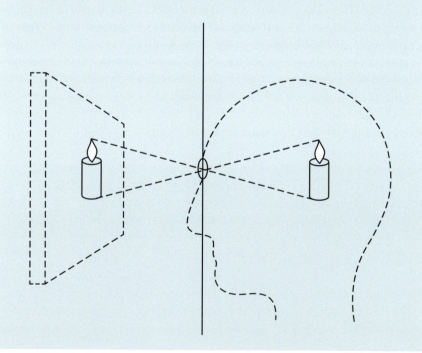

FIGURE 2.6
'Mental Images', diagram from W.J.T. Mitchell's *Iconology: Image, Text, Ideology* (1987, p.16). Courtesy of the University of Chicago Press.

permanent in any metaphysical sense; they are not perceived in the same way by viewers any more than are dream images; and they are not exclusively visual in any important way, but involve multisensory apprehension and interpretation.

[. . . One strategy is to examine how we put] images 'into our heads' in the first place by trying to picture the sort of world in which this move would make sense. I offer the figure [Figure 2.6] as just such a picture.

The figure should be read as a palimpsest displaying three overlapping relationships: (1) between a real object (the candle on the left) and a reflected, projected, or depicted image of that object; (2) between a real object and a mental image in a mind conceived (as in Aristotle, Hobbes, Locke, or Hume) as a mirror, *camera obscura*, or a surface for drawing or printing; (3) between a material image and a mental one.

[. . .]

If the half of the sketch here represented as 'mind' . . . were to be annihilated, the physical world, we tend to assume, would continue to exist quite nicely. But the reverse would not be the case: if the world were annihilated, consciousness would not go on (this, by the way, is what is misleading about the symmetry of the model). When we take the model, however, as an account of the way we talk about imagery, then the symmetry is not so misleading. If there were no more minds, there would be no more images, mental or material. The world may not depend upon consciousness, but images in (not to mention *of*) the world clearly do. This is not just because it takes human hands to make a picture or a mirror or any other kind of simulacrum (animals are capable of presenting images in some sense when they camouflage themselves or imitate one another). It is because an image cannot be seen as such without a paradoxical trick of consciousness, an ability to see something as 'there' and 'not there' at the same time. When a duck responds to a decoy, or when the birds peck at the grapes in the legendary paintings of Zeuxis, they are not seeing images: they are seeing other ducks, or real grapes – the things themselves, and not images of the things [see Figure 2.7].

But if the key to the recognition of real, material images in the world is our curious ability to say 'there' and 'not there' at the same time, we must then ask why mental images should be seen as any more – or less – mysterious than 'real' images. The problem philosophers and ordinary people have always had with the notion of mental images is that they seem to have a universal basis in real, shared experience (we all dream, visualize, and are capable, in varying degrees, of re-presenting concrete sensations to ourselves), but we cannot point to them and say 'There – that is a mental image.' Exactly the same sort of problem occurs, however, if I try to point to a real image and explain what it is to someone who doesn't already know what an image is. I point at Xeuxis' painting and say 'There, that is an image.' The reply is, 'Do you mean that coloured surface?' Or 'Do you mean those grapes?'

FIGURE 2.7 Edward C. Leavitt, *Still Life of Grapes* (1870). Courtesy of Post Road Gallery, Larchmont NY. Photo: David Bahssin. This nineteenth century painting is a wonderful example of *trompe l'oeil*. In his day, Leavitt was said to be one of the most renowned still life painters, though is now largely forgotten. His rendering of a bunch of grapes can be associated with an alleged contest in Greece, in the fifth century BC, between the painter Zeuxis and his contemporary Parrhasius. Zeuxis presented a painting of grapes that appeared so real and succulent that birds flew down to peck at them. Zeuxis then asked Parrhasius to unveil his painting from behind its curtain, only for Parrhasius to reveal the curtain itself was the painting. Subsequently Zeuxis was forced to concede defeat.

The image is both material and mental. This is true, for example, with the diagram shown in Figure 2.6. Mitchell notes how it is difficult to say whether or not we could mentally see the diagram before it is on the page; whether or not a mental picture enables the diagram to be drawn in the first place. Alternatively, Mitchell suggests, it is only through discussion and consideration of the terms such as 'boundary' that helps fashion the image. The argument, then, is that we 'cannot regard the diagram as something mental in the sense of "private" or "subjective"; it is rather something that surfaced in language, and not just my language, but a way of speaking that we inherit from a long tradition of talking about minds and pictures. Our diagram might just as well be called a "verbal image" as a mental one' (Mitchell, 1987, p.19).

The explanation of images being something we see as both 'there' and 'not there' at the same time, echoes the way we looked at the cartoon 'The History of Semiology' earlier in this chapter, and also relates to how different associations come to mind for an ecology of images. In the case of Figure 2.6, we could say we see a candle, though more accurately we might say it is a *picture* of a candle – however this requires we pay specific attention to the way it is drawn and the fact that it exists on paper, etc. When we look at pictures that accompany a narrative, and we are engulfed by the story, we are less likely to comment on how the picture is drawn or what colours and textures are adopted. Instead we accept – and enjoy – the image for what it is and as a way of viewing the story. There is an 'equation' of sorts here between the image itself, the manner in which is it made and transmitted (its medium) as well as the manner in which the viewer approaches or responds to the image, which in a sense is a bodily experience. So, for example, when we look at an image and see a 'coloured surface' we are responding (physically and cognitively) in a different way than if we see in the image a bunch of grapes.

The art historian Hans Belting echoes Mitchell's argument by pointing out: 'Images are neither on the wall (or on the screen) nor in the head alone. They do not *exist* by themselves, but they *happen*; they *take place* whether they are moving images . . . or not. They happen via transmission and perception' (Belting, 2005, pp.302–303). He adopts the terms 'medium' and 'body' to refer explicitly to the movement and plurality of the image. Thus, he explains:

> 'Images have always relied on a given technique for their visualization. When we distinguish a canvas from the image it represents, we pay attention to either the one or the other, as if they were distinct, which they are not; they separate only when we are willing to separate them in our looking. [. . .] We even remember images from the specific mediality in which we first encountered them, and remembering means first disembodying them from their original media and then reembodying them in our brain.'
>
> (Belting, 2005, pp.304–305)

Belting's use of the term 'medium' – or mediality – goes beyond the traditional distinction of form and matter (or content). We describe Leonardo da Vinci's *Mona Lisa* (c. 1503–1519) in terms of *form* as painted with oils on poplar, whilst its subject *matter* is a seated woman (with an enigmatic facial expression!). However, as Belting suggests, we can remember the image of the *Mona Lisa* without needing to refer to the original painting, indeed many people know of this image without ever having seen the actual painting, not least since it appears through all kinds of remediation and modifications (see Chapter 6). As Belting puts it: 'Visual media compete . . .

with the images they transmit. . . . The more we pay attention to a medium, the less it can hide its strategies. The less we take note of a visual medium, the more we concentrate on the image, as if images would come by themselves' (2005, p. 305). It is this competition, or oscillation between image and medium that is a key site (or sight) of enquiry for image studies.

However, in order to understand the relationship between image and media, it is also important we acknowledge the role of the body: 'It is our own bodily experience that allows us to identify the dualism inherent in visual media. We know that we all *have* or that we all *own* images, that they live *in* our bodies or in our dreams and wait to be summoned *by* our bodies to show up' (Belting, 2005, pp. 305–306). Belting describes our bodies as 'living mediums', through which we '*perceive, project,* or *remember* images and that also enables our imagination to censor or to transform them' (p. 306). Perhaps we can more readily relate to the idea of the body being a medium for spoken language, since the voice is a biological, acoustic phenomenon. Yet, the mediality of images goes beyond the visual realm. Language itself, for example, can serve as a medium for images, though equally this is a bodily experience. The idea of our body as 'living medium', which Belting traces back to Plato's distinction between speaking bodies and written language, raises important questions about the image, including its relationship to language (see Chapter 3), as well as the distinction between *sight* as a biological precept and *looking* as based upon a cultural history (see Chapters 6 and 7).

Summary

In this chapter we have come to understand the image from a variety of viewpoints, each seemingly constructing a system or categorization of the image. Yet, equally, with each attempt we find the image is not easily defined as any one singular thing. If we take the analogy of a camera lens moving out from a close-up to a wide-angle, even panoramic view, the chapter has effectively started with a single image and gradually opened up to reveal a wider set of contexts and connections. We began with the cartoon image of 'The History of Semiology'. Whilst on first glance it appears a fairly straightforward image, made up of simple graphical marks depicting an easily 'readable' scene, we find it opens out to different meanings depending on how we look at the relationship of elements, and from what associations we draw upon or feel it gives rise to. Any one single image does in fact exist in a wider 'ecology', which refers to the composition of different elements within an image, a wider set of associated images, and then the broader context within which images are made, transmitted and consumed. The additional lens of a 'family of images' helps to relate different image-types to different disciplines and discourses, which can lead us to think about different methods and motivations for making and using images. It also reveals why one account of an image need not necessarily relate to another, which can lead to confusions and disagreements, or just different interests.

We need to consider how as a viewer we come to look and take 'possession' of an image, which as Hans Belting argues relates to questions of image and media (including ourselves as 'living mediums'). The **mediality** of the image is, then, a vital component of study. In addition to opening up the contexts of any given image we can also circle back to body, to the viewing subject as the site upon which images are made and performed (see Chapter 6). The philosophical and conceptual ideas raised in this chapter continue to be developed in Chapter 3, with a particular focus on the relationship between text and image, which we will find relates to questions of interpretation, power and the status of visual knowledge. Part 2 of the book then looks in turn at various image-types, practices and cultures, with the view to further understand and elaborate upon the complexity of an ecology of images.

Further reading

Aumont, Jacques (1997) *The Image*, trans. by Claire Pajackowska. London: British Film Institute.

Belting, Hans (2005) 'Image, Medium, Body: A New Approach to Iconology'. *Critical Inquiry*, Vol. 31, pp.302–319.

Elkins, James (1999) *The Domain of Images*. Ithaca: Cornell University Press.

Elkins, James (ed.) (2007) *Visual Practices Across the University*. München: Wilhelm Fink Verlag.

Elkins, James and Naef, Maja (ed.) (2011) *What is an Image?* University Park, Pa.: Pennsylvania State University Press.

Manghani, Sunil, Piper, Arthur and Simons, Jon (eds) (2006) *Images: A Reader*. London: Sage.

Messaris, Paul (1994) *Visual Literacy: Image, Mind, and Reality*. Colorado: Westview.

Mitchell, W.J.T. (1987) *Iconology: Image, Text, Ideology*. Chicago: University of Chicago Press.

Mitchell, W.J.T. (1994) *Picture Theory: Essays on Verbal and Visual Representation*. Chicago: University of Chicago Press.

Mitchell, W.J.T. (2005) *What Do Pictures Want? The Lives and Loves of Images*. Chicago: University of Chicago Press.

Sontag, Susan (1979) *On Photography*. London: Penguin Books.

Stafford, Barbara Maria (1996) *Good Looking: Essays on the Virtue of Images*. Cambridge, Mass.: MIT Press.

IMAGE RESEARCH

The image researcher can be one of two things. Most commonly they will be some-one interested in examining and commenting on a specific image, or collection of images. In which case, a primary concern is how to locate images, as well as handling copyright permissions for reproduction. However, they may also be someone who uses and/or creates images as part of the process of research. The notes provided here are in the main concerned with the image researcher in the first sense, but a final section offers some brief remarks on image methodologies.

The search for images

The search for images can be somewhat circuitous, as images are not as easily classified and catalogued as text-based materials. As curator Christine Sundt (2002, p.67) explains, the image seeker will typically begin 'by browsing through books and magazines, using resources within reach with or without a specific image in mind'; and where this process proves limited, investigation is widened by referring to catalogues and published indexes, which more often than not requires the help of a skilled reference professional. Around the world there are many established picture libraries and image collections. Some collections are commercial, selling images or at least the rights to images. In other cases, collections can operate like museums or libraries with the aim to provide people with access to an array of pictures and information. Whilst the more commercial collections are well-organized, efficient businesses, picture libraries are often highly idiosyncratic in nature. Stephen Poliakoff's television film *Shooting The Past* (1999) offers an evocative and dramatic portrayal of an archetypal picture library threatened with closure. Eccentric staff of the library set about to reveal the inner secrets and stories held within the vast collection of photographs. The idiosyncratic process of accessing images is due in part to the fact that archival systems have often been 'conceived and constructed by whoever was in charge of the materials', and because 'classification systems for pictures were, and for the most part are still, lacking uniformity and conformity to any standard' (Sundt, 2002, p.67). It is frequently the case that any successful outcome has been due to 'the help of a resourceful information professional gifted with a photographic memory, homegrown finding aids, and a share of good luck' (p.67).

Today, picture libraries of a new kind have developed online. The social media site Flickr is probably the best known, with a reported 60+ million contributors and over ten million community groups. Arguably, we have yet to fully understand

FIGURE 2.8a and 2.8b The front and reverse respectively of a photograph of Yves St Laurent from the *Daily Herald*. Courtesy of the Science & Society Picture Library. Access to an image collection – such as a photography library – provides the unique experience of physically handling pictures. Typically we are interested in any given picture for what it shows, but image collections help remind us that pictures are also artefacts. Very often the physical condition of a picture can tell its own story, as too can the reverse of a picture. The back of a photograph, as seen here for example, can reveal all sorts of information that we would not get from the picture itself. Text and dates can be scribbled or typed on the back, and various signs of ownership and exchange can be revealed by stamp-markings and labels; as well as in this case signs of physical manipulation.

the true importance and inheritance of a 'collection' such as this – but clearly, our appetite to amass and organize pictures goes unabated. Nevertheless, whilst the Internet now provides unprecedented access to images, it remains difficult to locate and access images with accuracy. While the end-user can locate a wealth of images by freely entering keywords into a search engine, the images retrieved are dependent on the manner in which they have been 'catalogued' – and in a great many cases images on the Web have *not* been consciously indexed. In fact, images found on the Internet are often devoid of proper contextual information, even basic information such as author, title and date.

An example of the difficulty in locating images can be made with reference to Princess Diana, one of the most photographed persons of all time. The sheer number of pictures available means that it is by no means difficult to find her image on the Internet, even today long after her death. However, attempts to trace a specific image can prove difficult. One image of Princess Diana, seen here as part of a newspaper article (Figure 2.9), was used by a teacher for a classroom exercise. In the first

FIGURE 2.9

Guardian, Saturday 11 July 2009, pp.26–27. Text: 'Confessions of a tabloid hack', Wensley Clarkson. © Guardian News & Media Ltd, 2009. Photograph: Brendan Beirne.

instance it was found on the Internet and copied into a Word document. The teaching materials were later handed over to another teacher who made them accessible to students as an electronic resource. In this case it was possible to use the same digital file. However, there was then the idea to make the materials available as an 'open resource', to be accessible to anyone on the Internet. In order to achieve this it would be necessary to gain permission to use the image from the copyright holder. This proved extremely difficult. How can the image, which was originally obtained from the Internet with no contextual information, be traced to its creator or owner? Entering all sorts of keywords into Internet search engines returned many hundreds of results of images of Princess Diana, but never this specific image. It would have been possible to use many alternatives, yet none showed her being photographed – which in the context of the teaching materials was a significant reason for its initial selection. It seemed as if it would not be possible to trace the copyright holder of the image until quite by chance the teacher came across the exact photograph reprinted in *The Guardian* newspaper (Figure 2.9), many years after it was originally taken. This was a significant find, since newspapers always include an attribution to an image. In this case, at the end of the caption underneath the pictures it reads: 'photograph: Brendan Beirne'. Of course, it was still then necessary to research into the name and/or to contact the newspaper for further details. Finding the name is really only the start of a long process.

The version included here, from *The Guardian*, was scanned at high-resolution from the original newspaper. It required permission from both the attributed photographer and from *The Guardian*, since it is depicted here as laid-out in the newspaper. See below for more about copyright and permissions (see also Supplement III, Writing with Images, for more on quality and resolution). The example highlights a number of common factors, not least how serendipity plays a big part in image searches and also that the handling of images largely remains the preserve of professionals (in this case those working at *The Guardian* newspaper). Searching for images requires tenacity and a willingness to look across different media.

Searching by keywords

When trying to locate images through databases and the Internet it is useful to enter a range of keywords and it helps to think about specifying *layers* of information. It is important to recognize how text entries create hierarchies of information and that some methods work better than others. Consider the following example, given by the curator Christine Sundt:

IMAGE SEARCH

CHRISTINE SUNDT

FIGURE 2.10 Vincent van Gogh (1853–1890), *De Aardappeleters* [The Potato Eaters] (1885), Van Gogh Museum, Amsterdam.

- 'I'm looking for a picture of a group'
- 'I'd like it to be a family group'
- 'This family should be doing something that would be typical for a family, like sitting around a table with food in front of them, looking grateful for what they have to eat'

The hierarchy in this query demonstrates a thought process that proceeds from a general concept – the group – to the specific concept – a family sharing a meal together. One example of such a family group might be Vincent van Gogh's *The Potato Eaters* (1885), in which a peasant family from the Dutch town of Nuenen, wearing traditional costumes of the time and place, are seated around a table. The room in which they have gathered is dimly lit, illuminated only by the solitary lamp above them. Their humble meal consists of potatoes.

Keywords can help users formulate queries like those listed above for submission to an online search engine, but their effectiveness varies widely. The particular searcher's cultural background, education, and even verbal skills condition the choice of keywords used in an online search, not to mention his or her own native language. Most objects and concepts can be described using multiple terms or phrases in many languages or dialects. If an end-user happens to use a keyword different from the one in the information system being searched, he or she may miss items that are actually there.

(Sundt, 2002, pp.69–70)

It is evident in this example how the rich description of Vincent van Gogh's painting is unlikely to be captured by the kinds of keywords typically entered into a search engine or database. Also, the user needs to consider how they wish something to be represented. They may not want an art image for instance, or they may require an image of a particular period or region. All of these aspects need to be taken into consideration when making a search.

Searching by image

Despite huge advances in image recognition techniques and software, it remains the case that image search engines and databases are largely text-driven. In the future, however, it is likely *image-based* search engines will become more commonly available. The Google search engine, which has long provided a filter to search purely for images based on a text entry search, now also enables you to search *by image* itself – either by uploading a digital image file or by providing a URL for an image. Similarly, TinEye is an online search engine dedicated to searching the Web by image. The site describes itself as: 'a reverse image search engine. It finds out where an image came from, how it is being used, if modified versions of the image exist, or if there is a higher resolution version'. The user uploads an existing image or provides an address to an image online. The system then searches across the Internet for similar images. In doing so, it uses 'image identification technology rather than key-words, metadata or watermarks'. TinEye works by actively searching the Web for new images. It also accepts contributions of complete online image collections. The underlying principle is that the more it is used the more 'intelligent' and inclusive it becomes.

Ostensibly, TinEye can help overcome the kind of problem described above in trying to trace the source of the photograph of Princess Diana. In attempting a search, however, the results were less than satisfactory. Despite claiming to have searched 1.9185 billion images in 0.987 seconds, the site returned just three instances of an exact match. In two of these cases the links provided were no longer operative (N.B. while search engines can find materials previously available online, it does not automatically mean the user can still access them). The third option led to an unattributed use of the image and as it happened one of lower resolution. Clearly the role of image-based search engines remains speculative and does not necessarily refine the current idiosyncratic nature of searching for images.

Copyright and permissions

Copyright law protects the rights of 'authors' of *all* forms of creative work, including art, literature, music and drama, but also software design, gaming concepts, film and video, maps, diagrams and commercial packaging. The law ensures the right to charge a fee for the use of materials, but it also – and perhaps more importantly – protects the moral right of the author to control the context in which others use their work. It is not always the case a fee will be charged, but it is always necessary that consent is gained. Thus, when seeking the permission of a copyright holder, it is usually necessary to provide an explanation of how and where the work will be included. All of the images included in this book for example have been cleared for copyright – in doing so the publisher gave notification of the size of the image on the page and whether it is in colour or black and white. A small black and white reprint of an image will generally cost less than a colour image; and size and prominence is also an important consideration. The fee paid for an image used inside a book will generally be lower than if used as the cover of a book. The principle being that a cover image will generally be seen by far more people than an image inside a book. The publisher will also need to give details of the print-run and the scale of distribution. A book marketed internationally and of a high print-run will incur greater cost than if intended for distribution in a single region and/or of a small print-run. It is also common for a publisher to request both print and electronic rights, since most materials are now published in a range of formats.

Copyright holders do not need to make an explicit statement of ownership, which is one reason why it can be difficult to locate the right person or organization to request permission (as described with the example of the image of Princess Diana). Copyright permission, once granted, will be in accordance to specific terms of use, which generally restrict use to a single instance. Thus, each time you wish to use an image it is necessary to go back to the original copyright holder. If someone wished to reprint pages from this book they would need to contact the publisher, but they would also need to approach the original copyright holders of the images included. In other words, the permissions granted to use the images in the printing of this book are not transferrable to a third-party.

In gaining the rights to reprint an image, it is also necessary to obtain the image itself for use in reproduction. It is not always the case that the copyright holder can supply the image. Galleries or private owners, for example, generally hold artworks. In order to obtain permission it is necessary to contact the artist, or their representatives. It is then often necessary to contact a gallery or dealer who can supply a print or a digital file of the requested image. Thus, in addition to searching for the existence of images and copyright holders, it is also necessary to *locate* the image in a more 'physical' sense. In the case of prints or photographs, more than one gallery may hold the work; or similar versions of an artwork may exist. As such, versions of an image can be supplied from more than one place, but in most cases only one copyright holder can provide permission for use.

Image methodologies

In order to navigate through the complexities of researching images, it is highly recommended the researcher adopt their own system of recording ideas and information. Thus, just as we find with an artist's notebook (in which typically all kinds of thoughts and details are recorded about images, their colours, textures, associated texts and more besides), the image researcher should build up a scrapbook of information. The approach need not be systematic, since certain images and fragments of information may not be of immediate importance. However, some means of storing such information can make all the difference when trying to locate an image for a particular research project at a later time.

Of course, images can also be used in more systematic ways, as an explicit element of a methodological process. In Chapters 7 and 8, we will encounter a range of examples of scientific and informational imaging. Generally these images are visualizations of data, which can be the end result of an experiment or technical process, or used to communicate information. However, they are often only part of a more extensive unfolding process. The images – particularly scientific images – can often be very striking, yet in many cases they will be discarded once they have been used. The social sciences have also adopted various image-based methodologies. Again, it is often the case these images are not part of the final output of research, or at least not a central aspect. Instead, however, they can be central to the gathering of information. Photography and film, for example, are used in anthropology, education, sociology and legal studies (Prosser, 1998). In addition to working with archival materials, photography and/or drawing are commonly used as a productive tool for visual evidence and for documentation and fieldwork (Stanczak, 2007; Knowles and Sweetman, 2004; Sherwin, 2008; Howells and Matson, 2009). Of particular note, photo- and video-diaries are a powerful tool for gaining insights into social and cultural behaviour of individuals and communities (Chaplin, 2004; Latham, 2004; Holliday, 2007). In addition photo-elicitation has developed as a technique to enhance interviews, to help participants access latent memories and articulate ideas about how they think about the world around them and how they relate to social structures (Byrne and Doyle, 2004; Mauad and Rouverol, 2004; Clark-Ibáñez, 2007; Samuels, 2007).

Image research can mean many different things and involve a great variety of skills and knowledge. There is no one single approach to accessing, handling and using images. In some cases images are the 'things' we focus on for our analysis, in other cases they are a tool to aid further investigation. An informed understanding and critical awareness of what images are and what they are used for is crucial for effective image research – all of which takes time, experience and perseverance.

Further reading

Evans, H. and Evans, M. (2006) *Picture Researcher's Handbook: An International Guide to Picture Sources and How to Use Them*. Eighth Edition. Leatherhead: Pira International.

Howells, Richard and Matson, Robert W. (eds) (2009) *Using Visual Evidence*. Maidenhead, Berks.: Open University Press/McGraw-Hill Education.

van Leeuwen, Theo and Jewitt, Carey (eds) (2001) *Handbook of Visual Analysis*. London: Sage.

Pollard, E.B. (1986) *Visual Arts Research: A Handbook*. London: Greenwood Press.

Rose, Gillian (2012) *Visual Methodologies: An Introduction to the Interpretation of Visual Materials*. Third Edition. London: Sage.

Prosser, Jon (ed.) (1998) *Image-Based Research: A Sourcebook for Qualitative Researchers*. Philadelphia: Falmer Press.

Stanczak, G.C. (ed.) (2007) *Visual Research Methods: Image, Society, and Representation*. Los Angeles: Sage.

3 Image and text

The previous chapter considered the image as a complex and shifting phenomenon. We discovered any one single image can be understood to exist in a much wider ecology of images and that there are many different states of the image, making up a diverse 'family', which include the graphic, optical, perceptual, mental and verbal. This chapter continues along these lines, but pays specific attention to the relationship between text and image. Key points of interest include the role of language in interpreting the image; the purported rise of a contemporary image culture; the enduring (and often fraught) relationship between image and power; and formal distinctions and commonalities between image and text. The chapter begins with a consideration of what is termed the 'pictorial turn'. There then follows a brief history of **iconoclasm** as well as a return to Mitchell's 'Family of Images' to consider the potential root of all images as 'likeness', which again, importantly, blurs the boundary of 'the visual, pictorial sense of the image with an invisible, spiritual, and verbal understanding' (Mitchell, 1987, p.35).

It is important to note a distinction between 'image' (which can straddle a variety of forms, as shown with the family of images) and the visual image, or 'picture', which we can regard as a material object. The distinction between these two terms is not hard and fast. In everyday speech, for example, we would say: 'I can picture you in that suit', to imply one can imagine what the person would look like in certain attire. In this case, then, 'picture' would seem to refer to a more intangible experience of the image; and grammatically it would not be right to say 'I can image you in that suit' (Manghani, 2011, p.228). However, as we work through this chapter it is worth keeping note of the distinctions – explicit or otherwise – between the material image, such as a picture we might hang on the wall, and the image in a broader, conceptual sense. In both cases, of course, there is something we can refer to in contrast to text.

Pictorial turn

In 'Rhetoric of the Image' (1977, pp.32–51), Roland Barthes remarks:

> '. . . at the level of mass communications, it appears that the linguistic message is indeed present in every image: as title, caption, accompanying press article, film dialogue, comic strip balloon. Which shows that it is not very accurate to talk of a civilization of the image – we are still, and more than ever, a civilization of writing.'
>
> (Barthes, 1977, p.38)

As we will go on to see, a number of commentators would today take issue with Barthes' suggestion of a 'civilization of writing', and instead argue contemporary culture is dominated not by writing but by the image and the visual. However, it is worth keeping Barthes' comments to mind. The Internet, for example, is undoubtedly a multimedia domain, yet it is heavily dependent on text. Text appears on any given webpage and more crucially underpins the way we search online. Internet coding, tags, hyperlinks, menu navigation and search engines are all text-dependent. However, we might want to question whether text still dominates our experience and understanding of the world, or whether it is only a part of a broader media culture.

Bruce Millar (2004) argues unequivocally the twenty-first century has witnessed a shift towards a more visually literate audience. He suggests over the last 1000 years, 'artistic culture has been primarily literary; its people have entertained, defined and reflected themselves through poetry, plays and novels'. Whereas by the year 2000: 'it is possible to detect a profound and unprecedented shift: ours has become a visual culture, and it is the visual arts that seem best equipped to take the pulse of contemporary life, to describe the now' (2004, p.16). Millar writes specifically about British culture, but his remarks can relate to many other cultures, and not least globalized culture:

> 'Visual art takes its place seamlessly in the contemporary world's globalised economy, in which advertising and entertainment have given audiences around the world common sources of imagery and visual techniques. Literature has had an international reach for centuries – from the legacy of the classical authors to the passion for Shakespeare, but an image or design travels instantly and without the need for translation.'
>
> (Millar, 2004, p.20)

This account of a burgeoning visual culture and an audience increasingly adept at relating to and appreciating the visual arts connects with a wider discourse, which during the 1990s gave rise to the field of visual culture studies. Kress and van Leeuwen (2006a; see also 2006b, pp.16–44) describe a changing 'semiotic landscape', in which the place of language 'is moving from its former, unchallenged role as *the* medium of communication, to the role as *one* medium of communication' (2006a, p.120). In similar terms to Millar, Kress and van Leeuwen argue how a younger generation are more inclined to engage in visual media. In a comparison of science textbooks, for example, from the early and later parts of the twentieth century, Kress and van Leeuwen show (with the changing styles of page-layouts and information) how images have become 'the central medium of information, and the role of language has become that of a medium of commentary. Images (and this includes the layout of the page) carry the argument' (2006a, p.121).

We will examine visual culture in greater detail in Chapter 6, and the 'semiotic landscape' in Chapter 8. However, it is sufficient to say the debates from the 1990s onwards have raised important questions about the political, social and cultural status of images and the visual. The rising dominance of the visual (over the verbal) has led to concerns that it is 'a medium of entertainment as much as a medium of information', and that the '[visual] apprehension of facts displaces the concern with truth' (Kress and van Leeuwen, 2006a, p.121). Overall, however, Kress and van Leeuwen consider the shift from the verbal to the visual to result in both losses and gains. Different semiotic modes, they suggest, each have their potential and their limitations. Thus, it is more a question of needing to understand and have a grasp of the different modalities of image and text, than to consider any one form better than the other (Kress and van Leeuwen, 2006b, p.31). Crucially, however, the social valuation of knowledge in various spheres, such as science and education, has undergone massive change and that generally 'the authority of the transmitters of social values can no longer be taken for granted' (Kress and van Leeuwen, 2006a, p.122). Less hierarchical society and more extensive global flows of capital and information are part of the shift being described within contemporary visual culture. It is not just cultural and political boundaries which are said to 'dissolve', but semiotic boundaries too (2006a, p.120). Millar cites the British arts broadcaster Melvyn Bragg, who describes a new, ubiquitous visual literacy:

> 'Look at shop windows in the high street – they are full of well-designed stuff, the lighting, the look, the balance. No one is afraid of a shocking new look any more, and the new blocks of flats along the Thames that look like great hulls of ships have been built without any of the fuss you would have seen 15 years ago. Today, people want architects to design their cities, and they'll travel somewhere specifically to look at buildings.'
>
> (Bragg in Millar, 2004, p.20)

The array of new image-making technologies and modes of distribution, a changing audience, the intersection of 'high art' and everyday culture, a more sophisticated visual awareness and a blurring of categories and styles are key indicators of the shift towards a new visual culture. The impact of this change has been felt in traditional areas of study such as art history and literature, which have been challenged by the younger fields of media and cultural studies. Debates ensued around the prospect of and need for more interdisciplinary research methods, though equally these have revealed just how difficult it is to achieve. There are many competing claims on the nature and status of images and visual culture, which prove difficult to align (as subsequent chapters in this book show). Arguably, however, what does unite those interested in the image is a clear distinction between image and text. It is not in fact an easy distinction to define, but nonetheless the 'idea' of it – in various manifestations – is long-standing.

As we found in the preceding two chapters, various ways of thinking critically about the image exist (semiotics being a notable methodology), yet a definitive articulation of what an image is or what meaning it holds is difficult to pin down. By contrast, the concept of the 'text' or 'textuality' (even 'intertextuality') is deeply embedded in the practices of the human sciences, as well as extending into wider popular discourse. Models of textual analysis – which include linguistics, rhetoric, semiotics and psychoanalysis, etc. – have come to be at the centre of critical methodologies within the arts and humanities. As outlined with the brief history of semiotics in Chapter 1, this has allowed for the analysis of all manner of things, including for example film, performance and even sports being treated as cultural 'texts'. In fact, everything and anything has become subject to analysis by way of being a *text*, or held within *discourse*. As W.J.T Mitchell (1994, p.11) reminds us, the belief has been: 'Society is a text. Nature and its scientific representations are "discourses". Even the unconscious is structured like a language.' The 'text', then, underpins a whole way of thinking and interpreting our world, situating us in what the philosopher Richard Rorty (1979, p.263) describes as the 'linguistic turn'. Rorty's history of philosophy portrays a series of different underlying problematics, labelled as 'turns', starting with medieval philosophy concerned with *things*, enlightenment philosophy with *ideas*, and finally, contemporary philosophy with *words*, or language.

In response, and in light of growing interest in visual culture, Mitchell (1994, p.11) considers a new challenge to this history, suggesting, 'that once again a complexly related transformation is occurring in other disciplines of the human sciences and in the sphere of public culture' leading to a shift towards what he calls a visual or 'pictorial turn'. Developing along similar lines, the art historian Gottfried Boehm adopts the phrase of an 'iconic turn', which, like the pictorial turn, should not be taken as some new 'fashionable' idea. He writes: 'the "image" is not simply some new topic, but relates much more to a different mode of thinking, one that has shown itself capable of clarifying and availing itself of the long-neglected cognitive possibilities that lie in non-verbal representation' (cited in Boehm and Mitchell, 2010, p.9). In both cases, the implication is that 'visual experience or "visual literacy" might not be fully explicable on the model of textuality' (Mitchell, 1994, p.16). In fact, if anything, it is this principle that can be taken to be the 'foundational postulate to visual culture' (Mitchell, 1995, p.543).

Taken at face value, the pictorial turn can seem to equate to contemporary visual culture, such as described with a shift to the visual arts, the rise of a *new* 'semiotic landscape', or with the idea, as Nicholas Mirzoeff originally asserted in the first edition of *An Introduction to Visual Culture* (1999), that '[m]odern life takes place onscreen . . . Human experience is now more visual and visualized than ever before from the satellite picture to the medical images of the interior of the human body' (1999, p.1). However, visual culture as a shift in cultural production, as a new semiotic landscape, or as 'screen life', is not a wholly satisfactory corollary of the pictorial turn. Mitchell agrees that visual culture has greatly expanded to now underpin much of our lives. In fact, he accepts that the 'fantasy of a pictorial turn, of a culture totally dominated by images, has now become a real technical possibility on a global scale' (Mitchell, 1994, p.15). However, the more important point for Mitchell is to bring to the fore the *perennial*, ongoing problem or anxiety of pictorial representation, epitomized by the competing claims and interactions of both text and image. The point, then, is to think with more acuity about contemporary image culture through the lens of the pictorial turn, as it seeks to question how *both* text and image underlie constructs of knowledge and understanding – and have done so for many centuries.

Iconoclasm

As mentioned in Chapter 2, in *Simulacra and Simulation* (1994), the French cultural theorist Jean Baudrillard coins the phrase 'hyperreal' to refer to a **simulacrum** or image that 'has no relation to any reality whatsoever' (1994, p.6). The simulacrum comes at the end of an evolution of the image in four stages: (1) the image as a basic reflection of reality; (2) the perversion of reality; (3) the pretence of reality (whereby the image appears to be, but is not a copy of reality); and finally (4) the simulacrum. Baudrillard refers to the concept of god as an example of simulacrum. But most provocatively perhaps he applied the term hyperreal when commenting on the 1991 Gulf War, which he declared 'did not take place', being instead the product of media spectacle (Baudrillard, 1995). Baudrillard's theory of the simulacrum has been widely cited, not least as a way to account for postmodern culture. As noted previously, *Simulacra and Simulation* (1994) had a direct influence on the film *The Matrix* (1999) – indeed a dusty copy of the book appears briefly in one scene of the film.

While Baudrillard's account of the image can be said to have captured something about contemporary culture, the underlying concern about the power of the image harks back to biblical writing and early Greek philosophy; in particular, notions of **iconophobia** and **iconophilia** – the fear (or hatred) of images and the love of images respectively. Iconophobia relates to a deep mistrust of images, or certain kinds of images, and can be seen in the canonical writings of Plato to René Descartes, through to Karl Marx, Sigmund Freud and a whole swathe of twentieth-century thought (see Jay, 1994; Manghani *et al.*, 2006). Baudrillard's four stages of the image is derived from Plato's allegory or **simile of the cave** – one of the most influential comments on the image in the history of philosophy. For Plato, ordinary people are described as slaves chained in a dark cave witnessing in the firelight only shadows of what lies outside. Climbing out of the cave to 'enlightenment' is achieved only through rational thought, which provides the right way of 'seeing' (Plato, 1955, pp.278–283. The allegory establishes what is now a well-worn narrative from dark to light, from ignorance to enlightenment, and which significantly is linked to language (as the means of rational thought) usurping the image.

Throughout history **iconoclasts** have sought to denounce images, often by publicly breaking images or removing them from circulation. This impulse is found in early sections of the Bible and the Torah. Abraham, for example, literally smashes the idols in his father's shop in order to prevent people from worshipping false gods. In Genesis, image is afforded great importance with the line: 'God created man in his *own* image'. As a result prohibition surrounds the creation of images. In Exodus 20, God decrees: 'Thou shalt have no other gods before me. Thou shalt not make unto thee any graven image.' Moses is delayed in coming down from Mount Sinai to deliver this law to his people. In the meantime the people turn to Aaron to give them an idol – a physical representation of their God. Taking all of their gold possessions he fashions a golden calf and places it upon an altar for worship. Moses is warned by God of the people corrupting themselves and in anger – at the sight of dancing and reverie – he smashes the tablets of stone upon which are written the commandments. As David Freedberg (1989, p. 379) notes, '[Moses] breaks the verbal icons of the divine word', though he also destroys the idol. The episode poses an obvious tension between word and image, and significantly, through the various descriptions, makes explicit connection between **idolatry**, sensuality and sin; with the image considered a corrupting force.

FIGURE 3.1

Nicolas Poussin, *The Adoration of the Golden Calf* (1633–1634) © National Gallery, London.

The story of the commandments and the golden calf has been retold and depicted many times. Freedberg draws attention to two paintings, made a century apart. The first is by Luca van Leyden in 1530 and the second by Nicolas Poussin in 1634 (Figure 3.1). As Freedberg notes, the paintings 'bracket one of the greatest episodes of iconoclasm in Western history: the determined and violent wave of image-breaking that swept almost every town and village in the Netherlands during the extra-ordinarily intense last quarter of 1566' (Freedberg, 1989, p.385). Both paintings show 'the ultimate idolatry: a false image . . . surrounded by visible evidence of the debauched sensuality into which men and women fell as a result of their adoration of the artistic, manmade, golden substitute for the God they could never see' (p.378). The choice of subject matter replicated in these two paintings is not uncommon, whereas very few retellings choose to focus on the darkness of the punishment that Moses imposes upon the Israelites. In the two paintings, for example, '[e]xcept for the black cloud from which Moses descends in the background of both, neither picture gives an inkling of this horror; but in their portrayal of the relations between abandoned sensuality and idolatry they could not be more eloquent' (p.381). For Freedberg, there is a 'deep irony', since we 'admire . . . a picture which has as its subject the epitome of the negative consequences of looking, admiring, and adorning' (p.384). The irony is all the deeper since these paintings were not intended as religious, devotional pictures, but rather to showcase the ability of the painter. Adopting as their subject matter the sin of looking upon rich material idols, the paintings' 'virtues are purely visual, certainly not devotional' (p.384).

By contrast, the controversy over icons in eighth- and ninth-century Byzantium was far from a debate about artistry; rather it marked a crisis and deep conflict over the nature and uses of icons within social and political spheres. On the one hand iconoclasts – upholding the doctrine against 'graven images' – sought to purify the church of idolatry, while iconophiles considered the value of specific icons as a means to propagate ideas and maintain social order. Over the ages there has been a recurring pattern whereby some images are overturned by iconclasts in favour of other specific unifying political symbols, which themselves are later denounced. The Cultural Revolution in China and the rise and collapse of communism in Europe are fairly recent examples from the twentieth century. Further back, the English Civil War (1641–1651) is a prominent example, which was 'fought over the issue of images, and not just the question of statues and other material symbols . . . but less tangible matters such as the "idol" of monarchy and, beyond that, the "idols of the mind" that Reformation thinkers sought to purge in themselves and others' (Mitchell, 1987, p.7).

In the introduction to the catalogue of a major exhibition, *Iconoclash* (Latour and Weibel, 2002, pp.26–32), the sociologist Bruno Latour offers a classification of different types of iconoclasts, from those against *all* images, to those against only their opponents' images, as well as those wishing images not to ossify, but to keep circulating; and others breaking images unwittingly. He also suggests a category of those who mock or are sceptical of both iconoclasts and iconphiles – a kind of iconoclasm of iconoclasm! Significantly, however, what underlies iconoclasm is frequently the tension between the visible and invisible. In accordance with Plato's allegory of the cave, iconoclasts purport to possess a truth beyond the appearances of everyday, sensory reality. To mistake images for truths is considered a threat to the social fabric. Thus iconoclasm entails both a way of understanding the world and an ethical claim (as such it is no surprise Plato's allegory appears in his political text *The Republic*). As Mitchell puts it: 'The distinction between the spiritual and material, inner and outer image, was never simply a matter of theological doctrine, but was always a question of politics, from the power of priestly castes, to the struggle between conservative and reform movements (the iconophiles and iconoclasts), to the preservation of national identity (the Israelites' struggle to purge themselves of idolatry)' (1987, p.35).

FIGURE 3.2
Marcus Harvey, *Myra* (1995). © Marcus Harvey and White Cube. Photo: Stephen White. Courtesy of White Cube. All Rights Reserved, DACS 2012.

In today's media and celebrity culture we hear similar iconoclastic concerns regarding the inequities of power based upon an economy of false images. With a contemporary twist on the deep irony referred to above regarding the paintings of the golden calf, we can consider a painting by Marcus Harvey shown in the exhibition *Sensation* at London's Royal Academy in 1997. From a distance the painting appears to be a greatly enlarged version of the 'iconic' police photograph of Myra Hindley, imprisoned for her involvement in multiple child murders during the 1960s. On closer inspection it is apparent the painting is made up of the repetition of a child's handprint, used to create a mosaic of light and dark shades, replicating the dots of newspaper print. Unsurprisingly the painting caused a great deal of controversy and debate. Some consider it an insightful comment on the iconic power of the original photograph, with years of obsessive media reproduction. Others take it to be gratuitous, making cynical use of a potent (and for many an upsetting) image. John Molyneux draws out these complex issues in the following way:

> 'In so far as this particular image of Hindley possesses iconic power in our culture it is the media's constant use of it, not [Marcus] Harvey, that created it. When [British newspaper] *The Mirror* denounced the painting as a "disgrace" it plastered it all over its front page thus projecting it into 2 million homes. In other words, the fuss is not about the image itself but about making it into "art", or calling it "art". Does this mean paintings of monstrous people cannot be art or morally speaking ought not to be art? Where does that leave Holbein's Henry VIII portraits or John Heartfield's photomontages of Hitler and Goering? However, defending the "right" of the Academy to show Myra is not the same as proclaiming its great artistic merits.'
>
> (Molyneux, 1998)

Regardless of one's point of view, the painting is a reminder that the power of the image has far from waned despite our living in quite different times to that of the Byzantium era or other equally fraught periods. If the stakes seem a little lower, Mitchell suggests:

> '. . . it is not because [images] have lost their power over us, and certainly not because their nature is now clearly understood. It is a commonplace of modern cultural criticism that images have a power in our world undreamed of by the ancient idolaters. And it seems equally evident that the question of the nature of imagery has been second only to the problem of language in the evolution of modern criticism.'
>
> (Mitchell, 1987, pp. 7–8)

Image as likeness

While narratives around iconoclasm are arguably more pronounced, it is equally important to note how images and words bear a very rich history. In the preface to

Art, Word and Image (2010), a compendium covering 2,000 years of visual/textual interaction, Michael Leaman describes how Egyptian tombs were covered with both paintings and hieroglyphic commentaries. In thinking back to the remarks made in the introduction to this book on the need to bridge between thinking about and making images, it is worth noting those who painted the scenes on the Egyptian tombs 'were trained as scribes, and required to draw the hieroglyphic inscriptions as well' (Leaman in Hunt *et al.*, 2010, p.7). Leaman provides many examples of word and image through history, as follows:

> 'Roman buildings bore inscriptions on their facades celebrating the gods and the owners of those edifices. Babylonian and Etruscan haruspicy was solidified in clay and in bronze versions of animal livers respectively. Runes in Norway and Denmark in the Viking period were carved on stones, and rune stones acted as roadside memorials, with both magical and mundane messages. [. . .] When writing was manual, from the eighth century onwards illuminated manuscripts teemed with images and letters which could metamorphize into beasts or human forms, and by the fifteenth century images often took over the background and foreground of letters in such manuscripts to create illusions of space. Books of the Italian Renaissance continued this tradition but with the addition of perspectival images which turned the book into a quasi-theatrical space of transforming scenes as pages turned, sometimes with *trompe l'oeil* imagery which made them into multi-sided reflections of meaning. Lutheran images used words as propaganda; they were decorative as well as communicative and pedagogical. Images and prints of the Northern Renaissance contained such messages in interesting and innovative combinations, occasionally including speech bubbles which look just like those in today's cartoons.'
> (Leaman in Hunt *et al.*, 2010, pp.7–8)

Later comes the advent of printing in varying forms (woodcuts, engravings, etchings, the Gutenberg press and lithography), which leads to a vast dissemination of text and image, such as we are familiar with today (if with the volume ever increasing, not least with the means of virtual reproduction via the World Wide Web). Our long history of words and images can be said to reveal as much a positive view of images; captured well in Aristotle's famous remark that 'the soul's never thinking without an image' (Aristotle, 1965). Whilst it is not entirely fair to characterize Plato as a mere iconoclast, since all his writings grapple with the experience of images and poetry, his pupil, Aristotle, is generally credited with the counterview that images enable us to think and seek truth. In fact, according to Aristotle, images are instinctive. In his treatise on poetry, for example, he writes: 'The instinct for imitation is inherent in man from his earliest days', furthermore, 'inborn in all of us is the instinct to enjoy works of imitation'. Learning is pleasurable he writes, people 'enjoy seeing likenesses because in doing so they acquire information' (Aristotle, 1965). Aristotle's account of the image marks a trend that can be traced from the sixteenth century (when Aristotle's writing became widely read) to the present; and which includes the works of philosophers such as Immanuel Kant, Henri Bergson, and Ludwig Wittgenstein, as well as contemporary cognitive science (see, for example, Manghani *et al.*, 2006, pp.19–60).

The concept at the heart of Aristotle's account of the image and imitation is **mimesis**. The term can mean both the imitation and representation of nature, which inevitably has prompted a great deal of debate. For Plato, mimesis, as imitation, stood in contrast to diegesis, or narrative; so marking a difference between the verbal and the visual arts. Aristotle uses the term more broadly to encompass all means of imitation from the arts to mathematics. Crucially for Aristotle, mimesis describes a certain distance created by texts and images, which enable us to reflect on the world. It is through simulated representation, or mimesis, that we can respond to a whole range of experiences and ethical concerns. Mimesis is undoubtedly a complex term, though its very fluidity helps remind us of an important point about the image. As Mitchell explains, 'the very idea of an "idea" is bound up with the notion of imagery. "Idea" comes from the Greek verb "to see", and is frequently linked with the notion of the "eidolon", the "visible image" that is fundamental to ancient optics and theories of perception' (Mitchell, 1987, p.5). At this point, then, we can think back to the diagram in Chapter 2 of the 'family of images', in which Mitchell shows graphic, optical, perceptual, mental and verbal images rooted in the Image as likeness, resemblance and similitude. As such, we can consider the division of word and image to be less stable than we might previously have thought.

IMAGE AS LIKENESS

W.J.T. MITCHELL

(from *Iconology*, 1987, pp.31–36)

[The assumption is] that the literal sense of the word 'image' is a graphic, pictorial, representation, a concrete, material object, and that notions such as mental, verbal, or perceptual imagery are improper derivations from this literal sense, figurative extensions of the pictorial into regions where pictures have no real business. It's time now to acknowledge that this whole story could be told another way, from the standpoint of a tradition which sees the literal sense of the word 'image' as a resolutely non- or even anti-pictorial notion. This is the tradition which begins, of course, with the account of man's creation 'in the image and likeness' of God. The words we now translate as 'image' (the Hebrew *tselem*, the Greek *eikon*, and the Latin *imago*) are properly understood, as the commentators never tire of telling us, not as any material picture, but as an abstract, general, spiritual 'likeness'. The regular addition, after 'image', of the phrase 'and likeness' (the Hebrew *demuth*, the Greek *homoioos*, and the Latin *similitude*) is to be understood, not as adding new information, but as preventing a possible confusion: 'image' is to be understood not as 'picture' but as 'likeness', a matter of spiritual similarity.

[. . .]

The tension between the appeals of spiritual likeness and material image is never expressed more poignantly than in Milton's treatment of Adam and Eve as the *imago dei* [image of God] in the fourth book of *Paradise Lost*:

> Two of far nobler shape erect and tall,
> Godlike erect, with native honour clad
> In naked majesty seemed lords of all
> And worthy seemed, for in their looks divine
> The image of their glorious Maker shone,
> Truth, Wisdom, Sanctitude severe and pure,
> Severe, but in true filial freedom plac't.
> (*Paradise Lost, 4:288–294*)

Milton deliberately confuses the visual, pictorial sense of the image with an invisible, spiritual, and verbal understanding of it. Everything hinges on the equivocal function of the key word 'looks', which may refer us to the outward appearance of Adam and Eve, their 'nobler shape', nakedness, and erectness, or to the less tangible sense of 'looks' as the quality of their gazes, the character of their 'expressions'. This quality is not a visual image that looks like something else; it is more like the light by which an image can be seen at all, a matter of radiance rather than reflection, and to explain how this image 'shone' in 'their looks divine', Milton must resort to a series of predicates, a list of abstract spiritual attributes that Adam and Eve have in common with God – 'Truth, Wisdom, Sanctitude severe and pure' – along with a qualifying difference to stress that man is not identical with God: 'Severe, but in true filial freedom placed'. God in his perfect solitude has no need of filial relationships, but for his image to be perfected in mankind the social and sexual relation of man and woman must be instituted in 'true filial freedom'.

Is man created in the image of God, then, in that he looks like God, or in that we can say similar things about man and God? Milton wants to have it both ways, a desire we can trace to his rather unorthodox materialism or perhaps more fundamentally to a historic transformation in the concept of imagery which tended to identify the notion of spiritual likeness – particularly the 'rational soul' that makes man an image of God – with a certain kind of material image. Milton's poetry is the scene of a struggle between iconoclastic distrust of the outward image and iconophilic fascination with its power, a struggle which manifests itself in his practice of proliferating visual images in order to prevent readers from focusing on any particular picture or scene.

What lies *between* text and image is a point of contest that dates back over many centuries; evident on the opening pages of the Bible and in the Torah, for example, and of course explicit with the controversy over icons in the eighth-century Byzantium period. Having now placed the pictorial turn in its fuller historical and philosophical context, we begin to appreciate how images can be considered powerful and to bear a complex relationship to text; constantly oscillating, as captured beautifully with Milton's line, 'in their looks divine'.

Beyond the text . . .

The remainder of this chapter looks at the effects/affects of text and image in more detail. In his book *The Domain of Images* (1999), James Elkins suggests that those writing about and studying images tend to consider the relationship between text and image in one of two ways:

> 'One is the impossible ideal of the "pure picture" (the image unsullied by writing or any verbal equivalents, either in the object or in its interpretation): It gives meaning to concepts such as visuality, "visual meaning", and cognate terms . . . The other is the ideal – equally impossible in practice – of the picture as a substitute for writing, and hence a carrier of determinate meaning.'
>
> (Elkins, 1999, p.55)

Both these conceptions of the word-image dichotomy are merely ideals. They are each 'impossible' in practical terms, for reasons we have already started to explore when thinking about a wider ecology of images (in the previous chapter) and as developed by Mitchell's account of images as likeness (above). In everyday speech we tend to know what the difference is between an image and text. However, on closer inspection the distinction is not necessarily so easy to uphold. Those who wish to maintain the idea of a 'pure' picture will generally 'stress the untranslatable, uninterpretable meaning of pictures' (Elkins, 1999, p.55). This of course leaves us little to say about pictures, since we can only let them 'speak' for themselves (which of course is not a straightforward thing at all); and arguably this would seem to place images outside of the cultural context in which they are looked at, spoken about, exchanged, destroyed and manipulated. By contrast, the idea of the image as a 'carrier of determinate meaning' has given scope for a range of theorizing – with semiotics being one very obvious example. Semiotics, when applied to phenomena other than language, is predicated on the idea that while something might not be coded in the same manner as language, there is still nonetheless a system of meaning that can be revealed. A painting, for example, cannot be 'read' as one would read a sentence in a book, but nonetheless is thought to offer its own determinate meaning – the structure and iteration of which can potentially be understood and demonstrated to be a 'system' of painterly representation or expression (e.g. relating to a 'school of thought' and/or adopting key symbols or particular style). In practice, of course, this remains very difficult to sustain (see Chapter 4) and as suggested in the previous chapter (and above in reference to the pictorial turn) there is yet to be any definitive theory of the image. Elkins notes, for example, how 'Roland Barthes searches for moments in pictures that are ultimately different from what is "coded" and therefore socially significant', and yet like 'Odysseus's encounter with the sirens: Barthes listens to the call of the purely visual object, he approaches, and then he veers back into the safer waters of coded images' (Elkins, 1999, p.55).

The ongoing false starts in asserting a definite theory of images (which does not predetermine a 'reading' of the image) might at first seem frustrating. However, as we start to look at the different attempts to understand images (and their relationship to text) we begin to find that the difficulty and contradictions are themselves fascinating and revealing. It is through our actual existing engagement with images and text that we come to understand them, or at least experience and appreciate their richness. A playful account of the word-image dichotomy can be found in the children's book *On Beyond Zebra* (1955) by Dr Seuss. The book begins with a young child, Conrad, displaying his mastery of '*all* twenty-six letters' of the alphabet, proudly declaring: '. . . now I know everything *any*one knows / From beginning to end. From the start to the close. / Because Z is as far as the alphabet goes'. But Conrad is then taken by surprise when his friend reveals a whole series of alternative 'letters' beyond Z, telling Conrad: 'In the places I go there are things that I see / That I *never* could spell if I stopped with the Z . . . *My* alphabet starts where *your* alphabet ends!' On one level the book is simply a playful, and much loved rhyming nonsense story. But in the context of thinking about words and images it offers a nice illustration (quite literally) of how language can be highly flexible and unifying as a system of signification, but also have limits to its application. The idea of the story is that there are things beyond the scope of a commonly shared language.

On Beyond Zebra would seem to appeal to the idea of the picture 'as a substitute for writing'. It is a highly idiosyncratic 'system', but nonetheless the book gives us a vastly expanded alphabet – each page introducing a new, invented character to learn. It raises the idea of degrees of accuracy. Just as we can take measurements in centimetres or millimetres, with the latter offering greater precision, so potentially we can further calibrate our alphabet to allow for more finely tuned spellings. This is one way in which we can understand the idea of a 'language' of painting or film, which critics often refer to. These so-called languages might not be as clearly identifiable and stable as verbal language, but there is an appeal to the idea of a unique system of meaning, or code, which eventually we can read with some level of proficiency; and which typically artists and directors are considered to have mastered.

However, if we look again at the Dr Seuss book, we might make the opposite argument. *On Beyond Zebra* also gives rise to the idea of the 'pure picture', since each newly invented letter of the alphabet is meaningful only because of the wildly imaginative picture it accompanies. In other words, there is only an alphabet beyond the letter 'Z' because there is a whole world of newly invented *things* beyond 'zebra'. We are introduced to a weird and wonderful collection of unworldly creatures such as the Yuzz-a-ma-tuzz and the Sneedle; and it is only the pictures which make these 'real', as shared entities that we then wish to label. We can come up with a variety of schemes to label things, but essentially there is no easy way to theorize the 'pure picture' thesis. The pure picture exists in a unique way. We can experience it, but any attempt to translate or interpret it somehow takes us away from the experience. These are 'ideal' ways of thinking about images and as such remain unobtainable in practice. The example of *On Beyond Zebra* reinforces the point. However, it is not that we cannot experience pictures 'purely' as pictures or that they cannot be structured in some kind of 'meaningful' way, but that these incompatible ways of understanding the image do in fact co-exist, and in this case lend the book its humour. In other words, we cannot say there is one single way of addressing the image, nor can we assert a simple distinction between image and text, or systems of interpretation. Nevertheless, we begin to discern a variety of effects and affects associated with images, text and their combination.

Analogue and digital codes

'. . . can analogical representation (the "copy") produce true systems of signs and not merely simple agglutinations of symbols? Is it possible to conceive of an analogical "code" (as opposed to a digital one)?'

(Barthes, 1977, p.32)

One way of understanding the distinction between a 'pure' picture and a picture of 'determinate meaning' is to consider the distinction between the analogue and the digital. The meaning of 'analogue' is a person or thing seen as comparable to another – which relates to the word 'analogy', such as the analogy made in the previous chapter between environmental ecology and an ecology of images. It also, of course, relates to Aristotle's concept of mimesis, as discussed above. In the sciences, analogue signals or information are of a *continuously* variable physical quantity, such as voltage. In Barthes' case the idea of analogical representation refers to a copy that in its fullest sense would be a point-by-point reproduction of something. The ultimate 'copy' would be a clone; an absolute replica that does not need to translate one term into another, but simply is another existence of the thing copied. What happens in such a case is that there is no need for a system or code to translate between the original and the copy, which leads Barthes to suggest we would get only 'agglutinations of symbols'. It is an intriguing phrase. As a verb, to agglutinate means to 'firmly stick or be stuck together to form a mass'. This very visceral, material notion is pertinent to the idea of a biological clone. When used in the field of linguistics, agglutination means to combine words or parts of words without change of form to express compound ideas. In either case, whilst we may have new combinations of things, essentially there is only the compounding of one *thing* with another. Thus, Barthes is sceptical as to whether there is such a thing as an analogical 'code', since a code is a reduction or shorthand of something.

The English language uses just twenty-six letters in its alphabet in order to form some quarter of a million different words, which we use to represent things (and ideas) in the world. Language is *digital* code, since signals or information are

represented by *discrete* values (or digits). Typically, then, digital codes are made up of numbers or letters, which approximate the thing represented. Computers use the most rudimentary of digital codes: binary. All of the complex actions performed on a computer, whilst seemingly very fluid, colourful and rich, are actually all translated into a series of ones and zeros, which act like switches on and off. This is what enables computers to make very fast calculations and crucially for contemporary culture has meant we can copy files effortlessly, and without loss of information. Reducing graphics, text, sound and moving image to a simple series of ones and zeros allow us to make clones of our own, but only if translated back through a computer.

Consider the difference between an analogue and digital clock (see Figure 3.3). For a child, learning to tell the time is a complex, conceptual undertaking. It is not helped by the different ways in which analogue and digital clocks *show* the time. Generally, a digital clock does not show seconds, only hours and minutes, separated by a colon. Whereas an analogue clock often has a second hand, which we can watch as it moves 'through' time. Indeed, if we look patiently we can also watch the minute and hour hands as they too move through time, between the calibrated points on the clock face. The analogue clock face also visually shows the idea of quarter past/to and half past the hour, since, as if cutting a cake into quarters, you can quickly see the proportional relationship between the numbers. For a child this can be confusing. On a digital clock 'quarter past' shows as the number '15'. Of course, through experience (and by comprehending the mathematical logic) we come to understand the differences and eventually we barely notice them. Yet, the analogue clock shows time as a continuously changing variable and is a direct analogy of time – i.e. a minute is exactly how long it takes for the minute hand to move from one minute to the next, and its position on the clock face at any point during that minute will be proportionate to the time elapsed (assuming the clock is of a high precision design). By contrast the digital clock only shows the change from one minute to the next, with no in-between values. This is the essential difference between the analogical and digital code. Analogical representation shows not only a point-by-point copy of something, but all variables in-between.

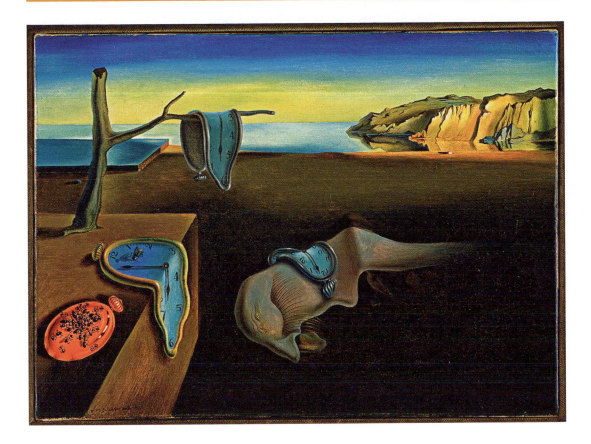

FIGURE 3.4
Salvador Dali, *The Persistence of Memory* (1931) © Salvador Dali, Funació Gala Salvador Dali, DACS 2012.

If a line of a drawing curves round to the right, a copy will look and feel the same. However, if we wish to chart the change of position we could use a grid referencing system – a digital code – to plot the change in position, without needing to fill in the detail between points. In the late 1980s, pop music production was shifting increasingly towards digital recording. At the heart of the studio was the sampler; a digital recording device that could endlessly copy, or replay, the sound recorded upon it. The sampler had a huge impact on the cultural production of music, making for a whole new aesthetic of cut and paste pop. Arguably, what fascinated people was both the fidelity of a captured sound and yet the seemingly effortless means to then manipulate and repeat the sound. Early on, samples were very short because it required huge amounts of computer memory to capture sounds at high quality. To make longer samples it was possible to reduce the sampling rate, but this would have an impact on the quality of the recording. If you imagine the smooth 'S' bend of a sine wave, a high quality sample would plot as many points along the curve. When played back, the human ear would generally not hear the gaps in-between. We can visualize this with the way photographs are reproduced in newspapers using many thousands of dots. Looking from a normal distance we generally only see a single image, but up close we can pick out the individual dots. Similarly, if we stand back from a mosaic we see the content of the picture, but up close we marvel at the little fragments used to make up its whole. At a lower sampling rate, fewer points are plotted along the line, hence a more approximated sound (or image) is formed. We are now accustomed to very powerful computers, with high sampling rates, giving the effect of seemingly 'pure' reproductions. Nonetheless, digital cultural production is indeed based upon digital code.

Of course, we have to remember even the analogue clock face is not without coding. Clocks are carefully calibrated with numbers placed accurately upon the face. This gives us the appearance of the duration of time as a spatial movement. All clocks, then, offer a system of reading time, except perhaps were we to possess an irregularly shaped clock face – such as those painted by the surrealist Salvador Dali. Such a clock is suggestive of a unique, analogical 'agglutinated' code; though this is precisely the reason for Barthes's query over the possibility of an analogical code, since there seems little point in having a 'code' that is unique and unrepeatable. Thus, at the heart of debates about text and image, about copies and originals, and analogue and digital codes, are questions about the transmission or translation of one state to another, of the difference between direct copies or systems of representation.

The cartoonist and theorist on comics, Scott McCloud, considers the spectrum of analogue to digital representation in terms of a difference between 'received' and 'perceived' (McCloud, 1994, p.49). Equating in some respects to Kress and van Leeuwen's (2006a; 2006b, pp.16–44) account of the semiotic landscape, McCloud argues pictures are *received* in an immediate sense, whereas text is *perceived* – it requires a system of reading, and takes more time to comprehend. There is a sliding scale, however, which he shows in a diagram (Figure 3.5) ranging from the photo-realistic to the idiosyncrasies of handwriting. The scale on one side, from the left to the middle, which gives different versions of a face, can be thought of as 'several slightly different progressions', from complex to simple; realistic to iconic; objective to subjective; specific to universal (McCloud, 1994, p.46). Mirroring such progressions, the spectrum from bold, typed text through to an individual's handwriting could be characterized as progressing from simple to complex, or widely-shared to specific, etc.

At all points along this diagram, whether referring to drawing, photo-realism, language, symbols and so forth, there are different means, or systems of representation. We learn all of the figures that make up the letters of the alphabet, and subsequently all of the words they can form. This seems quite understandable as a *system* of meaning. Yet we also learn how to draw. We learn about light and shade, outlines, foreground and background, as well as many nuances of graphic marks (see Chapter 4). It is through the experience of eye-to-hand coordination and through ways of understanding marks upon a page that we come to know how to 'read' or make a drawing; a young child is not able to 'read' a drawing in the way they can when they are older. There is, then, a system of meaning through drawing, though that does not mean it is then easy to *systemize*. Indeed there is much greater scope for individual signature styles, which we cannot necessarily learn as we do the alphabet. We might consider ways in which McCloud's distinction between received and perceived breaks down, but essentially it appears to capture a common way of thinking about the differences.

FIGURE 3.5

Pictures as 'received' and text as 'perceived' © Scott McCloud, *Understanding Comics: The Invisible Art*, New York: HarperPerennial (1994) p.49.

Anchorage and relay

In *Picture Theory* (1994, p.89n), Mitchell provides a brief note on three different typographic conventions that can be employed to designate different relations of text and image. We can write 'image/text', with a slash, to denote 'a problematic gap, cleavage, or rupture in representation'. The agglutination of 'imagetext' can be used to describe 'composite works (or concepts) that combine image and text', and, the use of a hyphen, as in 'image-text', 'designates *relations* of the visual and verbal'. These are useful conventions, delineating three different ways of thinking about text and image, but in themselves they are not necessarily easy to apply. For example, how should we describe Milton's evocative phrase 'in their looks divine'? It is clearly text, yet equally it conjures an image as well as comments on the visual. As an eloquent line of poetry we might not associate it with a 'rupture in representation'. Yet, as Mitchell suggests, this line 'deliberately confuses the visual, pictorial sense of the image with an invisible, spiritual, and verbal understanding' (1987, p.35). Ostensibly, it would be possible to label the phrase with any one or all three of these different conventions, image/text, imagetext and image-text.

The 'puzzle' of text and image is perhaps most famously illustrated with René Magritte's *Les trahison des images* (1929). This beguilingly simple painting evokes the continual oscillation of the relations of text and image (Foucault, 1983). The caption in the painting, 'Ceci n'est pas une pipe', reminds us that of course this is not a pipe – not a *real* pipe – but simply a picture of a pipe. Yet, we look again and nonetheless see a pipe; we can point to it as an account of what a pipe is. Perhaps, then, the text refers to itself. 'This', the text, is of course not a pipe. Indeed, the word 'pipe' is not a pipe. The pipe is the 'thing' that hovers above the writing. It is hardly a dramatic painting, yet it reveals something fundamental. We can consider it as a teaching aid (e.g. akin to an alphabet chart); in fact Magritte makes this explicit in *Les deux mystères* (1966), which includes the same image on a blackboard on an easel. Mitchell (1994, pp.66–67) suggests the painting helps teach us a 'negative lesson, an exercise in unlearning or deprogramming a set of habits which are second nature'. This leads him to consider the painting a 'metapicture' – as being a picture about picturing (see Chapter 6). It addresses the 'fundamental issue of the relation between pictures and texts and those who believe they know what that relation is, who think they know what to say about pictures, what pictures say' (p.67). Magritte's painting remains enigmatic about the relations of text and image. We are easily perplexed by its simplicity, unable to break out of the recursive relationship of words and pictures. Nevertheless, we can identify some further distinctions between word and image, and specifically ways of articulating their different modes of combining.

Further to his remarks on analogue codes, Barthes states all images as **polysemous**. In other words, as noted previously in this chapter, there is the coexistence of many meanings within the one image, of which we can choose some and ignore others. The polysemic nature of images suggests they can have multiple meanings, and leaves open the question as to which meaning we might settle on. Barthes suggests 'this question always comes through as dysfunction' (1977, p. 39) – here he is reflecting the long tradition of the image seen as both all-powerful yet weak in meaning, as discussed above in terms of the historical and philosophical precedents and with the enduring tensions of iconoclasm. The result, Barthes argues, is that 'in every society various techniques are developed to *fix* [the image] in such a way as to counter the terror of uncertain signs; the linguistic message is one of these techniques' (p. 39). Barthes introduces two key terms, **anchorage** and **relay**, which help specify the phenomenon of how language overlays the image.

ANCHORAGE

ROLAND BARTHES

. . . the text replies – in a more or less direct, more or less partial manner – to the question: *what is it?* The text helps to identify purely and simply the elements of the scene and the scene itself [. . .]. The denominative function corresponds exactly to an *anchorage* of all the possible (denoted) meanings of the object by recourse to a nomenclature. Shown a plateful of something (in an *Amieux* advertisement), I may hesitate in identifying the forms and masses; the caption ('*rice and tuna fish with mushrooms*') helps me to choose *the correct level of perception,* permits me to focus not simply my gaze but also my understanding. [. . .] Of course . . . anchorage may be ideological and indeed this is its principal function; the text *directs* the reader through the signifieds of the image, causing him to avoid some and receive others; by means of an often subtle *dispatching,* it remote-controls him towards a meaning chosen in advance. In all these cases of anchorage, language clearly has a function of elucidation, but this elucidation is selective, a metalanguage applied not to the totality of the iconic message but only to certain of its signs. The text is indeed the creator's (and hence society's) right of inspection over the image; anchorage is a control, bearing a responsibility [. . .] the text thus has a *repressive* value and we can see that it is at this level that the morality and ideology of a society are above all invested. (Barthes, 1977, pp. 39–40)

Both anchorage and relay can co-exist, though one or the other tends to be dominant. Barthes considers anchorage, or more simply the caption, to be the most frequent function of text in relation to the image. It is certainly a common feature of journalism, book publishing, advertisements, museum and gallery documentation and much else besides. As a theoretical term, anchorage has been widely adopted and used to describe not simply the explicit captioning of an image (such as a byline under a press photograph, or the plaque next to a painting) but also the less tangible and often dominant narratives and descriptors we bring to the viewing of an image (this is a subject we will consider in more detail in Chapter 5 on the photographic image). We could argue, for example, that many images of the American President Barack Obama were pre-empted or anchored by a discourse about race or the 'feel good factor' rhetoric encapsulated by his campaigning phrase 'Yes we can!'. The key point is that anchorage refers to how language controls our 'reading' of the image.

RELAY

ROLAND BARTHES

The function of relay is less common (at least as far as the fixed image is concerned); it can be seen particularly in cartoons and comic strips. Here text (most often a snatch of dialogue) and image stand in a complementary relationship; the words, in the same way as the images, are fragments of a more general syntagm and the unity of the message is realized at a higher level, that of the story [. . .]. While rare in the fixed image, this relay-text becomes very important in film, where dialogue functions not simply as elucidation but really does advance the action by setting out, in the sequence of messages, meanings that are not to be found in the image itself. (Barthes, 1977, p.41)

Relay refers to a more complementary relationship, though there can be various different 'weightings' between text and image. A story can be told mainly through the relay of text, in which case images play a more supportive role. Barthes refers to 'comic strips intended for "quick" reading' in which the story is predominately told through the text, but with the images adding details 'so that the hurried reader may be spared the boredom of verbal "descriptions"' (1977, p.41). Despite the term 'relay' having been widely adopted, Barthes actually says very little about this concept (the passage quoted above is really all he says on the subject). Thus, just as anchorage is understood to control the image and provide us with the 'right of inspection', so the concept itself has tended to be dominant. However, we can turn to a practitioner of the image, the cartoonist Scott McCloud, for a more expansive set of terms. He presents seven different ways of understanding the different weighting or balance between text and image. In McCloud's view the relations between words and images can be: (1) word specific, (2) picture specific, (3) duo-specific, (4) additive, (5) parallel, (6) montage, and (7) inter-dependent. Instead of written explanations, McCloud *shows* these differences in image-text form. Consult the comic strip panels (Figures 3.7–3.9) and then attempt to complete the task that follows.

153

FIGURE 3.7 © Scott McCloud, *Understanding Comics: The Invisible Art*, New York: HarperPerennial (1994) p.153.

154

155

FIGURE 3.9 © Scott McCloud, *Understanding Comics: The Invisible Art*, New York: HarperPerennial (1994) p.155.

TASK

Weighing Words and Images

Text and image are used in combination across all media, but the ways in which they work together (or act in tension) vary enormously. Select five different instances of text and image. You can choose from all manner of things, such as: a film or television clip, a scene from a play, a radio script, a storybook, a comic book, a cookery book, an encyclopaedia, a webpage, a newspaper article, an advertisement, consumer product packaging, a technical manual, a government or company report, an artwork, architectural design, etc.

In each instance try to characterize the relationship between text and image. Aim to record your analysis in both a pictorial and annotated fashion, and in doing so ask the following:

- Would you identify it clearly as an example of an image/text, image-text or imagetext? Or does it reflect different aspects through a combination of text and image?
- Would you describe the use of language in terms of anchorage or relay? Or a combination of the two?
- Would you define the relationship of text and image as: word specific, picture specific, duo-specific, additive, parallel, montage, or inter-dependent? If you feel more than one of these descriptors applies, show in detail how and where in your example you see the differences.

[handwritten margin note: depend on each other]

Image, text, notation

In paying attention to the difference between image and text, a difficulty arises from the fact that the dichotomy of word and image places emphasis upon the 'visual' or 'material' image. In this chapter, frequent reference has been made to pictures or visual artefacts, as opposed to the less tangible verbal, perceptual and mental images (i.e. the image types on the right-hand side of Mitchell's 'Family of Images', discussed in Chapter 2). There is constant difficulty in trying to define the domain of images with a single, precise term:

> '*Image* is fraught with issues of the propagation and reception of light rays, and it normally belongs to the discourse of vision. *Visual artifact* sounds like a prehistorian's term, or an anthropologist's, and it stresses the "material culture" of an object over its meaning. *Graphism* is technical-sounding and draws attention to the marks and traces that comprise the object.'
>
> (Elkins, 1999, p.82)

As explained at the start of this chapter, in relation to the pictorial turn, 'text' is also a term that has been used extensively, as applied to almost any object of analysis. Nevertheless, as Elkins points out, '[a]lthough it is meant as a neutral term, it is not – as evidenced by the fact that (written) texts do not get called *pictures* and *images*' (Elkins, 1999, p.83).

We cannot necessarily stop using common words such as 'image' and 'text', and of course very often the context in which they are used helps us distinguish between specific meanings. However, it is important to remain vigilant to what is being described. Elkins' approach is not to do away with the division of word and image, but to 'try to stop it from preventing us from seeing other relations between images' (Elkins, 1999, p.83). But what might that mean, or what else can we consider in relation to images? The dilemma in including in this book a chapter on 'image and text' is that it can constrain analysis by offering preconceived categories. Thus, in bringing this chapter to a close we need to acknowledge two main points. Firstly, the opposition of word and image is not a clear-cut distinction. Instead, it opens up far more (philosophical) quandaries about what we mean by the image. Secondly, there is arguably more to be gained by considering the combined phenomenon of 'image-text':

> 'Any sufficiently close look at a visual artifact discloses *mixtures* of reading and seeing. Everyday reading and everyday looking (say, reading this page, and watching images on television) are not pure acts, and so their "opposition" cannot comprise a binary pair. Any act of reading relies on a finite number of customs and strategies, and they are often at work in looking. The converse is also true: We look at images in various ways, in various orders, and at different speeds, and those ways of looking often come into play when we read. There are protocols of reading and looking, meaning signs by which we might recognize that we are reading or looking. Any visual artifact mingles the two, and so there is "reading" in every image and "looking" in every text.'
>
> (Elkins, 1999, p.84)

One of the underlying assertions of Elkins' *Domain of Images* (1999) is that '[t]hinking about images means being led into certain thoughts *by* images'. However, rather than consider images as simply separate from text, we need richer accounts of their interrelationship. Elkins offers a number of key terms in *Domain of Images*, which help open up a subtler spectrum of image-text upon which you can place many different occurrences of the image, mark-making or writing. In particular, he includes 'notation' as a third term. The philosopher Nelson Goodman provides a detailed theory of notation in *Languages of Art* (1968, pp.127–173), which seeks to define how nonlinguistic symbol systems can be quite different to language yet possess certain functional and systematic qualities. A music score, for example, 'is commonly regarded as a mere tool, no more intrinsic to the finished work than is the sculptor's hammer or the painter's easel' (Goodman, 1968, p.127). Yet music notation is not simply an aid to the performance of music. It *defines* a work, 'marking off the performances that belong to the work from those that do not' (p.128). In many respects the addition of a further term, making a triad of 'image, word, notation', raises yet further complications over definitions of the image – we will return to the subject in various guises in the remainder of this book, and in particular in Chapter 8 on images and information.

Summary

This chapter has looked in detail at the relationship between image and text. The notion of a 'pictorial turn' was evoked to suggest two things. Firstly, we have witnessed a shift towards a visual or image-culture. For Kress and van Leeuwen (2006a) this has meant a change in our 'semiotic landscape', whereby systems of information and modes of communication are increasingly dependent on the image, rather than text. A shift in the way we access, exchange and generate knowledge through visual communication has arguably changed the very nature of knowledge itself. However, the pictorial turn is not meant to describe only our contemporary situation. Mitchell's coining of the phrase the 'pictorial turn' is intended as a reminder of the perennial 'problem' or anxiety we attach to the image. Despite calling his book *Picture Theory* (1994), Mitchell is very clear, efforts to formulate an image theory are 'yet to be pictured'. In fact, he writes, '[if compelled] to imagine the shape of a new disciplinary formation that might emerge from efforts to theorize pictures and picture theory, it would have a thoroughly dialogical and dialectical structure, not in the Hegelian sense of achieving a stable synthesis, but in Blake's and Adorno's sense of working through contradiction interminably' (Mitchell, 1994, p.418). This, of course, echoes the different ways of viewing the image, image-systems, and family of images recounted in the preceding chapter.

A history of iconoclasm reveals some very real and hard-fought tensions which centre around the image, and the ways in which language has often come to define and confine the image. More broadly, the pictorial turn leads to a view we have of 'an overabundance of metalanguages for representation and that no "neutral" or "scientific" vocabulary (semiotics, linguistics, discourse analysis) can transcend or master the field of representation' (Mitchell, 1994, p.417). However, it is possible to consider different relationships of text and image. The second half of this chapter has considered various ways of articulating how different weightings of text and image can lead to different effects and meaning. Various terminology have been presented, such as 'analogue' and 'digital', 'anchorage' and 'relay', 'duo-specific', 'parallel', 'montage', etc. Hopefully you can start to adopt these terms when looking at your own examples, with the view to presenting a more nuanced analysis of the image.

Further reading

Barthes, Roland (1977) 'The Rhetoric of the Image' in *Image Music Text*, trans. by Stephen Heath. London: Fontana, pp.32–51.

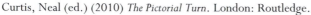

Curtis, Neal (ed.) (2010) *The Pictorial Turn*. London: Routledge.

Elkins, James (1999) *The Domain of Images*. Ithaca: Cornell University Press.

Elkins, James (ed.) (2009) *Visual Literacy*. New York: Routledge.

Foucault, Michel (1983) *This is Not a Pipe*, trans. by James Harkness. Los Angeles: University of California Press.

Goodman, Nelson (1968) *Languages of Art: An Approach to a Theory of Symbols*. London: Oxford University Press.

Hunt, J.D., Lomas, D., and Corris, M. (2010) *Art, Word and Image: Two Thousand Years of Visual/Textual Interaction*. London: Reaktion Books.

Jay, Martin (1994) *Downcast Eyes: The Denigration of Vision in Twentieth-Century French Thought*. Berkeley: University of California Press.

Latour, Bruno and Weibel, Peter (eds) (2002) *Iconoclash: Beyond the Image Wars in Science, Religion, and Art*. Cambridge, Mass.: MIT Press.

McCloud, Scott (1994) *Understanding Comics: The Invisible Art*. New York: HarperPerennial.

Manghani, Sunil, Piper, Arthur and Simons, Jon (eds) (2006) *Images: A Reader*. London: Sage.

Mitchell, W.J.T. (1987) *Iconology: Image, Text, Ideology*. Chicago: University of Chicago Press.

Mitchell, W.J.T. (1994) *Picture Theory: Essays on Verbal and Visual Representation*. Chicago: University of Chicago Press.

WRITING WITH IMAGES

When working on college assignments students frequently ask if they are 'allowed' to include visual images in their written work. What the query reveals is an anxiety about images. Interestingly it is not a worry over *how* to include images, i.e. from a technical point of view, but rather a question about the legitimacy of including images in the first place. Dissertations on visually rich topics from Japanese *ukiyo-e* prints to computer-generated imagery (CGI), tattoo art, Bollywood films, and nanoart, often banish images to the end of the assignment as appendix material. This handling of images would seem to hark back to a time when printing costs prohibited the reproduction of images, and/or more rudimentary printing processes required images to be handled separately. In fact it is still common in books to find colour images printed as 'plates' on high-grade paper and inserted at an arbitrary point in the book (usually without page numbering). However, printing and reproduction technologies allow for more sophisticated handling of both text and image, whether reproduced in full-colour or greyscale. Furthermore, word processor and graphic editing software have become increasingly powerful in manipulating and laying-out the page.

The question as to whether it is acceptable to include images should be re-framed. Not only do we need to ask how to handle images in a technical sense, but we should also be thinking about how images relate to and aid our understanding of a topic, and what different effects are achieved and for what purpose. We can consider three aspects: (1) placement; (2) adjustment or manipulation; and (3) output and quality.

Placement

In using images we need to consider their 'placement' – this might be on an exhibition wall, in a book, on printed packaging, on a video screen, or an online photo-gallery, etc. In the vast majority of cases this will involve thinking about the relationship between word and image, which, as we have seen in Chapter 3, is a complex subject. If we are hanging a picture on a wall, or uploading pictures to a shared online gallery we are likely to think about anchoring the meaning of the image through the use of a few lines of text. However, even in these simple cases, the nature of the text and its relative size and distance to the image makes for different effects. In more complex arrangements, when dealing with the printed page, we can make further choices about the weighting of words and images – so, for example, applying the concepts of anchorage and relay, or McCloud's seven categories of word-image relations (as outlined in Chapter 3).

FIGURE 3.10A Alice passing through the looking glass. Illustration by John Tenniel in Lewis Carroll, *Through the Looking Glass and What Alice Found There* (London: Macmillan, 1865).

FIGURE 3.10B Alice passing through the looking glass. Illustration by John Tenniel in Lewis Carroll, *Through the Looking Glass and What Alice Found There* (London: Macmillan, 1865).

One example of careful composition using both word and image can be shown with one of the best-known set of childrens' books, *Alice's Adventures in Wonderland* and *Through the Looking Glass*. While Alice herself might have bemoaned the lack of illustrations in her sister's storybook, the books she appears in as protagonist make fine use of pictures. The author of the *Alice* books, Lewis Carroll, included numerous drawings of his own in the early drafts of the books, as well as details of 'page placements, sizes and conditions of each illustration' (Wong, 2009, p.137). He also engaged in extensive correspondence with John Tenniel, the illustrator of the original published books.

> 'When it comes to the placement of the illustrations, it is interesting to see that Carroll makes significant allowances by altering the shape of the text to "fit" its illustrations. A surviving letter from Tenniel also demonstrates how Carroll yielded to several textual changes suggested by Tenniel, in particular the suppression of an entire episode.'
>
> (Wong, 2009, p.138)

FIGURE 3.11⃞
Alice's giant hand over the White Rabbit. Illustration by John Tenniel in Lewis Carroll, *Alice's Adventures in Wonderland* (London: Macmillan, 1865).

An illustration of Alice reaching out from inside the White Rabbit's house, where she is trapped having grown to an enormous size, is a good example of the interplay of text and image. Echoing the idea of being trapped in a confined space, the text borders the illustration on three sides. According to Wong, it is 'the kind of illustration that . . . allows a seamless, uninterrupted spatial flow of the narrative, while benefiting from the visual synchronized effects of text and illustration' (2009, pp.138–139). In fact, as Wong suggests, the illustration fits beside the text in such a way that 'even if one tries to read the narrative without looking directly at the illustration, the image lingers so enticingly within the peripheral vision that it seems to be effortlessly incorporated into the reading process' (Wong, 2009, p.140).

There are many other carefully considered techniques used in laying-out the *Alice* books. In *Through the Looking Glass*, the poem 'Jabberwocky' is printed in mirror writing, which at the time required first printing text and then before the ink dried electrotyping as a picture. In other words, in terms of production process, the poem is finally printed as an image, not as typed letters. There are also deliberate uses of the different sheaves of paper of the bound book. So, for example, in *Through the Looking Glass*, there are two almost identical illustrations of Alice going through a mirror to enter the Looking-Glass world. The pages are laid out with the same amount of text beneath the images, which are a mirror image of one another. The illustrations are printed on the recto and verso, or front and back, of the same leaf, so that as you turn the page it is as if you are witnessing Alice coming through the paper itself.

In *Alice's Adventures in Wonderland* the specific use of pages is used in a different way, but to equally good effect. Alice's second encounter with the Cheshire Cat is accompanied with two illustrations, but in this case placed on the recto side of two separate pages. In the first image we see both Alice and the Cheshire Cat, who sits – in full view – high up in a tree. As you turn the page however, on the next facing page, you see the very same tree but only a glimmer of the cat. Cleverly, then, as you turn the page it is as if you are a puppeteer lifting the cat out of the picture. However, of greater interest is the fact that Alice has disappeared entirely.

These examples from the *Alice* books show some rather subtle effects of text-image, with various modes of relay and inter-dependency, as well as careful consideration of the physical, bodily experience of reading. However, despite offering actual examples of how placement can be used creatively and intelligently, it is clear there are no simple templates one can apply from one project to another. The *Alice* examples highlight a unique, ongoing process of 'give and take' that is required in bringing text and image together. Effective placement requires thinking about what it is you wish to achieve and why, along with a willingness to experiment with different layouts. It is also worth considering how collaboration between a writer and illustrator or designer informs the process.

Adjustment

There are many simple processes and tools available for the creation, adjustment and manipulation of images. However, the ubiquity of digital technologies means that we are most likely to work with computers when handling both text and image. This is a very expansive topic, which goes beyond the remit of this book. The following notes provide a few starting points. Word processors are widely used, and the software has evolved to allow for the creation of quite complicated documents. However, there are noticeable limitations with how word processors handle the layout of a page, particularly the relationship between text and image. It can be very difficult to make fine adjustments to the spacing around images for example, and their inclusion often interrupts the flow of text in ways that are unsatisfactory. For more complicated page designs there are various desktop publishers. These provide far greater control over page-layouts and templates to enable the production of sophisticated posters, flyers, brochures, magazines, newspapers and books. In addition, there is various webpage design software dedicated to the creation of online

FIGURE 3.12A Alice and the Cheshire Cat. Illustration by John Tenniel in Lewis Carroll, *Alice's Adventures in Wonderland* (London: Macmillan, 1865).

media. The programs range in complexity, but generally need some level of study before they can be properly used.

Image-editing software are widely available. One of the best-known is the graphics and photo-editing software Photoshop, though there are many other derivative programs. In order to use these packages it is necessary to gain basic orientation of the controls and to work through tutorials – there are many self-help books, online tutorials and short courses. However, there are generic, commonly-used tools in image-editing which are relatively easy to master, allowing the user to crop, sharpen, re-scale, and rotate images, as well as to adjust colour balance, contrast, brightness and to remove red-eye (caused by the flash of a camera). Many of these tools are now available for use on a mobile phone and other portable devices – making the process of image capture and adjustment ever more accessible. One of the powerful features of digital imaging is that – like text – you can cut and paste elements to produce composite images. Generally, however, a higher degree of proficiency is required in order to bring elements together in a coherent and seamless fashion. Unlike text, joining visual elements creates many different effects and huge complexities of background and foreground, etc.

Software such as Photoshop have their own 'native' or proprietary file formats. These should be used when working on a complex design, to ensure all elements of the working process are saved, allowing for ongoing manipulation of the image. However, the file sizes are very large and are not recognized by other software such as word processors or web browsers. Thus, an important consideration when working with digital images is file format. If we include all of the proprietary formats (particular to software programs or image-capture devices), there are hundreds of different formats. However, there are two main types, either raster or vector images. The most common, generic file formats, PNG, JPEG, and GIF, are raster images, which can be displayed via most software and on the Internet. The JPEG format uses an algorithm to compress data, making it particularly suited for use on the Internet, since the smaller the file size the quicker it can be retrieved for display on the end-user's computer. File sizes can be reduced dramatically when using the JPEG format and often without much noticeable change in the quality of the image. If an area of an image displays a series of tones of a specific colour, compression can 'smooth' these out to a single tone, which in many cases need not undermine the information we take from the overall image. Inevitably, however, increasing the levels of compression leads to a poorer quality image (see below on resolution and quality of image). Other generic file formats, such as BMP, TIFF, and RAW, can save images uncompressed and are commonly used for digital photography. Vector graphics render images using a geometric description, which can be displayed smoothly at any scale. This is very different to raster graphics, which use a grid-system for plotting the image (see Sean Cubitt's 'Photography and Arithmetic' in Chapter 5). Vector graphics tend to be used in more professional software and is typically associated with 3D-rendering.

Overall, digital technologies have had a dramatic impact on the creation, adjustment, manipulation and storing of images. The processing of images has become more accessible and more powerful – and many techniques are transferable across different software. However, proper use of any image capture or editing hardware and software requires a period of familiarization and experimentation, as well as a clear sense of the desired outcomes.

Output

The final 'output' when using images can vary. You might work towards a print-based outcome such as an essay, report, book, magazine or catalogue. Or you might need to produce online materials for a static webpage, a blog or social media websites. Alternatively images can be used in presentations (using something like PowerPoint), as well as exhibited in their own right as visual artefacts. Each of these formats, and others beside, will dictate how you need to handle the image to ensure it can be best presented. Visual artefacts can be fashioned in all sorts of ways, according to different

FIGURE 3.12B The Cheshire Cat. Illustration by John Tenniel in Lewis Carroll, *Alice's Adventures in Wonderland* (London: Macmillan, 1865).

mediums. In each case the medium, materials and skills will lead to images of different sizes and quality.

When we refer to visual artefacts we generally assume an original version exists. However, in most cases we incorporate images into a larger piece of work or project, which requires a process of reproduction. Digital technologies have made reproduction very simple; however at the heart of any mode of reproduction is consideration for the resolution of the image and its fidelity to an 'original'. Resolution is measured in 'dots per inch' or DPI. When we look at any printed materials or video screens we see a variety of information – all of which is made up of tiny dots of ink or light rays. The greater the number of 'dots per inch' the greater the resolution. DPI is a measure of spatial dot density within an image. The same image – when looked at as a whole – will also have its own physical dimensions. So, for example, you could have two pieces of paper of the same physical size, each printed seemingly with the same photographic image. However, despite being the same physical dimensions the number of dots per inch in each case may be different. The untrained eye cannot necessarily tell the difference between resolutions within a similar range; however we soon start to notice discrepancies if we try to enlarge the image or use it at a higher grade.

When using images at a professional level it is important resolutions suitably match the mode of output and that appropriate colouring and image adjustment techniques are employed. In publishing print materials, especially when being handled by professional printers or publishers, the minimum recommended resolution

FIGURE 3.13 Reproductions of a detail from a photoetching of a Rembrandt print, as reproduced from James Elkins' *Visual Practices Across the University* (2007, pp.25–27), showing: (a) high-resolution scan of photoetching of original print; (b) same detail, scaled-up from the best reproduction in a book; (c) typical view of the same detail from of a classroom slide; (d) same detail again, but scaled-up from best available image on the Internet.

is 300 DPI. Anything below this figure can lead to the reproduction of 'fuzzy' or speckled images. However, when using digital media the higher the resolution the larger the file size. When sending illustrations to a publisher this might not matter too much, but when putting images into an online environment or even PowerPoint slide, file size starts to matter. An image scanned at 600 DPI will be of great value for creating print materials, but will dramatically slow down the loading of a web-page (and will not actually look any different on screen to an image of far lower DPI). Such an image will also make for a noticeable delay when moving between slides on a PowerPoint presentation.

In *Visual Practices Across the University* (2007), James Elkins reprints four different versions of a detail from a Rembrandt print (Figure 3.13), showing as follows: (a) a high-resolution scan from a photoetching of an original print, which shows much of the original's fine detail; (b) the same detail but scaled-up from the best repro-duction in a book; (c) 'the view a student in the back of a seminar room would have of the best slide of the print from the slide collection of the University of Chicago'; and (d) 'the best available image on the internet, which in many cases is all a student might be able to find' (Elkins, 2007 p.25).

Elkins uses these reproductions to make a point about the nature of enquiry in art history. He suggests: 'none of these images, except perhaps the last, would be an impediment to any of the existing art historical accounts of the print. What art history says about visual objects is routinely far less than what is contained in the objects' (p.25). Arguably, in other fields such as the sciences, degradation of the image might more readily render it unfit for use. A graph, for example, or the visual-ization of a molecule (which needs to evidence scale), may soon become unreadable if the quality of the image is diminished.

In simple cases, whether for an essay, a letter or email to a friend, or a classroom presentation, the best available image might simply be good enough. The important

point is to be able to communicate as effectively as possible about and/or with the selected image. Equally we need to ask *why* we might choose to use an image. You can look through this book and examine what is being said about the various illustrations, which perhaps in keeping with Elkins' comment is 'routinely far less than what is contained in the objects'. However, in the majority of cases the illustrations are important in developing an argument or in demonstrating something. It is possible to describe in words the four illustrations used here of the Rembrandt print, but nonetheless the images offer a much swifter and more detailed account.

PART 2

Image practices

The following five chapters provide accounts of specific image practices or cultures. In each case, the chapters aim to bridge theoretical and historical understanding with practical insights into the making, viewing and evolution of images and image-processes across a range of different domains.

4 Drawing and painting

This chapter considers arguably the most fundamental of image-making practices: drawing and painting. The discovery of European cave paintings dating back some 32,000 years remind us of humanity's deep-seated need and desire for mark-making and the rendering of images. Of course, the true purpose of paleolithic **cave paintings** remains unknown, and this chapter does not seek to address such a question. Instead, considering a more recent history, the chapter begins by offering some conceptual differentiation between drawing and painting. It then turns attention to ways in which we seek to make sense of art composition. Distinctions are made between what is legible, visible and visual in artworks. Following this, a critique of a semiotics of drawing and painting is explored, with specific reference to the notion of 'subsemiotic' marks.

The act of drawing

For John Berger 'drawing is discovery' (2005, p. 3). The act of drawing, he writes, 'forces the artist to look at the object in front of him, to dissect it in his mind's eye and put it together again; or, if he is drawing from memory, that forces him to dredge his own mind, to discover the content of his own store of past observations' (p. 3). Whilst drawing might appear to be a fluid action, the description Berger gives of both looking out to an object and 'dissecting' it in what he calls the 'mind's eye' would seem to describe something rather more complicated. As Berger adds: 'each mark you make . . . is a stepping-stone from which you proceed to the next, until you have crossed your subject as though it were a river' (p. 3).

The French philosopher Jacques Derrida was a guest curator in the early 1990s at the renowned Musée du Louvre, Paris. He organized an exhibition of drawings held by the museum under the title of *Mémories d'aveugle* [Memoirs of the Blind]. The exhibition brought together a series of drawings and prints that show blindness as a recurring motif. Derrida (1993) makes the case that the images are not simply representations of the blind, but self-reflexive accounts of drawing itself as blind. '[T]he blind man', he writes, 'can be a seer, and he sometimes has the vocation of a visionary' (p.2), a thought which he then combines with the act of drawing as 'an eye graft, the grafting of one point of view onto the other: a drawing of the *blind* is a drawing *of* the blind' (p.2). In other words, in order to draw it is necessary to look away or to bring a vision of something onto a different plane. The artist may literally draw a blind subject, but in order to bring pencil to paper there is inevitably a moment of blindness when the eye must look away from the subject and/or equally cannot see what goes on between the tip of the pencil and the surface it meets. Derrida brings together many images of the blind and blindness to elaborate on this idea, but essentially his statement – 'drawing is blind' – holds as a general argument of how meaning is mapped from one place to another in any act of mark-making:

> 'By accident, and sometimes on the brink of an accident, I find myself writing without seeing. Not with the eyes closed, to be sure, but open and disoriented in the night; or else during the day, my eyes fixed on *something else*, while looking elsewhere, in front of me, for example, when at the wheel: I then scribble with my right hand a few squiggly lines on a piece of paper attached to the dashboard or lying on the seat beside me. Sometimes, still without seeing, on the steering wheel itself. These notations – unreadable graffiti – are for memory; one would later think them to be a ciphered writing.
>
> What happens when one writes without seeing? A hand of the blind ventures forth alone or disconnected, in a poorly delimited space; it feels its way, it gropes, it caresses as much as it inscribes, trusting in the memory of signs and supplementing sight. It is as if a lidless eye had opened at the tip of the fingers, as if one eye too many had just grown right next to the nail . . . '
>
> (Derrida, 1993, p.3)

Roland Barthes also refers to drawing in terms of blindness (specifically in relation to the artist Cy Twombly, who we will consider later in this chapter). He goes further to suggest the history of painting has been subject to the 'repressive rationality' of vision. The eye, he writes, is related to reason and evidence, 'everything which serves to control, to coordinate, to imitate; as an exclusive art of seeing' (1985b, p.163; see also Chapter 6 on vision and visuality). Blindness, however, offers a different way of relating to the act of drawing – as a way of bringing together reflection and the body (or more specifically the hand). The blind man, Barthes describes, 'doesn't quite see the direction, the *bearing* of his gestures; only his hand guides . . . Or that hand's desire' (1985b, p.163). Barthes classifies this 'trajectory of the hand' as a controlled action, which in palaeography is termed *ductus*. In palaeography the analysis of handwriting is not based on the actual letters formed, but on the manner and direction in which the lettered strokes appear. Barthes considers Twombly's work as a prime example of the *ductus*, suggesting his is 'a writing of which only the leaning, the cursivity remains' (p.164).

Various art movements of the twentieth century led to 'artists reacting against the conventional assumption that the basis of drawing is visual perception' (Alphen, 2008, pp.60–61). The Surrealist principle of automatism is one clear example, since the hand is meant to rein free of conscious thoughts and visual guidance. Also, in the conceptualism of the 1960s, 'drawing was used as a weapon against the dominance of the retina in the visual arts. Robert Morris, for instance, produced a series of drawings in 1973 entitled *Blind Time* in which he completed self-imposed assignments with his eyes shut and within limited periods of time' (Alphen, 2008, p.61). Blindness (of the hand) describes the act of drawing as 'feeling one's way' in the production of forms. As we draw we invent drawing. Always at work in drawing is what Derrida (1993, p.2) terms *puissance* [potency], which can be said to mean that the 'power' of a drawing 'is not to be found in its persuasiveness, its effect or its goal (an image, for instance) but in a kind of underlying libido . . . a libido from which the drawing issues' (Alphen, 2008, p.61). Drawing in this sense is not simply marks upon a surface, but the manifestation of an underlying searching nature.

Taking a line for a walk

Drawing can be described as a fundamental pictorial act. David Rosand (2002, p.1) argues: 'To make a mark or trace a single line upon a surface immediately transforms that surface, energizes its neutrality; the graphic imposition turns the actual flatness of the ground into virtual space, translates its material reality into the fiction of the imagination'. Berger (2011) explains this process as a set of questions and answers. You 'question' the object (or model) you are drawing, he writes, 'in order to discover lines, shapes, tones that you can trace on the paper. The drawing accumulates the answers. Also, of course, it accumulates corrections, after further questioning of the first answers' (2011, p.8). What accrues through this process is difficult to pin down, but crucially, we can consider here the very formation of image, as an entity in its own right: 'At a certain moment – if you're lucky – the accumulation becomes an image – that's to say, it stops being a heap of signs and becomes a presence. Uncouth, but a presence. This is when your looking changes. You start questioning the presence as much as the model' (p.8).

The process of drawing as recounted by Berger is playfully described by the artist Paul Klee as taking a line for a walk. As we see from an extract here, the *Pedagogical Sketchbook* (1953) is made up of a series of drawings, or diagrams, designed to give methodical demonstration of the various effects of a line upon the page, and their combination. A single line, for example, when brought together with another becomes a picture, with various tensions, weightings, and even implied or imaginary elements. In another case, a single line, which as a figure has 'linear character', when moved through set points takes on a shape; its 'linearity is replaced by planarity'

TAKING A LINE FOR A WALK

PAUL KLEE

(from *Pedagogical Sketchbook*, 1953 [1925], pp.16–19)

An active line on a walk, moving freely, without goal. A walk for a walk's sake [. . .]

The same line, accompanied by complementary forms:

[. . .] Two secondary lines, moving around an imaginary line:

[. . .] A medial line which is both: point progression and planar effect:

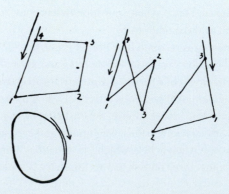

FIGURES 4.1–4.4
Paul Klee, line diagrams from *Pedagogical Sketchbook* (1973). Courtesy of Hattula Moholy-Nagy

FIGURES 4.5–4.6

Paul Klee, line
diagrams from
*Pedagogical
Sketchbook* (1973).
Courtesy
of Hattula
Moholy-Nagy.

In the process of being created, these figures have linear character; but once completed, this linearity is replaced by planarity.

Passive lines which are the result of an activation of planes (line progression):

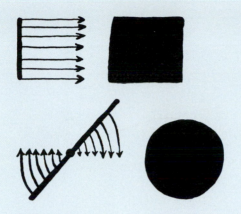

Passive angular lines and passive circular lines become active as planar constituents.

Walter Benjamin (2004) explains the effects Klee describes by arguing how background is conjoined with the line:

> 'The graphic line marks out the area and so defines it by attaching itself to it as its background. Conversely, the graphic line can exist only against this background, so that a drawing that completely covered its background would cease to be a drawing. This confers on the background a specific role that is indispensable for the meaning of drawing, so that in a drawing two lines can be related to each other only through the background . . .'
>
> (Benjamin, 2004, p.83)

As we'll go on to see, Benjamin begins to offer a distinction between drawing and painting – a drawing is inseparably linked to its background, whereas painting, he argues, has no background (or fills it entirely). Similarly, he also distinguishes the graphic line from the geometric line, which does not gain meaning through its interplay with the background. If we think of geometry examples in a mathematics textbook, the diagrams do not interrelate due to the spacing of the background. These are diagrams, not drawings. 'The identity of the background of a drawing', Benjamin writes, 'is quite different from that of the white surface on which it is inscribed. We might even deny it that identity by thinking of it as a surge of white waves (though these might not even be distinguishable to the naked eye)' (Benjamin, 2004, p.83).

These various accounts of drawing, based on lines, planes and their interactions, can be developed further with reference to an analysis of a painting by Cézanne by

Photograph of the
motif for Paul
Cézanne's *Jas de
Bouffan* (1885–1887),
from Erle Loran's
(1947) *Cézanne's
Composition: Analysis
of His Form with
Diagrams and
Photographs of His
Motifs*, Second
Edition. Berkeley:
University of
California Press.

Paul Cézanne, *Jas de
Bouffan* (1885–1887)
© Narodni Galerie,
Prague, Czech
Republic/Giraudon/
The Bridgeman Art
Library.

the artist Erle Loran. (NB: The account comes from a book-long study, *Cézanne's Compositions* (1947), which provides a series of accounts of Cézanne's paintings. Loran's aim in the study is to comment on Cézanne as an artist, to compare between what he observed and what he expressed when painting. For the purposes here, however, we can consider simply the dynamics of composition that Loran details.)

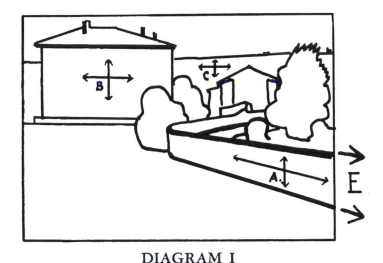

DIAGRAM I

FIGURE 4.9

Diagram I, from Erle Loran's (1947) *Cézanne's Composition: Analysis of His Form with Diagrams and Photographs of His Motifs*, Second Edition. Berkeley: University of California Press.

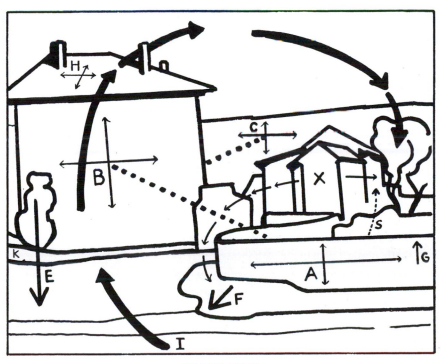

DIAGRAM II

FIGURE 4.10

Diagram II, from Erle Loran's (1947) *Cézanne's Composition: Analysis of His Form with Diagrams and Photographs of His Motifs*, Second Edition. Berkeley: University of California Press.

Figure 4.7 is a photograph of the scene of the *Jas de Bouffan*, which Cézanne painted between 1885 and 1887 (Figure 4.8). Figures 4.9 and 4.10, which Loran labels as Diagram I and II respectively, are schematics for the scene and the painting. Straightaway it is evident in the painting the house appears to lean to the left, which provides a dramatic quality to the picture. Loran describes the effect as giving the picture a 'somewhat haunted or deserted aspect to the scene' (1947, p.53). However he explains this in strict, formal terms:

> 'Cézanne's most important transformation of the motif [scene] becomes apparent when one compares the plane of the stone wall, marked with the axis bars and letter A in Diagram II, with the same wall, similarly marked, in Diagram I. In Diagram I it is obvious that there is no organization, no satisfying correlation between planes A, B and C. Plane A is the unruly element, as is emphasized by the arrows expanding beyond the frame at E, in Diagram I. Turning the wall, A, back so that it became parallel to the picture plane, as we see it in Diagram II, not only eliminated the forward rotation and expansion of the wall, but also brought plane A into relation with the two other basic planes, B and C. A satisfying tension now exists between planes A, B, and C, as is indicated by heavy broken lines . . .'
>
> (Loran, 1947, p.53)

Loran then goes on to suggest how movement is created through the spatial tension of planes A, B and C, indicated by the thick, circular arrows, which begin lower left (marked I). The eye is drawn upwards, with the house being the 'principal magnetic force', and the diagonal plane of the roof carries the movement into the sky region, which is then pulled downward, so returning in the direction of one's starting point. As well as the principal elements, various minor forces contribute to the 'balance between the house on the left and the complex volumes on the right' (p.53). So, for example:

> '. . . the vertical arrow E at the far left, pointing downward, indicates the dropping weight created by the leftward tilt of the axis of the house. An important tension exists between the dark tree, pierced by arrow E, and the grass shape at F in front of the wall, plane A. Of course, the tree is obviously rising in relation to the grass shape at F. With the left side of the house lower than the right side, there is consequently a slight rotation of the plane of the house; it comes out at the left, and at the right turns back into depth. But notice the subtle upward turn in the path just to the left of arrow E, at K. By turning this path upward [there is created] a feeling of space behind the house, even on the left, and has prevented too strong a profusion at the left side of the house. Place a finger over the lines to the left of the letter E, and a disturbing effect of too heavy and dropping weight in the house, which Cézanne has avoided, will at once become evident.'
>
> (Loran, 1947, p.53)

Loran also comments on the smaller house, marked X, which he describes as expanding to both right and left of the plane X. This, Loran argues, gives the buildings an extreme, distorted perspective comparable in some respects to Byzantine icon painting and modern, abstract art. The arrows peeling away from the mark X indicate this dual movement:

> 'The effect of the expanding walls is twofold. First, since both the left- and right-hand walls can be seen, the illusion of three-dimensionality, of "seeing around" the object, is increased enormously [. . .] The second function of the expanding walls is to create a return from the deep space to the original two-dimensionality of the picture plane. In no painting by Cézanne is this dualistic phenomenon more clearly evident. It can be studied extensively in Byzantine icon painting; in the abstract art of Picasso and Braque it is one of the favourite and most familiar devices, particularly in the drawing of tables.'
>
> (Loran, 1947, p.54)

Loran's account is concerned purely with how Cézanne's painting is 'drawn' – how lines, dimensions and shapes are composed and what dynamics they create. In this way, he draws attention to some fundamental ideas and experiences of composition, which we can experiment with in quite simple ways by making drawings ourselves and making sketches of existing paintings. However, in the section that follows, we will turn more specifically to the medium of paint and consider how painting differs from drawing.

TASK

Tracing Lines

(1) Copy Paul Klee's diagrams (from the extract 'Taking a Line for a Walk'). What experience do you have in drawing these lines and imaginary lines? Do you sense a change in form as you join up the points of the lines, or as you build up a series of lines to form a single plane? What does it feel like to 'take a line for a walk' – where might it take you?

(2) Select a drawing or painting, perhaps of a well-known artist. Then, using tracing paper, mark-out its compositional elements – i.e. how the picture is composed of lines, shapes and planes. Look back at Erle Loran's schematic diagram of Cézanne's *Jas de Bouffan* to help. Can you identify how elements complement each other or pose tensions in the picture? What are the most salient features of the composition?

What is painting?

For Berger, painting is associated with a 'finished' piece of work: 'Here you do not pass through your subject, but try to re-create it and house yourself in it. Each brush-mark . . . is no longer a stepping-stone, but a stone to be fitted into a planned edifice' (Berger, 2005, p.3). There are technical factors too. Paintings, we might argue, take longer, are generally of a larger scale, and need to simultaneously manage colour, quality of pigment, tone, texture, etc. (p.4). Berger also suggests that drawings, which frequently are only preparatory exercises, are private. Whereas paintings are for public showing. Complementing this view – albeit in a short, incomplete entry – Benjamin (2004b, p.82) suggests paintings are 'held vertically before the observer', whereas drawings are 'placed horizontally on the table'. His statement, which amounts to little more than a paragraph, is ambiguous, but begins to suggest how we read horizontally, and look vertically. Of course there are numerous examples that would contradict some or all of these specificities of painting. However, they point to an intuitive sense in which drawing and painting differ. Stephen Bann (1970), commenting on modern painting, for example, writes of the 'experimental painter' who is committed to 'a particular *path* of controlled activity, of which the works he produces remain as evidence'. Despite the suggestion here of the experimental, developmental nature of the painting, there is the sense of a larger 'project' of painting, whereby the 'direction in which the artist moves is at least as important as the individual statements which record the track that he has taken' (Bann, 1970, p.7).

For James Elkins (2000), drawing is a 'matter of touch', whereas painting represents a vast 'alchemy'. Quite different to concerns of the writing of art history, for example, which looks for meaning in paintings, Elkins reminds us of what is messy and unstable about the medium of paint:

> 'A painting is made of paint – of fluids and stone – and paint has its own logic, and its own meanings even before it is shaped into the head of a madonna. To an artist, a picture is both a sum of ideas and a blurry memory of "pushing paint", breathing fumes, dripping oils and wiping brushes, smearing and diluting and mixing. Bleary preverbal thoughts are intermixed with the namable concepts, figures and forms that are being represented. The material memories are not usually part of what is said about a picture, and that is the fault of interpretation because every painting captures a certain resistance of paint, a prodding gesture of the brush, a speed and insistence in the face of mindless matter: and it does so at the same moment, and in the same thought, as it captures the expression of a face.'
>
> (Elkins, 2000, pp.2–3)

Benjamin (2004, p.85) describes a painting as a picture with no background and no graphic lines. Instead, he argues, 'painting is a medium'. He explains the phenomenon as follows: '[No] one color [is] ever superimposed on another, but at most appears in the medium of another color. And even that is often difficult to determine, so that in principle it is often impossible to say in many paintings whether a color is on top or underneath' (p.85). Benjamin explains that the 'reciprocal demarcations of the colored surfaces' of a painting are not based on graphic lines, but that forms appear *through* the layering and interplay of paint. It is true that painters often sketch outlines before painting. However, 'such composition has nothing to do with drawing' or at least the only instance in which it does, where colour and line coincide, is with watercolours. In this case, 'pencil outlines are visible and the paint is put on transparently. In that case the background is retained, even though it is colored' (p.85). Presumably, then, for Benjamin watercolours can be *both* drawing and painting simultaneously.

The full significance of describing painting as a medium (as differentiated from drawing) comes into focus with the contrast Benjamin makes between 'sign' and 'mark'. An immediate difference he notes is that 'the sign is printed on something, whereas the mark emerges from it' (p.84). He gives Christ's stigmata, blushing and birthmarks as examples of marks. Furthermore, as well as asserting 'the realm of the mark is a medium' (p.84), a crucial difference is that 'signs are intentionally made by a subject whereas marks just emerge or appear' (Alphen, 2008, p.66). According to Benjamin, then, the difference between drawing and painting is based on the difference between signs and marks. Drawing is an intentional act of mark-marking, whereas in painting the composition is indirectly created. The painter places colours upon a surface, but 'does not create their differential values . . . only utilises them. They have to be accepted as they emerge or appear' (Alphen, 2008, p.67).

Putting aside Benjamin's rather idiosyncratic use of the terms 'sign' and 'mark', there are numerous problems in asserting a rigid distinction between drawing and painting. As we will consider at the end of this chapter, there are numerous ways in which drawing comes *through* complex layers of mark-making, so being closer to the mark as medium. Drawing as a more intentional act than painting is overly forced, but nonetheless, Benjamin's account does usefully bring out subtle differences in how one physically handles pencil and paint, etc. Also, importantly, the mark as medium reveals what Benjamin refers to as the 'problem of painting' (though we might extend this to the problem of picturing), whereby we must acknowledge 'a picture can have a composition even though this cannot be reduced to a graphic design' (2004, p.85). Benjamin tries to solve this problem by considering the relationship between the word and the picture, which we will return to in more detail below, when first considering the relationship between legibility and the visual, and then finally the notion of subsemiotics. Before doing so, however, it is worth exploring in more detail how a diversity of mark-making – even in a contained set of examples – produces some quite fundamental differences.

de Kooning, Pollock and Twomby . . .

On adjacent walls in a gallery of the Art Institute of Chicago you can view Willem de Kooning's *Excavation* (1950) and Jackson Pollock's *Greyed Rainbow* (1953). If either of these paintings are seen in isolation we might say we observe a similarly complex interplay of mark-marking; or even controlled chaos. But next to each other we quickly see how they differ. Pollock is well-known as the innovator of action painting, which is strongly associated with **abstract expressionism** (with some critics even using the terms interchangeably). His paintings were achieved not with a brush, but with paint itself and the action of the body. Pollock 'painted' with the canvas flat on the ground. He would physically move about the frame whilst dripping and throwing paint; as if entering into the canvas itself. As we see with the example of *Greyed Rainbow*, the results made for bold, colliding, and energetic markings.

De Kooning's *Excavation* is again understood as an example of abstract expressionism (and is painted in the same period), yet it is very different. Here the mark-making, whilst equally complex and without pattern, appears rather more deliberate. We see also erasure, or the 'digging out' of marks and forms (hence the

FIGURE 4.11

Willem de Kooning, *Excavation*, 1950 © The Willem de Kooning Foundation/ ARS, New York and DACS, London 2012.

title of excavation), which has the effect in places of the picture eroding, folding in on itself. Yet elsewhere, with various bold markings and outlines, the picture appears *almost* to surface with clarity and vigour. A seemingly precarious construction, the painting oscillates around a critical moment: it is on the verge of total collapse, yet equally nears the forming of a clearly structured picture. Looked at in this way, de Kooning's painting is a picture *about* representation; about the threshold of meaning. It presents the question: when does a picture become a picture, and when is it simply a series of incoherent markings? (The caption besides the painting as featured in the gallery adds to this reading. It notes neorealist film as an underlying influence, so alluding to the fact the painting is an abstraction *from* the world, or at least a filmic world. There is, then, a clearly intended relationship to ideas about representation.)

By contrast, Pollock's work is about the body. It does not so much represent the body, however, but rather has recorded, or traced its gestures in a compounded fashion — like a saturated tape-loop. At risk of being reductive, we might argue Pollock externalizes the internal temporality and motion of one's own body. Whereas de Kooning's *Excavation* internalizes (in the frame of the painting) the act of representation, which is a move to externalize something.

To further this 'drama' of mark-making — elaborating on the sheer diversity achieved *through* what Benjamin refers to as the absolute mark — we can look at

FIGURE 4.12

Jackson Pollock, *Greyed Rainbow*, 1953 © The Pollock-Krasner Foundation/ ARS, New York and DACS, London 2012. Photography © The Art Institute of Chicago.

FIGURE 4.13

Cy Twombly, *The First Part of the Return from Parnassus*, 1961 © The Art Institute of Chicago.

another painting hanging in the same gallery as *Greyed Rainbow* and *Excavation*. As you turn a corner from these paintings Cy Twombly's *The First Part of the Return from Parnassus* (1961) comes into view. We can make partial comparisons with both Pollock and de Kooning. Like the latter, Twombly's work – through a series of marks and erasures – shows a similar oscillation of forms appearing but which do not quite coalesce. As Barthes suggests, Twombly's work 'is decipherable, but not interpretable; the strokes themselves may well be specific, discontinuous; even so, their function is to restore . . . *vagueness*' (Barthes, 1985b, p.160). Like Pollock, what Twombly shows is gesture – his is another kind of action painting. Barthes defines gesture as the 'surplus of action. The action is transitive, it seeks only to provoke an object, a result' (1985b, p.160). However, for Barthes, whilst Twombly *shows* gesture, '[w]e are not asked to see, to conceive, to savour the *product*, but to review, to identify, and, so to speak, to "enjoy" the movement which has ended up *here*' (Barthes, 1985b, p.164). Unlike Pollock's whole bodily engagement in painting, for Twombly it is 'the trajectory of the hand, and not the visual perception of its work' (Barthes, 1985b, p.164); the process described earlier in this chapter with the term *ductus*. Barthes defines Twombly's work through the distinction between product (the mark) and producing (or marking), which like a child 'playing' (without rules) is about 'the *process* of manipulation, not the object produced' (Barthes, 1985b, p.172).

Twombly's work presents further considerations, distinctive from the work of Pollock and de Kooning. Firstly, going by Benjamin's definitions of drawing and painting, we are presented with a confusion as to the nature of Twombly's work. There are graphic lines and background, making his work more drawing than painting. Yet equally, his mark-making displays painterly qualities, in which marks appear in the medium of other marks. One way of understanding the work is as graffiti (graffiti as and on modern art). Rosalind Krauss writes: 'Twombly took up graffiti as a way of *interpreting* the meaning of Action Painting's mark and most particularly that of Pollock's radically innovative dripped line' (1994, p.118). Reference to graffiti helps explain the notion of background in Twombly's work. Barthes suggests graffiti is constituted not through its inscription or message, but the background (the wall, the surface, etc.): 'it is because the background exists fully, as an object which has already *lived*, that such writing always comes to it as an enigmatic surplus: what is *in excess*, supernumerary, out of place – that is what disturbs the order of things' (Barthes, 1985b, p.167). In effect Twombly works upon the already existing canvas (surface) of modern art, disturbing its order.

However, aside from blending both drawing and painting, Twombly's work is particularly distinctive as a kind of writing, or what Barthes calls 'the *allusive* field of writing', for Twombly 'retains the gesture, not the product' (Barthes, 1985b, pp.158, 160). Thus, Barthes explains: '. . . what appears to be writing in [Twombly's] work is born from the surface itself. [. . . T]here is the texture of paper, then the stains, the hatchings, the tracery of strokes, the diagrams, the words. At the end of this chain, writing loses its violence; what is imposed is not this writing or that, nor even the Being of writing, it is the idea of graphic texture' (1985b, p.162). The 'image' of 'graphic texture' that Barthes discerns in Twombly's work is certainly evocative, and not least raises all sorts of questions about the relationship between writing, drawing and painting.

Beyond the legible

The account of the paintings given above are in effect narratives that make sense because they sit within a master narrative of modern art criticism (which, for example, makes it possible to evoke concepts such as action painting, and abstract expressionism). While Benjamin argued the picture is only a set of marks which come *through* the painting, he also adds it is through language – how we come to name the picture – that the 'composition' is created (2004, pp.85–86). In its heyday, it was thought semiotics, the science of signs (as discussed in Chapter 1), would elucidate painting as a language; 'to put the picture's signifiers on one side and its signifieds on the other, and to systematize their rules of substitution and combination' (Barthes, 1985b, p.149). Drawing on the work of Jean Louis Schefer (1995), Barthes suggests rather than ask the 'rigged question' as to whether painting is a language, we need consider the *connection* between the picture and language. He suggests this connection *is* the picture itself: 'The picture . . . exists only in the *account* given of it; or again: in the total and the organization of the various readings that can be made of it: a picture is never anything but its own plural description' (Barthes, 1985b, p.150).

This plurality of the picture fits with the notion of an ecology of images (discussed in Chapter 2), except Barthes imposes the domination of language. He breaks with the idea of the semiotic 'model' against which to measure pictures, but nonetheless, in reference to Schefer (1995), he looks to a form of *writing with* the picture: 'the work of reading (which defines the picture) is radically identified with the work of the writing: there is no longer a critic, not even a writer talking painting, there is the *gramatographer*, someone who writes the picture's writing' (Barthes, 1985b, p.151). Whilst seductive an idea, this conjoining of picture and writing fundamentally refers to a picture's *writing*. We might say Twombly's graphic textures look from the other end of the spectrum, as someone who 'pictures writing's pictures'. Yet, here again, writing remains the underlying principle of legibility.

What happens, then, if we simply try to look at paintings without language – what might we see? The art historian and philosopher Georges Didi-Huberman provides one response to such a question, with an insightful account of a fresco in the monastery of San Marco in Florence, painted around 1440 by a Dominican friar, Fra Angelico. The fresco is located in a small whitewashed room, or cell, and is regarded as an important work of **Renaissance painting**. It depicts the scene of the Biblical story of the Annunciation, in which the angel Gabriel tells the Virgin Mary that she will conceive and become the mother of the Son of God. Didi-Huberman leads us first through the all too usual 'reading' of the image as a *representation* (making for the picture's plural description to follow Barthes terminology), followed by a more immediate response to the fresco as a visual experience – so treating the work as a *presentation*. In doing so, he delimits what is 'legible', 'visible' and 'visual' in the work.

THE LEGIBLE, VISIBLE AND VISUAL

GEORGES DIDI-HUBERMAN

(from *Confronting Images: Questioning the Ends of a Certain History of Art*, 2005, pp.11–17.)

It is with the emergence of its representational details that the fresco, little by little, will become truly *visible*. It becomes so in Alberti's sense, which is to say that it sets about delivering discrete, visible elements of signification – elements discernible as *signs*. It becomes so in the sense familiar to historians of art, who today strive to distinguish the master's own hand from that of his students, to

FIGURE 4.14 Fra Angelico, *The Annunciation*, c.1440–1441. Fresco. Florence, Monastery of San Marco. It is important to note, the fresco is situated deliberately next to a small, east-facing window, which provides the only light into the room. In the first instance, the effect of the light is to obscure the presence of the fresco. Gradually, however, as one's eyes adjust, it becomes clear – and yet, as Didi-Huberman notes, what is revealed is largely only the whitewash of the wall, since the fresco 'consists only of two or three stains of attenuated color placed against a slightly shaded background of the same whitewash. Thus where natural light besieged our gaze – and almost blinded us – there is henceforth white, the pigmentary white of the background, which comes to possess us' (2005, p.11). Of course, today, in visiting the artwork you will be only one of a series of tourists who have arrived to the monastery, which is now transformed into a museum. Such an 'experience', Didi-Huberman suggests, prompts us to look in a certain way, offering up the artwork as a series of visible signs, which in turn allows it to be 'legible'.

judge the coherence of the perspective construction, to situate the work in Angelico's chronology as well as in the stylistic landscape of fifteenth-century Tuscan painting. The fresco will become visible also – and even primarily – because something in it has managed to evoke or 'translate' for us more complex units, 'themes' or 'concepts', as Panofsky would say, stories or allegories: units of knowledge. At this moment, the perceived fresco becomes really, fully visible – it becomes clear and distinct as if it were making itself explicit. It becomes *legible*.

[. . .]

But let's try to go a bit further. Or rather let's stay a moment longer, face to face with the image. Quite soon, our curiosity about details of representation is likely to diminish, and a certain unease, a certain disappointment begin to dim, yet again, the clarity of our gazes. Disappointment with what is legible: this fresco presents itself as the most poorly and summarily recounted story there could be. No salient detail, no discernible particular, will tell us how Fra Angelico 'saw' the town of Nazareth – the 'historical' site of the Annunciation – or help us to situate the meeting of the angel and the Virgin Mary. There's nothing picturesque in this painting: it's as taciturn as they come. [. . .]

[However . . .] if the *visible* and the *legible* are not Fra Angelicos's strong points, that is because his concern was with, precisely the *invisible*, the ineffable. If there is nothing between the angel and the Virgin in his Annunciation, that is because the *nothing* bore witness to the indescribable and unfigurable divine voice to which Angelico, like the Virgin, was obliged to submit completely. Such a judgment clearly touches upon something pertinent to the religious, even mystical status of the artist's work in general. But it refuses to understand the means, the *material* in which this status existed. It turns its back to the specifics of painting and fresco.

At this point in his account Didi-Huberman suggests we have reached the limits of a semiotics that has only three categories: the visible, the legible and the invisible. The legible, he writes, is of an 'intermediary status', since it is concerned only with translatability. Thus, it appears we are left with two choices. Either we can accept what is visible and offer some description of the 'world' that it depicts. Or, we can 'view' the invisible, and so refer to a metaphysics beyond the frame of the painting, which in this case relates to a religious discourse.

There is, however, an alternative to this incomplete semiology. It is based on the general hypothesis that the efficacy of these images is not due solely to the transmission of knowledge – visible, legible, or invisible – but that, on the contrary, their efficacy operates constantly in the intertwinings, even the imbroglio, of transmitted and dismantled knowledges, of produced and transformed non-knowledges. It requires, then, a gaze that would not draw close only to discern and recognize, to name what it grasps at any cost – but would, first, distance itself a bit and abstain from clarifying everything immediately.

[. . .]

We must return . . . to what is simplest, in other words to the obscure self-evidences with which we began. We must momentarily leave behind everything that we thought we saw because we knew what to call it, and return henceforth to what our knowledge had not been able to clarify. We must return, then, this side of the represented visible, to the very conditions of the gaze, of *presentation* and figurability, that the fresco proposed to us at the outset. Then we will remember our paradoxical sense that there wasn't much to see. We will remember the light against our face and above all the omnipresent white – the *present white* of the fresco diffused throughout the space of the cell. What to make of this glare, and what to make of this white? The first constrained us initially to distinguish *nothing*, the second hollowed out all spectacle between the angel and the Virgin, making us think that Angelico had simply put *nothing* between his figures. But to say that is not to look, it is to be satisfied with what we're supposed to see. Let's look: there's not nothing, because there's white. It isn't nothing, because it reaches us without our being able to grasp it, and because it envelops us without our being able, in our turn, to catch it in the snare of a definition. It is not *visible* in the sense of an object that is displayed or outlined; but neither is it *invisible*, for it strikes our eye, and even does much more than that. It is material. It is a stream of luminous particles in one case, a powder of chalky particles in the other. It is an essential and massive component of the work's pictorial presentation. Let's say that it is *visual*.

We can apply Didi-Huberman's terms to another, more contemporary example, in this case a painting by Paul Klee, titled *Haupweg und Nebenwege* (1929), meaning 'main way and byways'. The painting – as it is made *visible* to us – is made up of horizontal bands of colour, of oranges, blues and greens, which build up a series of vertical patterns, with one main pathway just off centre and a series of contributory tracks; all of which appear to be move towards a distant horizon. The painting begins perhaps to take on some form of *legibility*. If a little haphazard and misshapen, the painting presents a grid, like a map of a myriad set of fields, perhaps leading out to the sea. The sense of movement into the distance, pronounced by the central 'main' pathway, leads our eye into the picture as if we might readily know how to 'read' it – as if the vertical and horizontal lines provide a 'system' of navigation. We think we are heading somewhere, yet quickly the other possible pathways soon distract our eye and we begin to doubt the very idea of a 'main way'. As with Didi-Huberman's account, Klee's painting returns us to the 'very conditions of the gaze, of *presentation* and figurability'. The painting provides a *visual* experience. Indeed, surely the unique quality of any picture as opposed to the sentence is that we are at liberty to roam its surface without losing the 'meaning'. Klee's painting explicitly reminds us of this experience at the very point of looking at it.

FIGURE 4.15

Paul Klee, *Haupweg und Nebenwege* (1929). Courtesy of VG Bild Kunst.

TASK

Between the Legible, Visible and Visual

Visit an art gallery, museum or place of worship. Select an exhibit and spend some time studying it. Attempt to apply Didi-Huberman's terms of the legible, visible and visual to your experience of the exhibit. You might begin with information that is provided, whether with a caption on the wall, or an informational booklet. Further still, you can make some preparatory notes prior to your visit by looking up information in books and/or online. Based on your 'reading' of the exhibit you will no doubt have a sense of key ideas or narratives which are being told – how are these ideas and narratives made visible? Are there certain 'units' of meaning, whether themes, concepts or symbols? Do you find tensions with what can and cannot be made visible? Having thought about the exhibit in these ways, try to step back from what you think you see because of the information you have acquired. What 'strikes your eye' as you look at the exhibit? What comes to mind before you even start to attempt to articulate a response? What does the 'material' object present to you, what is it that is made *visual* as you stand before it? What happens as you try to record or articulate your response (whether in writing or by talking to someone else)?

Above and below the line

If we try to respond purely to the 'visual' in a painting or drawing, as discussed above, or Benjamin's idea of marks coming through the medium of paint, how are we to know what we are looking at? Arguably, there needs to come a point when the image is legible to us, when the marks become signs. One response to this problem has been the application of **visual semiotics** (Bal and Bryson, 1991). The literary theorist Mieke Bal explains visual semiotics as a reading of a painting (or other visual media) which is 'primarily *visual*, but . . . at the same time *meaning oriented* and focused on *meaning production*' (Bal, 1996, p.578). She draws explicitly upon the semiotics of Peirce (see Chapter 1), in particular his notion of semiotic process. Thus, for Bal, an important principle of visual semiotics is that visual details push an initial 'passive gaze' and 'dynamize the activity of the viewer' (Bal, 1991, p.4). So, for example, in looking at a picture your line of vision might chance upon a seemingly insignificant detail, which has the effect of unbalancing any previous unity of meaning, making one aware of 'looking' at the picture, as well as of a possible re-interpretation (Bal, 1996).

In *Reading 'Rembrandt'* (1991), Bal considers an ink drawing by Rembrandt, *One of the Magi Adoring the Infant Jesus* (Figure 4.16). As the title suggests the picture portrays one of the wise men come to pay respects to the infant Jesus, as told in the Nativity story. However Bal wonders why there is only one adorer, not three; and she suggests no detail of the man actually identifies him as a 'king' or 'wise man'. Bal offers an alternative account, which importantly is motivated by a visual detail in the picture. Thus, she activates a different reading, but one based on looking at the picture itself, rather than overlaying a prior commentary of her own devising. Bal draws our attention to a specific mark in the drawing: 'The feet of the baby are continuous with a very bold line, almost a blot of ink, between the woman's thighs' (Bal, 1991, p.210). This blot, she argues, is there to be seen and yet by itself is apparently 'meaningless'. She calls such a mark **subsemiotic**, by which she means it is *potentially* semiotic (Bal, 1996, p.576). The idea of the subsemiotic mark is that it contributes to the construction of a sign, yet in itself is not a sign (rather it resides just below the line of what is meaningful):

'. . . stylistic variation, light and dark, composition, or more technical aspects like brushstrokes, paint thickness, and lines are not, a priori, signs in themselves; not any more than in a literary text sheer ink on the page, mere punctuation

marks, and syntactic structures are. Although they are part of what make us interpret the work, we do not give them meaning in themselves . . . '

(Bal, 1991, p.400, n.16)

In the example Bal gives of the adoration, the semiotic potential of the blot at the centre of the picture is activated by combining with other aspects. Bal notes the man 'does not look up to the child the story wants him to adore. He is not kneeling either; he is squatting. He has his hands ready to take the baby and put it into his lap' (Bal, 1991, p.211). Bal suggests this 'meaningless' blot can lead us to process the scene as one of delivery, as much as adoration:

'The woman is "right now" pulling the baby out of her body and handing it over to the elderly man. In other words, this fabula is not congruent with the iconographically recognizable scene, which in fact tends to obliterate rather than emphasize the [specifically visual elements, and would have no use for the blot]. Yet it is a fabula, and if it needs to bracket the official story temporarily, it certainly does not contradict that story, but only conflates the Nativity with the Adoration; by representing both in one scene, they shed an unexpected light on both.'

(cited in Bal, 1996 p.577)

The concept of subsemiotics has prompted debate (see Elkins, 1995; 1996; 1998; Bal, 1996; and Manghani, 2003). One criticism of Bal is that she looks too selectively. As Elkins (1996, p.593) suggests, 'it is also true that subsemiotic elements are those she declines to interpret' (for example, what might we say about the overworked lines at the top-left of the man's shoulder?). Elkins describes Bal's approach with an analogy of making popcorn: 'one by one meaningless subsemiotic marks pop, becoming meaningful signs. In the end, whatever fails to pop is thrown away' (Elkins, 1996, p. 593). We could say what is discarded in Bal's analysis constitutes the picture *as* picture (or the visual as Didi-Huberman terms it) as much as her meaningful signs. In this light, a properly visual semiotics would need to find some way of acknowledging and even incorporating *all* 'meaningless' details.

Elkins attempts extremely close readings of graphic marks in pictures in order to unveil distinct modes of mark-making out of what he notes must always be a massive taxonomy. Each 'distinct non-semiotic structure' is put forward to further a discussion of 'what really goes on in a picture'. For example, in a drawing by Michelangelo (Figure 4.17), he examines the *contorno* – 'a serpentinate braiding of marks that is at once a mark in itself and many marks supporting a single mark. The part does not exist without the whole and vice versa' (Elkins 1995, p.858). As Elkins explains: 'Michelangelo often began with dull chalks, sketching rapidly and schematically, and then went more slowly and forcibly with a freshly sharpened chalk, so that the last lines were sharper and darker than the others' (1995, p.848). Thus, he went back over the contours, always altering and correcting but *not* erasing. In the drawing we can discern various different shapes and positions of the cross as well different expressions of the figure of Mary. These are subtle details, which might well suit a reading Bal would make of the image. Elkins, however, suggests 'the drawing is wilder than that, since most of what happens to the body of Christ is nonsemiotic' (Elkins, 1996, p.598) – or we could say subsemiotic, if without assuming its potential as being a sign, or part of a sign.

'His body, for example, is far from clear even as a body. It is wrapped in a thickened air made of faint lines, and those lines spread out and dissipate into the blank paper as if the figure were trembling in a tub of water and sending tiny ripples out to either side. There is a place on the figure's right flank where its flesh ends the highlights of the armpit, chest, and hip are distinctly marked but that may not be the end of the body, since there are several sharp contours incised just beyond. (One is just to the left, where there should be nothing but air.) In effect, Christ's body seems to continue into a soft darkness for several

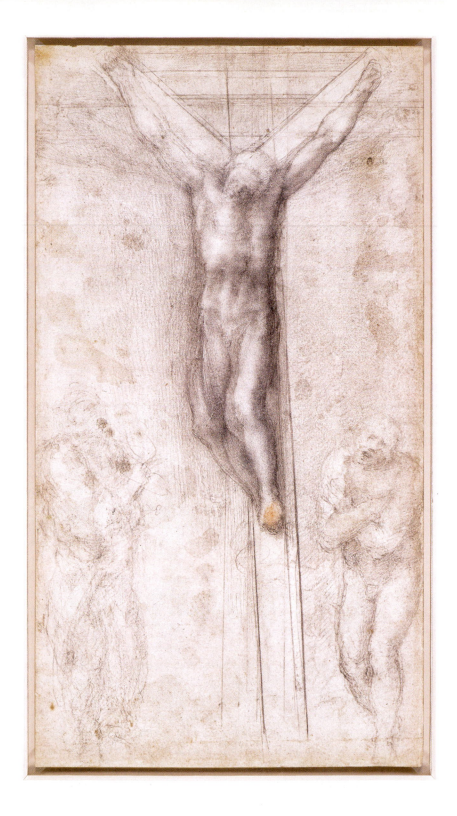

inches before it begins to lighten and fade. And even then, at a distance that seems to be a foot or more from the body, imperfect echoes of the ribs and the hip continue outward, until the atmosphere itself takes on the form of the torso and abdomen. On the right side of the sheet, the straight cross seems to clear the air, and Michelangelo has given the page some texture with light parallel strokes rising diagonally upward from the ruled line. But on the left the short marks are not parallel to one another; they are slightly turned, so that each set is aligned to a portion of the body. They follow the curve of the hips, move up the chest, and turn outward with the arm. Below, they fall straight from the knees like rainwater.

These are not traces of earlier, monstrously large versions of the body but echoes or anticipations of it, as if the body were congealing out of empty atmosphere. There is no determinate contour on either side of the body; the flanks are slurred in darkness and are also broken, divided into incompatible segments. One especially strong line on the figure's right side dives down from the armpit and curls around the ribs, but it cannot be continuous with the line that seems to border the abdomen. That line hooks around the pelvis in an impossibly tight curve, breaking again before it meets the softer arc of the thigh.'

(Elkins, 1996, pp.598–599)

Elkins' approach is to describe the picture in close detail (in effect by carefully following marks wherever they lead). In this example of the Michelangelo, he seeks to show the complexity of the contorno *before* we attribute it semiotic value, or at least as it oscillates in and out of meaning:

'*Contorni* work against sense by denying the viewer any single solution, any unambiguous form that can carry a determinate meaning. In a way the marks in a *contorno* work together to create a single, fused form that is more powerful than any that could be done with a single outline; but at the same time they are disunified and slip free of any unitary reading. I would say much the same about the watery darkness [Bal describes] between the woman's legs in the Rembrandt drawing. Perhaps it can be seen as a sign, and perhaps it makes sense to read it as a birth canal, but even if we choose to do so, the mark is also a place where Rembrandt's brush passed several times, trying to draw something – or some things – no longer entirely legible. Even aside from any guesswork about what they might have been, or whether they were representational, or even consciously intended, there is the fact that the blot also smears any potential reading.'

(Elkins, 1996, p.599)

A significant facet of Elkins' account – in contrast to Bal – is an interest in the materiality and practicality of mark-making. Through very close inspection, he tries to account for how marks are made, and/or, as Benjamin might suggest, how marks work themselves through a medium. Of course, one result of placing this kind of emphasis on marks has arguably 'left more exacting questions about graphic marks to the domain of practical criticism, so that the people who are said to understand marks best are other artists, and the most incisive critiques are taken to be other paintings instead of texts' (Elkins, 1995, p.822). The underlying principle of this book has been to find a bridge between practical and theoretical criticism, but, with the view it is very difficult to achieve — as these accounts reveal of even the most fundamental mark-making of drawing and painting.

Summary

This chapter has sought to elucidate ideas about drawing and painting as fundamental practices of image-making. There has been a deliberate attempt to avoid too much influence from art history — which is the dominant field of study, but which is often overly concerned with the *interpretation* of images. In trying to offer a practical understanding of drawing and painting, the chapter begins with outlining some distinctive qualities. So, for example, drawing has been characterized as a more exploratory medium, in which, to take Paul Klee's famous line, one can 'take a line for a walk'. Painting, on the other hand, has been characterized as a medium more associated with a 'finished' work. Crucially painting is described as being suspended in a medium. As a result, Benjamin argues there is no background or graphic lines to painting, instead one colour or form is superimposed in another. These considerations are explored with specific reference to major artists of the twentieth century, Willem de Kooning, Jackson Pollock and Cy Twombly. The second half of the chapter is concerned with how we make 'sense' of or 'read' art composition. Georges Didi-Huberman's account of the legible, visible and visual in Fra Angelico's fresco provides an initial consideration of attentions we can give to the 'system' of mark-making in artworks. The chapter concludes with a critique of a semiotics of drawing and painting, which is explored through a debate between Mieke Bal and James Elkins on the subject of 'subsemiotic' marks. The illustrations they offer reveal very subtle readings of the mark-making in artworks, which brings into focus the ongoing tension between theoretical criticism and image practice.

Further reading

Bal, Mieke (1991) *Reading 'Rembrandt': Beyond the Word-Image Opposition*. Cambridge: Cambridge University Press.

Bal, Mieke and Bryson, Norman (1991) 'Semiotics and Art History'. *Art Bulletin*, Vol. 73, pp.174–208.

Bann, Stephen (1970) *Experimental Painting: Construction, Abstraction, Destruction, Reduction*. London: Studio Vista.

Barthes, Roland (1985) *The Responsibility of Forms: Critical Essays on Music, Art, and Representation*, trans. by Richard Howard. New York: Hill and Wang.

Berger, John (2005) *Berger on Drawing*. Cork: Occasional Press.

Berger, John (2011) *Bento's Sketchbook*. London: Verso.

Derrida, Jacques (1987) *The Truth in Painting*, trans. by Geoff Bennington and Ian McLeod. Chicago: University of Chicago Press.

Didi-Huberman, Georges (2005) *Confronting Images: Questioning the Ends of a Certain History of Art*, trans. by John Goodman. Pennsylvania: Pennsylvania State University Press.

Duff, Leo and Davies, Jo (eds) (2005) *Drawing – The Process*. Bristol: Intellect.

Elkins, James (1998) *On Pictures and the Words That Fail Them*. Cambridge: Cambridge University Press.

Elkins, James (2000) *What Painting Is: How to Think Abut Oil Painting, Using the Language of Alchemy*. New York: Routledge.

Garner, Steve (ed.) (2008) *Writing on Drawing: Essays on Drawing Practice and Research*. Bristol: Intellect.

Klee, Paul (1953 [1925]) *Pedagogical Sketchbook*, trans. by Sibyl Moholy-Nagy. London: Faber and Faber.

Rosand, David (2002) *Drawing Acts: Studies in Graphic Expression*. Cambridge: Cambridge University Press.

5 Photography

Photography has multiple beginnings. As early as the fourth and fifth centuries BC, the Chinese philosopher Mo Di and Greek mathematicians Aristotle and Euclid produced descriptions of a pinhole camera. However, it was not until the early 1800s that the first proper cameras were made, based upon the development of chemical photography in the 1820s. Today, digital algorithms have largely overtaken the distinctive chemical process. Yet, still, photography can be defined by the capturing of light for purposes of image-making. This chapter does not provide a history of photography, nor does it seek to offer an all-encompassing theoretical account (on both counts, a vast literature is available). Instead, the chapter examines a set of specific research themes. Broadly based around questions of public and private viewing, the chapter considers photography and social commentary, the relationship of writing and photography (specifically the production of the photobook and photo-essay), and digital photography, or the post-photographic era. To begin, however, the chapter outlines the paradox of photography to faithfully record a scene, yet equally remove it from its original context.

The paradox of photography

A commonly held view of photography is that it does not simply represent some-thing, but rather *presents* to us 'the scene itself, the literal reality' (Barthes, 1977, p.17). The case can be made as follows:

> 'From the object to its image there is of course a reduction – in proportion, perspective, colour – but at no time is this reduction a *transformation* (in the mathematical sense of the term). [. . . T]here is no necessity to set up a relay,

that is to say a code, between the object and its image . . . Thus can be seen the special status of the photographic image: *it is a message without a code.'*

(Barthes, 1977, p.17)

The photograph would seem to offer a 'pure' representation, or a 'message without a code'. Following Peirce's division of signs (1932, pp.134–173; see also Chapter 1), we might initially consider the photograph an icon. 'Photographs, especially instantaneous photographs', he writes, 'are very instructive, because we know that they are in certain respects exactly like the objects they represent'. However, Peirce actually considers the photograph an indexical sign, because they point to the existence of something in space and time. The photographic resemblance of something is 'produced under such circumstances that they were physically forced to correspond point by point to nature' (Peirce, 1932, p.159). In other words, photographs are a visual equivalence to the demonstrative pronouns 'this' and 'that', which 'call upon the [viewer] to use his powers of observation, and so establish a real connection between . . . mind and object' (p.162). Nonetheless, we know photographs can be used for ideological purposes. One only has to think of the use of photography in advertising or election campaigns and other overt political activities.

FIGURE 5.1
Nazi Book Burning, Opemplatz, Berlin, 11 May 1933. Courtesy of the Imperial War Museum.

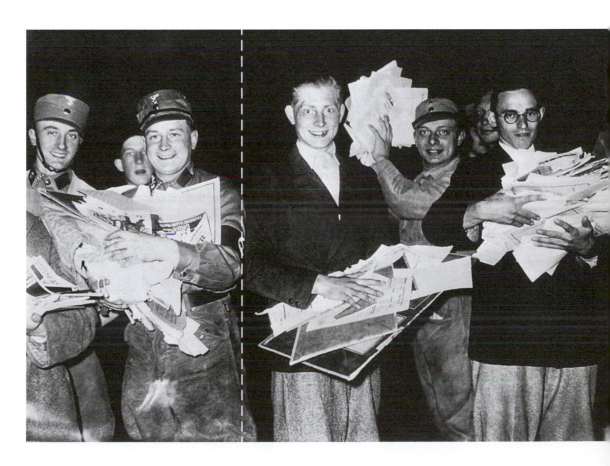

A portion of a photograph appears in Berger and Mohr's *Another Way of Telling* (1982), the quality of which indicates or *connotes* an old photograph. It is in fact an image from the 1930s. The part of the image they reprint shows a group of three men smiling and clutching papers (on the right-hand side of Figure 5.1). It seems a fairly innocuous image. Yet meaning quickly invades when the caption is provided: 'Nazis Burning Books'. Suddenly the image becomes something completely different, something sinister and unpleasant. As Berger and Mohr (1982, p.88) write: '[t]he ambiguity of a photograph does not reside within the instant of the event photographed: there the photographic evidence is less ambiguous than any eye-witness account'. There is nothing ambiguous about the photograph, it is a picture of three men staring straight at the camera. The caption, however, brings to the fore a problem in our ability to know the 'full picture'. The point they make is itself illustrated by seeing the original un-cropped photograph (Figure 5.1), in which a solider wearing a Nazi uniform can clearly be seen as part of the wider group of men. As Berger and Mohr describe, photography yields a 'historical discontinuity'. In this case, for example, our reading of the time is potentially misplaced by the fact this is just a single, cropped frame of an ongoing event. Unlike the story-teller, painter or actor, 'the photographer only makes, in any one photograph, a single constitutive choice: the choice of the instant to be photographed. The photograph, compared with other means of communication, is therefore weak in intentionality' (Berger and Mohr, 1982, pp.89–90).

As we will go on to see, John Berger and Jean Mohr have a particular interest in making alternative use of the photograph. They wish to harness its indexical power for raising social consciousness. They were strongly influenced by the writings of Walter Benjamin. In his essay 'A Small History of Photography' (1997) – originally written in 1931 – Benjamin notes how the photograph, as the 'reflection' of reality, hardly reveals anything about reality. Instead, in order for the photograph to offer critical commentary, it is necessary to construct meaning around the photograph – to build up meaning from a variety of components, of words and images and their arrangements and combinations. For Benjamin, this led to the idea of constructing meaning from a variety of cultural 'fragments'; to include everything around us from half-torn posters, graffiti, phrases upon the radio airwaves, film clips, shop-window displays, as well as books and papers. Thus, Benjamin highlights the importance of a certain visual literacy:

> '. . . photography turns all life's relationships into literature, . . . "The illiteracy of the future", someone has said, "will be ignorance not of reading and writing, but of photography". But must not a photographer who cannot read his own pictures be no less accounted an illiterate? Will not the caption become the most important part of the photograph?'
>
> (Benjamin, 1997, p.256)

We find the photograph presents a strange paradox. On the one hand, it appears to capture or 'index' reality as it is. The photograph is irrefutable evidence of something that once really existed. Yet on the other hand, any one single photograph lacks meaning, or rather can be interpreted in different ways. 'Captioning' the photograph – in a whole variety of ways – is seen to be particularly useful in appropriating and re-contextualizing meaning.

Writing with photographs

There is a rich tradition of bringing text and photographs together as either a **photobook** or **photo-essay**. Parr and Badger describe the photobook in the following way:

> 'What is a photobook? This may seem a redundant question with an obvious answer. A photobook is a book – with or without text – where the work's primary message is carried by photographs. It is a book authored by a photographer or by someone editing and sequencing the work of a photographer, or even a number of photographers. It has a specific character, distinct from the photographic print, be it the simply functional 'work' print, or the fine-art 'exhibition' print. However, while this might serve as a basic definition, it is not that simple. The photographer/author [can be] considered here as auteur (in the cinematic sense – the autonomous director, who creates the film according to his or her own artistic vision), and the photobook treated as an important form in its own right.'
>
> (Parr and Badger, 2004, p.7)

Parr and Badger go on to cite the Dutch photography critic Ralph Prins, who describes the photobook as 'an autonomous art form, comparable with a piece of sculpture, a play or a film. The photographs lose their own photographic character as things "in themselves" and become parts, translated into printing ink, of a dramatic event called a book' (cited in Parr and Badger, 2004, p.7).

The photo-essay, as we'll come to below, echoes these descriptions of the photobook, though we might say a photobook is generally longer than a photo-essay and bound as a book. As with any book it is a 'thing' in itself, something you can hold in your hand. However, photobooks are not necessarily widely distributed and some are considered more as works of art, available in limited supply. The photo-essay refers to all kind of publications that adopt the *form* of the essay, and can include photobooks. Photo-essays come in all sorts of shapes and sizes and often include ephemeral publications (typically appearing in newspapers and magazines). Of course, publications such as magazines always make use of photographs and text, so what is distinctive about the photo-*essay*? W.J.T. Mitchell (1994b, pp.281–322) provides a comparative account. He suggests the 'classic examples of this form (Jacob Riis's *How the Other Half Lives*, Margaret Bourke-White and Erskine Caldwell's *You Have Seen Their Faces*) give us a literal conjunction of photographs and text – usually united by a documentary purpose, often political, journalistic, sometimes scientific (sociology)' (Mitchell, 1994b, p.285). He also mentions how the photographer

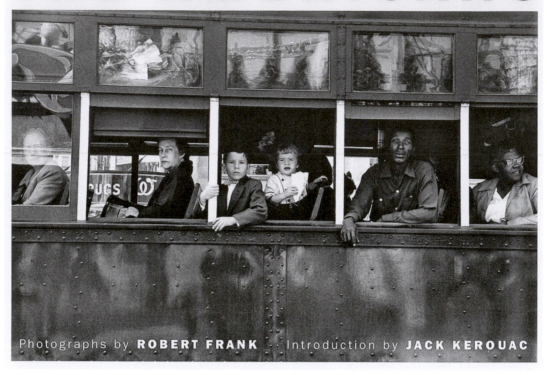

THE AMERICANS

Photographs by **ROBERT FRANK** · Introduction by **JACK KEROUAC**

FIGURE 5.2

The Americans by Robert Frank. Published by Steidl/www.steidl.com

Eugene Smith (1918–1978) argued that 'the photographic series or sequence, even without text, can be regarded as a photo-essay' (Mitchell, 1994b, p.286). A seminal example is Robert Frank's *The Americans* (first published in 1959, see Figure 5.2), which provides a subtle (and dark) portrait of America of the 1950s (see Greenough, 2009). The book has a very rigid, clean-design template. Each double-spread is the same, with a photograph from Frank's road-trip across America on the right-hand page, and a single-line caption on the left-hand page.

These well-known examples, including Frank's *The Americans*, are all published as books. Mitchell, however, refers to them as photo-essays because they are *essayistic*. The word *essay* comes from the French infinitive *essayer*, 'to try' or 'to attempt' and it is this more modest idea of attempting to write about something and by implication being able only to begin to cover a subject that is so typical of essay writing. The essay is usually a short piece of non-fiction writing, generally with an 'expository' aim, i.e. the author attempts to inform, explain, describe or define a subject to the reader. However, essays are often experimental (in regards both to form and content), they can be narrative in style, and can be quite subjective in tone, especially when written from the author's personal point of view. Thus, the photo-essay can be understood to be its own specific genre. Mitchell defines three key aspects:

'The first is the presumption of a common referential reality: not "realism" but "reality", nonfictionality, even "scientificity" are the generic connotations that link the essay with the photograph. The second is the intimate fellowship between the informal or personal essay, with its emphasis on a private "point of view", memory and autobiography, and photography's mythic status as a kind of materialized memory trace imbedded in the context of personal associations and private "perspectives". Third, there is the root sense of the essay as a partial, incomplete "attempt", an effort to get as much of the truth about something into a brief compass as the limits of space and writerly ingenuity will allow. Photographs, similarly, seem necessarily incomplete in their imposition of a frame that can never include everything that was there to be, as we say, "taken". The generic incompleteness of the informal literary essay becomes an especially crucial feature of the photographic essay's relations of image and text. The text of the photo-essay typically discloses a certain reserve or modesty in its claims to "speak for" or interpret the images; like the photograph, it admits its inability to appropriate everything that was there to be taken and tries to let the photographs speak for themselves or "look back" at the viewer.'

(Mitchell, 1994b, p. 289)

The suggestion of 'incompleteness' as a 'crucial feature of the photographic essay's relations of image and text' refers to something open-ended and potentially thought-provoking about the photo-essay. However, a further significant and distinctive feature of the photo-essay (and photobook) is the deliberate *sequencing* of photographs to create a 'dramatic event' as described above. Different to the work of a picture editor or layout designer of a magazine (or other print-based publication), who typically introduce images to liven up the page for the reader, the photo-essay is the work of an author, or perhaps a specific collaboration between a writer and a photographer. An explicit aim is to garner meaning through the use of *both* words and images. The most crucial aspect of the photobook or photo-essay is that the collective meaning of images becomes more important than the individual meaning of each image. Regardless of the quality of images used, it is 'the way in which they are choreographed [that] creates an astonishing work. In the true photobook each picture may be considered a sentence, or a paragraph, the whole sequence the complete text' (Parr and Badger, 2004, p. 7).

TASK

Photo-Essay Review

Select an existing *print-based* photographic essay. It can be a well-known published photobook, such as James Agee and Walker Evans' (2006) *Let Us Now*

Praise Famous Men; Malek Alloula's (1986) *The Colonial Harem*; John Berger and Jean Mohr's (2010) *A Seventh Man*; or Jacob Riis' (1998) *How the Other Half Lives: Studies Among The Tenements Of New York*. Or it might be something less well known, perhaps a book you have come across or an article in a magazine. Whatever you choose, try to make sure it fulfils the definitions of a photo-essay provided in this chapter.

Spend some time 'reading' the photo-essay to get a feel for what it is trying to say/show and consider carefully how it brings words and photographs into combination (think back to some of the observations about text and image in Chapter 3). Following this, try to adopt the same style and format to either extend or critique the ideas raised in your chosen book or essay. So, for example, if you were to look at Berger and Mohr's *A Seventh Man*, originally written in the late 1960s about the plight of migrant workers, you could think about how the ideas compare or differ to today's context of migrant workers and the global economy. In creating your photo-essay you may want to re-use photographs from the original, find them from other sources or create your own.

Photography and social commentary

In the 1950s, photography was still in its infancy as a serious artform worthy of large institutional backing. In 1955, however, the Museum of Modern Art in New York put together a landmark exhibition, *The Family of Man*. It was an ambitious project, with around 500 images finally selected from 2.5 million submitted photographs. The exhibition 'proposed photography as a means through which the alarming tensions and uncertainties of the Cold War era could be seen in a wider context of human values' (Marien, 2006, p.308). Its curator, Edward Steichen, sought to highlight 'human consciousness rather than social consciousness', with the view to illustrate 'the essential oneness of mankind throughout the world' (Steichen, 1955, p.3).

While individual images were not manipulated, the exhibition formed a spectacle of 'everyday' techniques of montage:

> 'As on the pages of an illustrated magazine, individual photographs are recontextualised into new chains of meaning. Photographs become interchangeable units of meaning. *The Family of Man* uses these techniques to construct an interactive framework for the photographic image, rather than using the public space of the exhibition to confer value on the individual author . . . This was a radical move, aligning photography with mass culture's reliance on the rapid reading of anonymous images . . .'
>
> (Roberts, 1998, pp.124–125)

Reactions of those attending the exhibition were 'overwhelmingly positive', though 'some photographers objected to Steichen's transformation of their work into

tonally harmonized, standard-format prints' (Marien, 2006, p. 309). These objections relate to a more general criticism over the ideological message of the exhibition. Roland Barthes, for example, was highly critical of the American-led moralizing and sentimentalizing post-war liberal humanism (it is worth noting, the exhibition was partly funded by the Coca Cola corporation).

> 'Everything here, the content and appeal of the pictures, the discourse which justifies them, aims to suppress the determining weight of History: we are held back at the surface of an identity, prevented precisely by sentimentality from penetrating into this ulterior zone of human behaviour where historical alienation introduces some "differences" which we shall here quite simply call "injustices".'
>
> (Barthes, 2009, p. 122)

Roberts (1998, pp. 122–126) usefully explains more of the historical and philosophical context to Barthes' critique:

FIGURE 5.3

Installation view of the exhibition 'The Family of Man', on view January 24–May 8, 1955 at The Museum of Modern Art. Gelatin silver print. Photographic Archive, The Museum of Modern Art Archives, New York. Photo by Rolf Petersen. © 2012 The Museum of Modern Art, New York.

'Barthes's attack on the *The Family of Man* is one of the first — if not the first — post-war critique of photographic truth to reinscribe the problem of the subject. Who is talking? Who is the image being addressed to? And on what terms? Barthes's eventual construction of a theory of ideological interpellation — or the presence of myth as Barthes was to call it — produced a seismic shift away from a positivist model of photography in which images *reflect* the world to a social one. That is, the purported truthfulness of the photographic image is no less coded than other kinds of visualisation. For Barthes the photograph does not *represent* reality, but *signifies* it.'

(Roberts, 1998, p.126)

Similarly, Berger stresses the importance of what an image *signifies*, rather than simply what it (re)presents to us. While he is equally critical of the sentimentality of the exhibition, Berger is positive about Steichen's curatorial approach to *The Family of Man*, suggesting the arrangement of the exhibition like a 'family album' is close to what he himself considers to be a fruitful approach in using photography for public

FIGURE 5.4
John Heartfield, 'Der Sinn des Hitlergrusses: Kleiner Mann bittet um große Gaben. Motto: Millionen stehen hinter mir!' [The Meaning Behind the Hitler Salute: Little Man Asks for Big Donations. Motto: Millions Stand Behind Me!], 1932. Courtesy of the David King Collection © The Heartfield Community of Heirs/VG Bild Kunst, Bonn and DACS, London 2012.

discourse (Berger, 1997). One aspect of the exhibition that no doubt appeals to Berger is the 'straight' use of photography. Aside from cropping the image and their placement within the overall flow of the exhibition, at no point are attempts made to physically manipulate or combine the photographs. Thus, for Berger, '[t]he meanings of the photograph lie in how they are reconstructed discursively, and not in the discursive extraction of their truth content *from* the image' (Roberts, 1998, pp.134–135). This latter idea describes the art of photomontage (Ades, 1986). John Heartfield is probably the best-known artist of this genre. A German artist, Heartfield was a member of the influential Berlin DADA group in the 1920s and 1930s and produced political photomontages, which attacked the Nazi regime and unsurprisingly were banned by the rule of the fascist state.

Photomontage is frequently used for political satire and commentary, and remains a popular art form. Take for example, Peter Kennard and Cat Phillipps's 'Photo Op' (Figure 5.5), which superimposes two images to satirize the former British Prime Minster Tony Blair. The latter was also the subject of a photomontage (Figure 5.6) by the artist Richard Hamilton (whose earlier collage-work we examined in

FIGURE 5.5
Peter Kennard
and Cat Phillipps,
'Photo Op', 2005
© kennardphillipps

Supplement I). In addition to photomontage, we might also consider other imaging styles that physically manipulate the image in ways that echo the principle of montage. In Chapter 3, Marcus Harvey's *Myra* portrait (Figure 3.2) was an example of how a painter is able to build up a picture in the way that a photograph is made up of tiny dots — and in doing so offer a critique of photographic reproduction itself. We might also think of how graffiti artists, such as Banksy, 'place' photorealistic images into the physical environment — which in a sense create living montage (and which frequently have an afterlife as photographs).

It is interesting to consider the differences at stake between Berger's work and that of photomontage, whether in the usual sense of the term, or even in a more expanded sense. Berger would no doubt be sympathetic to the political intentions

of the examples given here, but ultimately he considers them 'incomplete'. He writes:

FIGURE 5.7
Banksy, 'Maid' graffiti, London, 2006.

> 'You can use photography in all kinds of agitprop ways, you can make propaganda with photographs – you can make anti-capitalist propaganda, anti-imperialist propaganda. I wouldn't deny the usefulness of this, but at the same time I think the answer is incomplete. It's like taking a cannon and turning it round and firing it in the opposite direction. You haven't actually changed the practice, you've simply changed the aim.'
>
> (Berger, 1997, p.45)

Berger himself has used images in his work for critical purpose. However, in wanting to achieve more than simply changing the 'aim', Berger argues the need to put the photograph back into the context of a social experience and to respect the way memory functions, which runs not in a unilinear fashion, but *radially*.

RADIAL CONTEXT

JOHN BERGER

The problem is to construct a context for a photograph, to construct it with words, to construct it with other photographs, to construct it by its place in an ongoing text of photographs and images. How? Normally photographs are used in a very unilinear way – they are used to illustrate an argument, or to demonstrate a thought which goes like this:

Very frequently also they are used tautologically so that the photograph merely repeats what is being said in words. Memory is not unilinear at all. Memory works radially, that is to say with an enormous number of associations all leading to the same event. The diagram is like this:

If we want to put a photograph back into the context of experience, social experience, social memory, we have to respect the laws of memory. We have to situate the printed photograph so that it acquires something of the surprising conclusiveness of that which was and is. There are a few great photographs which practically achieve this by themselves. Any photograph may become such a 'Now' if an adequate context is created for it. In general the better the photograph, the fuller the context which can be created. (Berger, 1997, p.46)

Obviously it is not possible to literally place a photograph back into its original context, but Berger argues for a new context that is achieved through a 'constructed narrated time' (1997, p.47). Contrary to this approach, however, is the photo-journalistic use of photography, which equally seeks to provide social and political commentary. **Photojournalism** refers to the use of images as a means to reporting events and news and should be distinguished from other forms of photography, such as documentary photography, street photography (Scott, 2007) or celebrity and news photography. Photojournalists are reporters who provide the 'first filter of reality, selecting the moment and the composition which fits whatever it is he feels is the essence of the story' (H. Evans, 1997, no page number). Typically, photo-journalistic images are distinctive for their *timeliness* (to be current and worthy of news), *objectivity* (to offer accurate representation, regardless of events) and sense of *narrative* (images need to offer explanation and tell stories, i.e. to be 'readable'). While the latter two qualities of objectivity and narrative would seem to be equally pertinent to photo-essays, photojournalism is very different. The pressure to deliver up-to-date, dramatic images is certainly one difference, but also the tendency to use just a single image to tell a big story is crucially very different. It contrasts sharply with Berger's attempts to re-contextualize images by constructing alternative sequences of images.

In *Pictures on a Page*, Harold Evans (1997), a former editor of *The Sunday Times* and *The Times*, notes how even with a predominance of moving image media, 'imaginative directors of documentaries will use a still image in preference to film when they can exploit the singularity of the still by dwelling on a detail or pulling back for dramatic revelation' (H. Evans, 1997, no page number). As an example, Evans considers Kenneth Jarecke's singular and explicit photograph of a soldier killed in the Gulf War in 1991. The image caused outrage when it was printed in the UK in *The Observer*. In America it was effectively censored by a picture editor who took it 'off the wire' as soon as it was sent through the Associated Press news agency. It was only months later that a magazine finally printed it as part of an article about the limits of war photography (H. Evans, 1997, no page number). Arguably, despite the wall-to-wall coverage of 24-hour news and the pressures brought to bear for visual exposure of the war, the absence of a single photograph of this kind made acceptable 'the lethal felicity of designer bombs as some kind of video game'. Jarecke's photograph, however, was different: 'Once seen, it has a permanent place in one's imagination . . . The moving image may make an emotional impact, but its detail and shape cannot easily be recalled . . . Anyone who saw that still photograph will never forget it' (H. Evans, 1997, no page number).

The ethics over whether or not to publish the photograph are certainly complex. For Berger, as noted above, the usefulness of the single, still image remains 'incomplete'. While his use of photography is not timely in the way that photojournalism strives to be, we can consider its strength to lie not only in the use of pictures to say something poignant about issues such as war and conflict, but equally to say something about how the same images we consume can lend themselves to a variety of different readings. In the extract 'Radical Context', Berger offers his reflections on how he worked with the photographer Jean Mohr to create what he regarded as a more 'radial' and discursive approach.

In terms of a wider 'ecology' there are aspects of Berger's account that we might not fully recognize today. There are various assumptions made about beauty and the quality of images that are deeply subjective, yet here posed as quasi-objective (for a critical commentary on Berger and Mohr's approach to storytelling and the photo-essay, see Scott, 1999, pp.251–291). Nonetheless, the account is valuable precisely because it reveals the tensions that exist (and processes undertaken) when attempting to work purposefully with photographic materials.

WAYS OF REMEMBERING

JOHN BERGER

(from Evans, Jessica (ed.) *The Camerawork Essays*, 1997, pp.48–49)

FIGURE 5.10 'Old woman in market, Greece'. By kind permission of Jean Mohr.

FIGURE 5.11 *Madonna* by Perugino.

FIGURE 5.12 'Wall above bed in Barracks, Switzerland'. By kind permission of Jean Mohr.

FIGURE 5.13 'Peasant girl working in field'. By kind permission of Jean Mohr.

In A Seventh Man, one particular photograph portrays three migrant workers (Figure 5.12). These men work long hours underground and live in 'wooden barracks', sleeping on bunk beds. What is striking about the photograph is that the walls of the room in which the men sit are covered with pornographic pictures. Images of naked women, in alluring poses, literally cover the room like wallpaper. In presenting a documentary account of migrant workers, John Berger and Jean Mohr thought it was important to use this picture. First of all, they suggest, because it was like that, second because it is, 'in a sense, an indirect index of the sexual deprivation suffered by these men'. The difficulty, however, lay in how to use the photograph.

[. . . Y]ou put that picture on a page and what does it say? How is that image going to work? It first, maybe, approves of the virulent sexism of the images stuck up. We tried juxtaposing that picture with pictures of the men's faces, it doesn't work because it doesn't really mean anything – it really only adds the personalities of these people. We tried putting in a photograph of something in the street, some sex shop in the street where the bourgeois of the city go. But again that says it is okay the petty bourgeois go to the sex shop the same as the migrant workers. It doesn't help. I'm not saying that the solution we found is the ideal one, but finally we found a photograph of an old peasant women in her village who could have been the mother of any of those workers – in fact she wasn't – but she could have been. It is a picture of a mother, quite influenced in some respects by Catholic iconography with the Madonna, and so on. The kind of picture that one of those workers might have carried around with him. It had a kind of icon value, it was sacred. We then put next to it, not a photograph at all, but a reproduction of a Madonna, a painting by Perugino. There begins to be a juxtaposition between idealized maternity and real maternity – that's to say a woman of 45 looking like 65 and probably with eight children. Then we turned the page and in that context we put the picture of the barracks with the sexy pictures all round. Beginning to relate, to talk about a life story, beginning to talk about women in more than one dimension, beginning to talk about the experience of those men. And then finally we chose to put opposite the barracks picture an extraordinary photograph that Jean took of a young polish peasant girl – at that time totally uninfluenced and untouched by sexist consumerist glamour, who at the same time has a very beautiful face, young and questioning, the exact opposite in fact of the women in the barracks picture but corresponding very likely to one of the girls in the village. Now with those four pictures we perhaps began to put back the first one – that is to say the barracks one – in context.

TASK

Ways of Remembering

Select a photograph that you think is striking in a way similar to how Berger describes the photograph of the men in the barracks in the extract from 'Ways of Remembering'. The image you select should relate to a specific social or political concern. (Perhaps choose from one of the following suggestions: The Veil, Global Economics, Size Zero, Global Warming, Suburban Youth, Ethical Shopping.)

Around your chosen image attempt to place a further 3–4 images or photographs. In placing the images try to achieve a newly contextualized reading of your original photograph. In addition, write a short commentary to describe the motivations behind your choices and layout. The images you use for this task can be your own or taken from magazines, newspapers and the Internet (though aim to use pictures of reasonable and comparable quality).

Photographic memory

As we have seen, Berger acknowledges the importance of the private engagement with photographs. Indeed, probably the most common and meaningful experiences with photographs come when handling our own personal photographs and family albums, etc. Photographs create discontinuity because the images are literally 'taken' out of context. Private photographs, however, maintain greater continuity with our experiences and our memories of people, places and events. Nevertheless, the problem in trying to relate to ideas about personal memory is not only that our thoughts are private, but also they are generally fleeting thoughts, which are difficult to share. The novelist Marcel Proust (1871–1922) famously captures the experience of memory in his multi-volume novel *À la recherche du temps perdu* [*In Search of Lost Time*]. In a much-cited passage, the narrator is struck by a distant memory as he tastes a biscuit dipped in his tea; though the more he repeats the action (which is seemingly the original source of the memory) the less vivid the memory appears to be (Proust,

2002, pp.47-50). Proust beautifully captures the sensation of what is termed an **involuntary memory**: a memory that arises without you having consciously recalled it, a memory that is often incomplete, yet somehow potent and intriguing; a certain in-between space when you are fully aware you cannot quite remember something. A phrase commonly used when we 'feel' close to recalling something (yet can't quite recall it) to mind is 'it's on the tip of my tongue'!

Proust's account of memory is frequently cited in commentaries about photography – often as the antithesis of how a photograph fixes a moment in time. Roland Barthes makes reference to Proust in *Camera Lucida* (1981) – a book both about photography and about his private mourning for his mother. In sifting through old photographs Barthes describes how he had no hope of 'finding' his mother:

> 'I expected nothing from these "photographs of a being before which one recalls less of that being than by merely thinking of him and her" (Proust) . . . I was not sitting down to contemplate them, I was not engulfing myself in them. I was sorting them, but none seemed to me really "right": neither as a photographic performance nor as a living resurrection of the beloved face.'
>
> (Barthes, 1981, pp.63–64)

Nonetheless, there is one image – which he calls the Winter Garden photo – in which Barthes claims somehow to 'find' his mother again. The photograph is of his mother when only 5 years old:

> 'I studied the little girl and at last rediscovered my mother. The distinctness of her face, the naïve attitude of her hands, the place she had docilely taken without either showing or hiding herself, and finally her expression . . . all this constituted the figure of a sovereign *innocence* . . . all this had transformed the photographic pose into that untenable paradox which she had nonetheless maintained all her life: the assertion of a gentleness.'
>
> (Barthes, 1981, p.69)

As with the recalling of a distant memory noted by Proust's narrator, Barthes here sees something in the photograph of his mother that goes beyond the single photograph and says something about her as a person, throughout her life. The experience Barthes describes in looking at the Winter Garden photograph would seem to chime with the private experience of photographs that Berger suggests we need to translate for public, social purposes. Yet, at the same time, Barthes makes it clear just how difficult a task it is. He claims he cannot reproduce the photograph of his mother, as it would be meaningless to anyone but himself. In a sense, then, *Camera Lucida* is a book that can only be read by its own author. Yet, like Proust, Barthes is able to communicate and share with us the fact that a private and meaningful engagement with the photograph exists. The book results in an unusual blend of personal and theoretical writing.

Arguably, there is something overly sentimental about the work of both Barthes and Berger (see respectively: Elkins, 2011; Scott, 1999, pp.251–291). They both

FIGURE 5.14 *The Stock*, from Roland Barthes' *Camera Lucida* (1981, p.104). Or is it the 'Winter Garden' photograph'? Barthes writes: 'I cannot reproduce the Winter Garden Photograph. It exists only for me. For you, it would be nothing but an indifferent picture' (1981, p.73). Diana Knight suggests we should not take Barthes at face value. 'If *Camera Lucida*', she writes, 'recounts a "true story" of Barthes refinding his mother in a photo of her as a child, then the photo must surely be the one reproduced later in the text with the title "The Stock" ("*La Souche*"). If the mother as child is younger than five, and if she and her brother stand with their grandfather (rather than alone in a conservatory), her pose, her expression, and the position of her hands exactly match Barthes' description of the Winter Garden photograph. It is therefore my belief (or my fantasy) that the Winter Garden photo is simply an invention, a transposition of the "real" photo ("The Stock") . . .' (Knight, 1997, p.138).

privilege a private experience of the photograph, as if somehow it possesses more meaning and enables a more immediate re-connection with our past and with others. Their work is suggestive of something beyond the mere indexicality of photograph, though this is never defined in substantive terms. Of course, it is important to note private, family photographs can be considered equally in ideological terms. Thus,

146

while photography is frequently described as a democratic art, Clive Scott argues we 'should rather speak of the domestication of art' (1999, p.229). By this he refers to a double logic, whereby:

> 'The presence of the family-snap mode in tabloid newspapers, or indeed in fashion magazines, banalizes the extraordinary, brings it within reach of the quotidian and demythicizes photographic "reality". By the same token, these generical interferences allow the family snap to invert the process and make claims of extraordinariness for the banal, a strategy which informs pub-table narrative art.'
>
> (Scott, 1999, p.229)

In many respects, his observations aptly describe the phenomena of 'ordinary' people becoming celebrities and the mechanism by which the recording of the mundane in reality TV can be transformed into apparently extraordinary spectacle. Essentially, Scott is interested in bringing out the social value of private photographs. The family album, he notes, is 'a form of publication, consecrating and enshrining family memory and family history, for the benefit of the larger community' (p.229). He refers to the artist Jo Spence, whose exhibition 'Beyond the Family Album' (1979) makes the case for the controlling mechanism of the family album, typically by *not* recording many aspects of family life and instead only really concentrating on the usual festive and signature events of family life such as holidays and birthdays, etc. (see J. Evans, 1997, pp.237–261; and Roberts, 1998, pp.199–215). Thus, as Scott explains, for Jo Spence 'all photographs are, to a greater or lesser degree, "fictions", subject to a visual rhetoric' (1999, p.230).

Not only is it apparent that our private, personal feelings in relation to pictures of the past are difficult to assess and share, we can equally come to the conclusion there is no such thing as a private photograph, because every time the shutter is released the person looking into the lens has potentially only lent themselves to its 'social game'. Scott describes this as to 'connive in the reinforcement of stereotypes and roles' (Scott, 1999, p.237); though he suggests we do this involuntarily. Scott also draws attention to the fact that 'the family album carries within it the mechanisms of its own deconstruction' (p.231), not least by the fact that photographs can literally fall out of the collection. He goes on to consider the manner in which family albums can order and re-order to render different meanings. Today the physical photographic print has largely been surpassed by the intangible digital print, which has again dramatically altered our ability to capture and share images of ourselves, of others, of events and places and things.

Post-photographic era

In *The Reconfigured Eye* (1994b), William J. Mitchell identifies the early 1990s as the start of the 'post-photographic era', in which digital imaging begins to supplant the role of traditional photography in a wide range of professional and cultural

FIGURE 5.15 Jo Spence, from 'The Picture of Health?' (1982) © Jo Spence. Courtesy of Museu d'Art Contemporani de Barcelona. In her exhibition 'Beyond the Family Album' (1979), Jo Spence explored the significance and aesthetics of amateur photography. In effect she re-wrote, or re-staged her family photo album. The work comprised a series of collages made up of existing family photographs; her own photographic re-staging of the scenes they depict; and various biographical texts. Deconstructing the family album in this way, the collages bring into view both what the family album typically portrays as well as what it excludes. In 'The Picture of Health?' (1982) Spence took her methodology and aesthetic a stage further, exhibiting a series of photographic responses to her treatment for breast cancer. Taking her own patient's perspective, the work raised important issues about power dynamics within medical practice, with Spence drawing particular attention to what she considered the role of healthcare institutions in the infantilization of patients. In the image shown here, a documentary photograph has been surrounded by Spence's fragmented body which had been written on and staged for the camera in a phototherapy session.

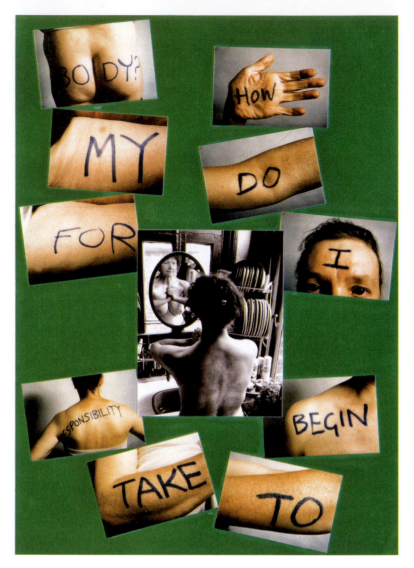

contexts. The phrase 'post-photographic' is revealing. It suggests something that comes after photographic technology, yet it not quite willing to let go of what we consider to be the nature and experience of photography. As Lev Manovich puts it:

> 'The logic of the digital photograph is one of historical continuity and discontinuity. The digital image tears apart the net of semiotic codes, modes of display, and patterns of spectatorship in modern visual culture – and, at the same time, weaves this net even stronger. The digital image annihilates photography while solidifying, glorifying and immortalizing the photographic. In short, this logic is that of photography after photography.'

(cited in Murray, 2008, p.153)

The double-logic of the post-photographic has fuelled lots of interest in trying to re-formulate what we take photography to be, but equally it has proved difficult to offer definitive statements. So, for example, we can consider the following:

> 'If an image is captured with a digital camera, there is no chemical process as with analog photography. Instead, the image is recorded by photosensitive cells and never exists except as bits. Is such an image a photograph or a computer graphic? If the image began as a conventional photograph and was scanned into the computer and digitally retouched, is it then a photograph or a computer graphic?'
>
> (Bolter and Grusin, 2000, p.105)

There is no one right answer to these sorts of questions. Instead we have to take into account the context of use of any given 'photograph'. In some cases the use of digital technology is explicit and so can reveal photography always to be a process of manipulation and reproduction. In other cases, the digital retouching of a photograph – typically on the front of magazines – aims to retain the idea that we are being presented with 'the scene itself, the literal reality' (Barthes, 1977, p.17). The digital photograph is ostensibly an indexical sign, though digital manipulation opens up whole new possibilities. The advent of computer photorealism, however, pushes at the limit of defining the photographic and the relationship between old and new technology. In fact it potentially undermines the very concept of photography as a 'transparent' recording of things in the world:

> 'If [computer specialists] could achieve perfect photorealism, then they could create "photographs" without natural light. An image could be synthesized to meet the viewer's desire for immediacy without the need for the objects in the image to have existed or to have been together at any time . . . Complete success in computer photorealism would make nonsense of the term *photorealism*, because no one could any longer believe in a causal connection between the image and the world.'
>
> (Bolter and Grusin, 2000, p.106)

The post-photographic era reveals the potentially disturbing fact that we now can never quite tell whether or not a photograph has been digitally altered. We can find it difficult to free ourselves of the habit of seeing the photograph as a point-by-point index of 'something' (elsewhere) in the world. However, as Bolter and Grusin go on to argue, 'altered images become a problem only for those who regard photography as operating under the logic of transparency' (2000, p.110). Of course, traditional photography has a long history of altered images – including a great deal of political imagery as well as, for example, the more playful (but no less deceptive) Cottingley fairy photographs taken in 1917. Conversely, the digital photograph can be just as transparent as the analogue one. There are important considerations we can make regarding image-capture technology (which we will come to shortly), but

FIGURE 5.16 *Kodak Film* © Todd Siechen, RealEyz Imaging. 'A computer graphic of a Kodak film box and canister is almost perfectly photorealistic. It is successful because it recalls a special genre of photography, common in advertising, in which surreal colors and textures and the absence of extraneous detail serve to focus our attention on a featured commodity. This genre of photography does not correspond to anything we see in daily life (except on billboards and in magazines), and precisely for that reason the computer image seems so [convincing] . . . The content of the image is photographic film, while the technique remediates photography. We notice that the canister is empty, and the roll of film appears already to have been shot. The playful suggestion is that photographic film is no longer needed because computer graphics can now imitate perfect photography. This

image reveals . . . the double logic of remediation: by representing the desire for immediacy in the shape of a film canister and roll, the image insists on the reality of media as objects in the world' (Bolter and Grusin, 2000, pp.129-130).

arguably the digital capturing of light is no more or less artificial than the traditional chemical process of photography. As such, '[i]t is a purely cultural decision to claim that darkening the color values of a digitized image by algorithm is an alteration of the truth of the image, whereas keeping an analog negative longer in the developing bath is not' (Bolter and Grusin, 2000, p.110). We can understand the post-photographic in terms of what Bolter and Grusin describe as a process of **remediation** – whereby we reflect the properties of one medium in another (typically the old in the new) in an attempt either to foreground mediation or the opposite to affect a sense of immediacy (as if free of mediation). The concept of remediation – discussed further in Chapter 6 – can be said to complement the understanding of an ecology of images, which – as examined in Chapter 2 – prompts a contextual and interconnected analysis of the image. Nonetheless, we can still identify important distinctive features of digital photography, both in terms of behaviour associated with it and also the limits of the technology itself.

By the end of the 1990s digital technologies had become more and more ubiquitous for personal, domestic and entertainment uses. The market for digital cameras properly takes off from the year 2000 as prices fell. By 2004, '28 billion digital photos were produced. That number represents 6 billion more photos than were shot on film, even though twice as many people owned film-roll cameras than digital' (Murray, 2008, p.152). Digital photography has enabled us to take many more images at any one time, since, unlike the roll of film, memory cards in cameras can hold a huge amount of data; typically storing more pictures than we can comfortably keep track of. Added to which, of course, digital cameras make it possible to delete images as quickly as we have made them. Digital technology thus engenders a different kind of relationship to both operating the camera and our sense of having 'caught the moment'. However, unlike the production of traditional photographs, digital pictures are not so readily handled physically; there are certainly no negatives to digital photographs as we associate with roll film pictures, but also digital photography is frequently viewed on screens rather than as paper-based prints. As a result, our experience of the photograph can be very different, more akin to a performance than an object:

> 'Many digital images . . . are never printed but appear only as transient screen displays. In other words they are replayed from digital data . . . exactly as musical performances on digital compact disc are replayed. When used in this way, digital image files are more closely analogous to [music] recordings than to negatives or printing plates. They represent the latest stage in the long evolutionary development of images as objects into images as performances – a transition away from images realized as durable, individually valuable, physically rooted artefacts (frescoes, mosaics, and murals), through portable easel paintings and inexpensive prints, to completely ephemeral film projections and video displays.'
>
> (Mitchell, 1994b, pp. 78–79)

The idea of photography being more analogous to music recording is further pronounced with online and mobile technologies. Almost all mobile phones now have a built-in camera and there are numerous ways to share images across the Internet. An attraction of social media would seem in part to be the ease with which it is possible to share photographs. In many cases, when people upload their pictures to social media sites, the photographs are not placed on static web pages, but instead are embedded in a constantly updating timeline – so further heightening their ephemeral and intangible status.

When disseminated via social media, digital photography becomes something closer to a broadcast medium. In contrast to the family photo album, which acts like a private archive, the online environment leads to private memories being made public. Thus, where before we might have shared holiday snaps amongst close friends and provided contextual information by pointing at elements in the image, the distribution of photographs via social media makes a spectacle of our private sphere and alters the way we contextualize past events. It is easy to read this negatively, as a diluted experience – particularly if we think of photography as a medium for preserving 'lost time' (in a Proustian sense). Most literature on photography deals with ideas of history, memory and loss. Susan Murray (2008), however, suggests we can think of photography in additional ways. In her study of online photo-sharing, she argues, 'the introduction of digital photography and accompanying websites such as Flickr have created an additional function to photography that has much more to do with transience than with loss' (Murray, 2008, p. 154). The proliferation of online photo-sharing groups, often with very specific rubrics under which photos can be submitted, leads Murray to consider a very different 'landscape' in which photography now appears. On the one hand there can be a greater sense of collective production and dissemination of pictures, but also there is more emphasis on individual interests, elements of the 'everyday' and even obscure or surreal sightings. Murray describes, for example, a group on Flickr dedicated solely to images of houses made of bottle glass (which is linked to another group on the site dedicated to photographs relating to recycling).

The use of digital photography and photo-sharing marks a definite shift, with photography now seemingly 'less about the special or rarefied moments of domestic/family living (for such things as holidays, gatherings, baby photos) and more about an immediate, rather fleeting display of one's discovery of the small and mundane' (Murray, 2008, p.151). In addition, whilst amateur photography has a long history, it is now possible for more and more people not only to create and distribute photographs, but also to comment on them with ease and authority. Murray does not necessarily suggest these new practices are 'inherently more emancipatory, progressive, or participatory', but she does argue they define a 'shift in our temporal relationship with the everyday image, and have helped alter the way that we construct narratives about ourselves and the world around us' (2008, p.151).

From an aesthetic point of view the ease of manipulation and dissemination of digital images can be argued to have given rise to a myth of a new kind of *depth* to the photograph. In *What Photography Is* (2011), James Elkins writes about the physicality of photographs – including the dust, scratches and finger-marks that can appear on them. However, he also notes that we don't tend to think of photographs as surfaces, but rather use them 'to help us think of ourselves and our world' (2011, p.38). They are viewpoints upon another world, whether of the past or just of an elsewhere. Yet, digital photography, computing and the display screens apparently lead to new possibilities *in* the image. William Mitchell describes how the computer-graphics pioneer of the 1960s, Ivan E. Sutherland, 'realized that electronic displays do not *have* to take the etymological implication of "perspective" – viewing as "seeing through"', and instead considered how they can 'dispense with the bounding frame, break open the plane, and allow redirection of the gaze' (Mitchell, 1994b, p.79). Using only the crude technology of the day, Sutherland developed the prototype of what we would now recognize as a virtual reality helmet. Such technology has gone on to promise 'architects the possibility of walking through geometrically modelled proposed buildings, astronomers the possibility of flying through radar-scanned planetary landscapes, and surgeons the possibility of seeing "through the skin" by superimposing on patients' bodies three-dimensional displays generated from ultrasound or MRI scanner data' (Mitchell, 1994b, p.80).

Fully immersive virtual reality environments have not really come to fruition in the way that was once predicted, however 3D-rendering in films and virtual reality effects on gaming consoles have become increasing popular and widespread. While often working with photorealistic imagery, the various media are of course based upon computer-animated models. Nevertheless, the idea of a photographic image 'interior' has entered into popular discourse. We can recall, for example, a well-known scene in Ridley Scott's *Blade Runner* (Scott, 1982) in which the protagonist 'loads' a photograph into his Esper machine, asking it to scan its surface as he searches for a 'clue'. The distinctive feature of this machine is its ability for image *enhancement*, to convert from low-grade to high-grade resolution; which in fact would mean sharpening the focus of something that previously had not really (or rather, digitally) existed.

The fictional technology of the Esper machine represents an imaging apparatus now prevalent in popular consciousness. It appears in various forms in a wide range of film and television productions; obvious examples can be made of police, espionage and forensics dramas. Its function (usually at pivotal moments in the diegesis) is to mine the depths of an image to reveal a vital clue. The ability to search through the interior of an image and/or to enhance the quality of an image is based on a fallacy. If you click repeatedly on the 'zoom' icon in any image-editing software, as you move 'deeper' into a computer-generated picture, all you really get to see are increasingly abstract images of colour block formations. In fact, with each click of the button, you are generating on screen whole new images. The bottom line, however, is a pixel landscape divided up by a uniform grid. When taken in isolation,

FIGURE 5.17 Varying effects of pixilation. William J. Mitchell, *The Reconfigured Eye: Visual Truth in the Post-Photographic Era,* Photograph p.68 © 1992 Massachusetts Institute of Technology by permission of the MIT Press. 'There is an indefinite amount of information in a continuous-tone photograph, so enlargement usually reveals more detail but yields a fuzzier and grainier picture. [. . .] A digital image, on the other hand, has precisely limited spatial and tonal resolution and contains a fixed amount of information. Once a digital image is enlarged to the point where its gridded microstructure becomes visible, further enlargement will reveal nothing new: the discrete pixels retain their crisp, square shapes and their original colors, and they simply become more prominent' (Mitchell, 1994b, p.6).

a single pixel 'depicts nothing in particular — merely "light thing" or "dark thing"' (Mitchell, 1994b, p. 67). It is as if we reach the limits of what was referred to in the previous chapter as the 'subsemiotic'.

The difference between an analogue and digital photograph ties in directly with the arguments made in Chapter 3 regarding the difference between image (analogue) and text (digital). If anything, then, the analogue photograph offers more sense of an 'interior' – it is 'an analog representation of the differentiation of space in a scene: it varies continuously, both spatially and tonally' (Mitchell, 1994b, p.4). By contrast, the digital image uniformly divides up the picture place 'into a finite Cartesian grid of cells (known as *pixels*) and specifying the intensity or colour of each cell by means of an integer number drawn from some limited range' (p.5); the benefit of which is that the 'resulting two-dimensional array of integers (the *raster grid*) can be stored in computer memory, transmitted electronically, and interpreted by various devices' (Mitchell, 1994b, p.5). Arguably, then, whilst a digital image may look just like a photograph, 'it actually differs as profoundly from a traditional photograph as does a photograph from a painting. The difference is grounded in fundamental physical characteristics that have logical and cultural consequences' (Mitchell, 1994b, p.4). Thus, along with the need to interpret photographs for what they show, we also need to pay attention to what we mean or think we mean by the *photographic* itself. As Sean Cubitt suggests, in the account given here, this will mean giving further thought to the fundamental physics and 'mathematics' of photography, and in turn how we understand the image in a complex technological, aesthetic, political and economic nexus.

PHOTOGRAPHY AND ARITHMETIC

SEAN CUBITT

A characteristic of nineteenth-century print technologies was their randomness. Aquatint, lithography and photography adopted their textures from chance: the lie of sand on a rocker, the pockmarks in stone or scrubbing of aluminium sheets, and the spatter of silver halide molecules. Something seems however to have lured photography towards its twenty-first-century arithmetic destiny.

The challenge was to extract multiple copies from photographs which seemed destined to give just one. In 1855, Poitevin disclosed the light-sensitive properties of gelatine bichromate, which hardens when exposed to light. Dark areas stay soft and can be washed away, leaving an embossed surface to print from. The British pioneer of photography, William Henry Fox Talbot, had already invented a technique – the calotype or Talbotype – for making multiple copies of a negative. Now, in the 1850s, he introduced a muslin screen to help transfer the image to a matrix of dots (it is a constant in printing that flat fields of ink always bubble and smear: dots, or the cross-hatching of older techniques, hold the ink better than any flat surface). The still near-random, organic texture of textiles was not yet rigid enough to support the development of the mass-produced photograph. The magazine and newspaper industries began to include more and more photography after the pioneering first mass halftone news photo in 1873. Industrial control of inks, on these scales and speeds of production, brought in the idea of using screens not of cloth but made from two sheets of glass, each scored with horizontal lines, laid at right angles to each other and at 45 degrees to the horizontal.

The point of the 45 degrees was that the human eye spots horizons easily, and is more likely to construe a diagonal array as continuous. So the question is: why move to the horizontal? The first challenge was to mass-produce photographs. The second was to get them moving at the same tempo as the news itself, the tempo of the ubiquitous telegraph system of the late nineteenth century. Wire photography was pioneered at the same time as the earliest fax, but the first viable, quality, near-instantaneous transmission happened only in 1935. The image was scanned by the sender, and the receiver had to print it out in exactly the same order. For maximum efficiency, the scanners read the image horizontally – otherwise they would have sent a diamond-shaped image with a lot of blank area around it. This first horizontal scan became the norm for all electrical and electronic images, in the cathode ray tubes (CRTs) of television, and then in computer monitors.

CRTs, like old photography, are molecular media: the phosphors are sprayed randomly on the inside of the tube's screen. When scanned, they light up not in neat rows but as they happen to lie, and the light from an illuminated molecule can flood over the area of an unilluminated one. Using shadow masks, this softening was diminished, and the greys appeared as a result more black. Then LCD, LED and plasma came in, while slide projectors gave way to digital projectors. Now all images are made of strict lines, rigidly laid out, and connected in intricate ways to the fundamental functioning of the computer.

These displays, known as raster displays, simplify the image data sent to them. They convert it into an average value for the colour over the area of a single square pixel. The computer sends, in theory at least, an address ('45 pixels across and ten rows down') accompanied by a six-figure code for its colour value. Actually this numerical system makes it possible to send averaged descriptions for large areas of the screen, visible whenever you look at backgrounds in televised or Internet-transmitted photographs, with rare exceptions. In fact, this arithmetic system of image-management allows managerial ideas to enter the circulation of images at every level. Each pixel, or great blocks of pixels, can be treated statistically to provide the most efficient delivery, regardless of other values – truth, beauty, ethics. All images are composed of the same unit arrays.

The alternative? Many other imaging systems and instruments for sensing light exist, and many are in use for scientific and engineering purposes. They have been rigorously excluded from the increasing standardization and normalization of digital images in general and digital photography in particular. Whenever images travel, from broadcasters to TVs, or down the wires of the Internet, or between celnet masts, or for that matter transferred from the photo-sensitive chip to the storage on board the camera, or downloaded to hard-drive or opened in a software application, images lose data. They also, step by step, conform to the industrial norms, and with them the aesthetic and cultural standards, of a system engineered for maximum efficiency and maximum profit.

Why should that matter? For two main reasons. In the twenty-first century, we experience the world more and more through screens. We gossip with friends, catch entertainment, and learn about the world, through screens which literally frame what we see. Knowing how and why they work the way they do is smart, because it makes you alert to the possibility of being manipulated. But we also feel things through our screens. The word 'aesthetics' means art, but it also, in the old Greek root, means feeling: how we experience the world and our place in it. The aesthetic – the look and feel – of screens has changed subtly over the last hundred years, becoming an ever more rigid grid, locking our visual sensations into a numbered universe where every colour can be swapped for any other, and where the law that everything can be counted is made to apply not just to money but to everything we can capture in a photograph.

The photograph has become arithmetic; and its display is now caught in a fine-meshed, highly rectilinear net. Whatever it first looked like, this is how images look from now on. Unless, of course, we go back a little, and look again at the randomness we started with, or forward to the alternative geometries which computer graphics have made available, even if they too can only ever be seen on raster screens. Before we can take back control over our own sensations, we need control of our media. Before we can change the world, we have to change how we perceive it. Understanding that we actually see the world through very square eye-glasses is the first step to taking them off.

Summary

This chapter has explored specific ideas and practices of photography. Photography we have seen has a unique ability to record a scene as it is presented in its continuity. Yet equally, in fixing the image, photography produces discontinuity, pulling a scene out of its immediate context. This 'paradox' of photography poses both a problem and a set of possibilities for social commentary and creative endeavours. The chapter looked at different attempts to combine word and image, notably the form of the photobook and photo-essay. The collaborative work of writer John Berger and photographer Jean Mohr provides one model for practically handling the process of 'writing with photography'. There are certainly no set rules or methods, but none-theless, their careful consideration of placing words and images together brings to light a dynamic process involved in working with photography as a vehicle for social commentary. The chapter also raised questions about photography and memory, a topic that then becomes further complicated by the advent (and ubiquity) of digital photography. Our so-called 'post-photographic era' presents whole new challenges in how we ought to think about photography – not least: what it is, and what it does for us.

Further reading

Ades, Dawn (1986) *Photomontage*. London: Thames and Hudson.

Batchen, Geoffrey (1999) *Burning with Desire: the Conception of Photography*. Cambridge, Mass.: MIT Press.

Berger, John and Mohr, Jean (1995) *Another Way of Telling*. New York: Vintage International.

Bolter, Jay David and Grusin, Richard (2000) *Remediation: Understanding New Media*. Cambridge, Mass.: MIT Press.

Cubitt, Sean (1998) *Digital Aesthetics*. London: Sage.

Elkins, James (2011) *What Photography Is*. New York: Routledge.

Evans, Jesscia (ed.) (1997) *The Camerawork Essays: Context and Meaning in Photography*. London: Rivers Oram Press.

Mitchell, W.J.T. (1994) 'The Photographic Essay: Four Case Studies' in *Picture Theory*. Chicago: Chicago University Press, pp.281–322.

Mitchell, William J. (1994) *The Reconfigured Eye: Visual Truth in the Post-Photographic Era*. Cambridge, Mass.: MIT Press.

Modrak, Rebakah and Anthes, Bill (2010) *Reframing Photography: Theory and Practice*. London: Routledge.

Parr, Martin and Badger, Gerry (2004) *The Photobook: A History (Volume 1)*. London: Phaidon Press.

Parr, Martin and Badger, Gerry (2006) *The Photobook: A History (Volume 2)*. London: Phaidon Press.

Roberts, John (1998) *The Art of Interruption: Realism, Photography and the Everyday*. Manchester: Manchester University Press.

Scott, Clive (1999) *The Spoken Image: Photography and Language*. London: Reaktion Books.

Sontag, Susan (1979) *On Photography*. London: Penguin Books.

Wells, Liz (ed.) (2000) *Photography: A Critical Introduction*. Second edition. London: Routledge.

6 Visual culture

The phrase '**visual culture**' appears sporadically in literatures of the twentieth century, generally referring to cultures of practice and consumption associated with a range of visual artefacts and experiences. However it is not until the 1990s that visual culture becomes a defined subject and area of study. Nicholas Mirzoeff's *An Introduction to Visual Culture* (1999; 2009) and edited volume *The Visual Culture Reader* (2002) were pivotal in establishing visual culture as a properly interdisciplinary field. Like cultural studies, which 'sought to understand the ways in which people create meaning from the consumption of mass culture', visual culture can be said to 'prioritize the everyday experience of the visual from the snapshot to the VCR and even the blockbuster art exhibition' (Mirzoeff, 1998, p.7). In one of the key introductions to *The Visual Culture Reader* (2002, pp.24–36), Irit Rogoff characterizes the emergent field in the following way:

> 'At one level we certainly focus on the centrality of vision and the visual world in producing meanings, establishing and maintaining aesthetic values, gender stereotypes and power relations within culture. At another level we recognize that opening up the field of vision as an arena in which cultural meanings get constituted, also simultaneously anchors to it an entire range of analyses and interpretations of the audio, the spatial, and of the psychic dynamics of spectatorship. Thus visual culture opens up an entire world of intertextuality in which images, sounds and spatial delineations are read on to and through one another, lending ever-accruing layers of meanings and of subjective responses to each encounter we might have with film, TV, advertising, art works, buildings or urban environments.'
>
> (Rogoff, 2002, p.24)

The scope, ambitions and complexities of visual culture are evident from this citation. Crucially, images 'do not stay within discrete disciplinary fields such as "documentary film" or "Renaissance painting", since neither the eye nor the psyche operates along or recognises such divisions' (Rogoff, 2002, p.26). Instead we can understand (and study) visual culture as experienced in a more fluid and complex manner; like a 'scrap of an image', for example, which 'connects with a sequence of a film and with the corner of a billboard or the window display of a shop we have passed by, to produce a new narrative formed out of both our experienced journey and our unconscious' (Rogoff, 2002, p.26).

Rogoff's account of the image fits with the idea of an ecology of images, as outlined in Chapter 2 of this book. A number of studies have taken this approach, particularly in looking at public, iconic imagery of the twentieth century (Buck-Morss, 2000; Hariman and Lucaites, 2007; Manghani, 2008) and the more contemporary 'imagefare' of the war in Iraq (Mirzoeff, 2005) and the associated 'War on Terror' (Mitchell, 2011). Nonetheless, an important criticism levied against visual culture studies is the potential to privilege an *abstract* interest in the visual. As Carol Armstrong (1996, p.27) has argued, the objects of study can come to be viewed 'not as particularized *things* made for particular historical uses, but as exchanges circulating in some great boundless and often curiously ahistorical economy of images, subjects, and other representations'. In other words, visual culture can be said to place a pre-determined structure, albeit a 'fluid interpretive structure' (Mirzoeff 1998, p.11), *before* the visual object. (For more on this 'problem' of visual culture, see: Bal, 2003; Manghani, 2003; 2008, pp.67–91.) Despite these concerns, however, the field of visual culture has developed a rich and critically engaging account of image culture(s). In this chapter, we look at some of the key terms and problematics.

Reproduction and remediation

Reproduction is a complex term, which we can use in various different ways. We most readily think of reproduction in terms of technical, mechanical means of reproduction such as the printing press and photography (as well as now digital copying), since these technologies have marked important shifts in the scale and range of cultural exchange. However, it is worth keeping in mind a much wider historical view. Marita Sturken and Lisa Cartwright make reference, for example, to the copying of scrolls in the Egyptian historical period of the New Kingdom. Funerary scrolls, they note, 'previously rendered only for the coffins of dead pharaohs and court members began to be copied more widely and placed in the coffins of those who were not nobility' (2009, p.190). In this case the copying was done by hand, with artisans working in specialist funerary workshops using ink on papyrus. Nonetheless, just as we find with mechanical reproduction, there is an underlying link between reproduction and a potential democratization of art and communications. Indeed, the political connotations of the term reproduction are significant. The concept of reproduction, or the copy, relates directly to iconoclasm (see Chapter 3), whereby prohibitions mark out dividing lines between preserving and disrupting the social order. In Marxist theory, the term reproduction 'is used to describe the ways that cultural practices and their forms of expression reproduce the ideologies and interests of the ruling class' (Sturken and Cartwright, 2009, p.183).

Walter Benjamin's (1992) essay, '**The Work of Art in the Age of Mechanical Reproduction**', originally written in 1936, is still one of the most widely read commentaries on our culture of reproduction (indeed the essay has itself been reproduced many times!). Benjamin describes how the new media of photography and film came to alter irrevocably our idea of the 'original' artwork. Take for example Leonardo da Vinci's *Mona Lisa*, which is one of the most recognizable paintings in the world. It was completed some time between 1503 and 1519. The portrait measures just 77cm × 53cm and hangs in the Louvre, in Paris, behind bulletproof glass. The painting has survived over 500 years and bears with it a cult of the artist: it is an original artefact, the indelible handiwork of a revered Italian Renaissance polymath. Benjamin refers to the original, one-of-a-kind artwork as bearing an **aura**: 'Even the most perfect reproduction of a work of art', he writes, 'is lacking in one element: its presence in time and space, its unique existence at the place where it happens to be' (Benjamin, 1992, p.214).

Yet, the uniqueness of the *Mona Lisa* cannot be the only reason for its enduring legacy. Indeed many older paintings survive. Like many artworks, the painting is mostly known to people through reproductions – which in this case include not just illustrations in art books, but a wide array of merchandise, from postcards to refrigerator magnets. The effect of all these reproductions is to alter the meaning of the painting. Echoing Benjamin's essay, John Berger explains how due to mechanical reproduction, an artwork 'now travels to the spectator rather than the spectator to the painting. In its travels, its meaning is diversified' (Berger, 1972, p.20). Of course it is still possible to view the original artwork. Yet, arguably, rather than being a picture to be viewed, it has become an event, or rite of passage. On any given day it is necessary to jostle with a large crowd all peering at the picture, many recording it digitally on their cameras (bringing it closer than the original can allow) – and with gallery attendants quietly ushering people in and out of the room to ensure a constant flow of 'spectators'. The point, then, in our age of reproducibility, is that whether or not we look at an original or the reproduction we can no longer look without the fact that 'the uniqueness of the original now lies in it being the original of a reproduction. It is no longer what its image shows that strikes one as unique; its first meaning is no longer to be found in what it says, but in what it is' (Berger, 1972, p.21).

The *Mona Lisa* is one very clear example of the layered phenomena of visual culture. It fits, for example, with Rogoff's account of the image (cited at the start of this chapter), which in transition produces new narratives. The painting was not in fact widely appreciated until as late as the mid-nineteenth century, when those associated with the Symbolist movement reinterpreted its subject matter as depicting the 'feminine mystique'. In an essay written in 1869, the critic Walter Pater described the portrait of the woman as the embodiment of *eternal* femininity:

FIGURE 6.1
Mona Lisa
(c.1503–1519),
Louvre Museum,
Paris, France.
Courtesy of
Getty/Wire Image.
Photograph: Barry
King.

'. . . older than the rocks among which she sits; like the vampire, she has been dead many times, and learned the secrets of the grave [. . .] The fancy of a perpetual life, sweeping together ten thousand experiences, is an old one; and modern philosophy has conceived the idea of humanity as wrought upon by, and summing up in itself, all modes of thought and life. Certainly Lady Lisa might stand as the embodiment of the old fancy, the symbol of the modern idea.'

(Pater, 1986, p.80)

Arguably, this textual reproduction or reading of the painting has been most influential in our making a virtue of the enigmatic smile of the sitter.

We can argue the iconic status of the *Mona Lisa* is found in and generated through its many re-inscriptions. Any Internet search will reveal a profusion of adaptations and spoofs. Perhaps the most famous and defining of these is the parody by one of the most influential modern artists of the twentieth century, Marcel Duchamp. In his work *L.H.O.O.Q* (1919), Duchamp makes explicit reference to the painting's reproduction by using a cheap postcard version of the image, which he defaces with a moustache and beard. The title of his work, when read aloud sounds out (in French) as 'Elle a chaud au cul', which translated means 'she has a hot ass'. Everything about

the work is designed to mock the original, and its reinsertion into the 'art world' is as much a comment on that domain as it is on the original painting. However, if we accept Duchamp's work as a radical gesture, we have to accept it is only made possible by first acknowledging the reverence of the original – in effect, it serves to further reinforce the significance of Leonardo's painting.

The copying and repurposing of images raises questions about ownership and copyright (see Sturken and Cartwright, 2009, pp. 204–212; see also Supplement II, Image Research). These concerns are further heightened in our 'age' of virtual, or digital reproduction. Yet, the new, digital technologies also reveal continuities with modes of reproduction, or what Bolter and Grusin (2000) refer to as **remediation**. Unlike Benjamin, they do not consider new media necessarily to break from the aesthetic and cultural principles of earlier media. In fact, they argue new media frequently define themselves by paying homage to, rivalling, and/or refashioning earlier media. For example, Bolter and Grusin note how 'digital photorealism defines reality as perfected photography, and virtual reality defines it as first-person point-of-view cinema' (2000, p.55). It is also evident that people entering into the online 3D virtual world of Second Life, seek to identify themselves to others through 'real world' social markers, such as a home, clothing and everyday accessories – despite the fact that none of these things have any real significance to what you can do in the virtual 'physics' of the online domain. Whilst we might typically find examples of how new media remediate older media, Bolter and Grusin point out the process can go the other way too:

> 'Older media can also remediate newer ones. Television can and does refashion itself to resemble the World Wide Web and film can and does incorporate and attempt to contain computer graphics within its own linear form. No medium, it seems, can now function independently and establish its own separate and purified space of cultural meaning.'
>
> (Bolter and Grusin, 2000, p.55)

The concept of remediation adds further nuance to Benjamin's account of repro-duction. Bolter and Grusin suggest, for example, 'remediation does not destroy the aura of a work of art; instead it always refashions that aura in another media form' (2000, p.75). The account given above of Duchamp's parody of the *Mona Lisa* would seem to attest to this view. There are two specific 'logics' of remediation according to Bolter and Grusin (2000), which date back at least to the Renaissance and the invention of linear perspective. On the one hand we seek for a medium to offer transparent *immediacy*. In other words, we wish for the apparatus of a medium to disappear from view, leaving us only with the message it delivers. Virtual reality and 3D films remain somewhat cumbersome with the need to wear various headgear in order to experience their effects (though home gaming consoles are becoming increasingly sophisticated with the recognition of movement, etc.). These new media represent our clear desire for immediacy, for a 'real' experience; and this desire is present in all other media.

The second logic of remediation is *hypermediacy*, which represents our opposite desire to foreground the act of mediation. In terms of digital media, Bolter and Grusin suggest 'the practice of hypermediacy is most evident in the heterogeneous "windowed style" of World Wide Web pages, the desktop interface, multimedia programs, and video games' (2000, p.31). When television refashions itself in terms of the Web it adopts a form of hypermediacy. Contemporary news practices, for example, particularly with the advent of global 24-hour news production, have led to a foregrounding of the gathering and transmission of news information. The television screen now offers multiple views and layers of information (such as scrolling texts superimposed on the screen). Bolter and Grusin also explain hypermediacy with reference to Richard Hamilton's *Just What is it That Makes Today's Homes so Different, So Appealing?* – which we encountered in Supplment I of this book. They write:

'Just as collage challenges the immediacy of perspective painting, photomontage challenges the immediacy of the photograph. When photomonateurs cut up and recombine conventional photographs, they discredit the notion that the photograph is drawn by the "pencil of nature" . . . Instead, the photographs themselves become elements that human intervention has selected and arranged for artistic purposes. Photographs pasted beside and on top of each other and in the context of other media, such as type, painting, or pencil drawing, create a layered effect that we also find in electronic multimedia. We look at Richard Hamilton's *Just What is it That Makes Today's Homes so Different, So Appealing?* . . . its cluttered space makes us aware of the process of construction. We become hyperconscious of the medium in photomontage, precisely because conventional photography is a medium with such loud historical claims to transparency.'

(Bolter and Grusin, 2000, p. 38)

Remediation relates to the double logic in Benjamin's essay on the artwork in the age of mechanical reproduction. Photographic reproduction serves to break the aura of an artwork 'by eliding or erasing the distance between the work and its viewer' (Bolter and Grusin, 2000, p. 74). Benjamin, we might suggest, considered mechanical reproduction to satisfy our desire for transparent immediacy. As people jostle to see the *Mona Lisa* they can pull the painting (and its significance) closer to them by capturing its image on their cameras. Yet, equally, 'Benjamin's mechanical reproduction also seems to evoke a fascination with media. In the case of film, he describes the viewer as distracted by the rapid succession of scenes, as simultaneously entranced and aroused by the mediation of film' (Bolter and Grusin, 2000, p. 74).

Furthermore, Bolter and Grusin remind us that it is not simply the copying of images we need to consider, but also the citing and re-citing of media too. We can think here of Marshall McLuhan's slogan 'the **medium is the message**', from *Understanding Media* (1997 [1964]), by which he meant that 'the "content" of any medium is always another medium. The content of writing is speech, just as the written word is the content of print, and print is the content of the telegraph' (1997, p. 8). Mitchell (2005, pp. 201–221) echoes aspects of McLuhan's medium theory and of remediation, to remind us that images 'cannot be assessed without some reckoning of the media in which they appear'. The difference, for example, of image and picture, 'is precisely a question of the medium. An image only appears in some medium or other – in paint, stone, words, or numbers' (p. 203). As Bolter and Grusin would assert, we can find these different media are not always as distinctive as we are led to believe.

Vision and visuality

Having considered the image in terms of reproducibility, and revealed a blurring of boundaries between media, it is important we situate the viewing subject. On the one hand we assume vision is universal; while we might suffer impairments to our vision, in broader, evolutionary terms we all share the same biological capacity to see. On the other hand, however, we attribute all kinds of 'ways of seeing' and modes of representation that are culturally and historically specific (Davis, 2011, pp.11–42). We might label the difference as being between vision and **visuality**, with the latter referring to culturally specific ways of seeing, or forms of representing the world. This formulation is however a little rigid. In the preface to *Vision and Visuality* (1988) Hal Foster writes:

> 'Although vision suggests sight as a physical operation, and visuality sight as a social fact, the two are not opposed as nature is to culture: vision is social and historical too, and visuality involves the body and the psyche. Yet neither are they identical: here, the difference between the terms signals a difference within the visual – between the mechanisms of sight and its historical techniques, between the datum of vision and its discursive determinations – a difference, many differences, among how we see, how we are able, allowed, or made to see, and how we see this seeing or the unseen therein.'
>
> (Foster, 1988: ix)

As much as this neat formulation defies simple reductionism, it equally raises many questions. Martin Jay, one of the contributors to *Vision and Visuality*, has come to query the idea of a discrete '**scopic regime**', which apparently needs to be understood 'as analogous to the various forms of life that have become known as distinct cultures in the anthropological sense of the term' (Jay, 2002, p.268). Put another way, he asks: 'is it ever possible to disentangle vision from . . . "discursive determinations"? Are the views we have of the world, in short, always like the intellectual "worldviews" . . . ?' (Jay, 2002, p.268).

The notion of **realism** lays perhaps the strongest claim to being both how we see (vision) and a historically and culturally informed set of conventions for under-standing and depicting the world (visuality). Generally, there is an assumption that realistic images reproduce things as they 'really' look. Photographs are frequently described as being more realistic than paintings due to the mechanical means of reproduction that physically captures the light emanating from the object depicted. Furthermore, as Sturken and Cartwright suggest, '[r]ealism is an important aspect of our sense of ethics as citizens in a world in which images proliferate as forms of communication and expression. We expect photojournalists to observe the conventions of realism when they document events for news stories. When they don't, we object' (2009, p.141). Yet, as they go on to explain, realism can be linked to a diverse set of conventions and approaches. Even abstract images can be consid-ered in terms of realism. So, for example, the action painting of Pollock considered in Chapter 4, whilst labelled a work of abstract expressionism, can be said to generate a 'more direct, uncensored release of inner feelings of the artist and that the marks on the canvas would express these feelings without direct pictorial symbolism' (Sturken and Cartwright, 2009, p.170).

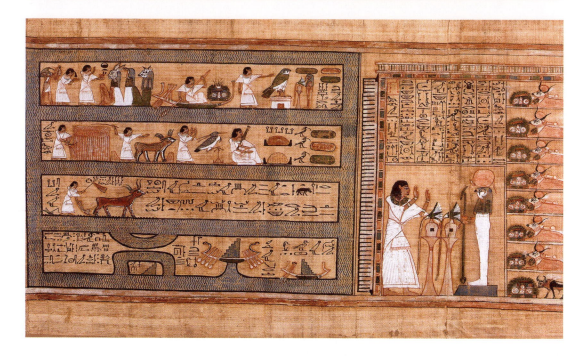

FIGURE 6.3

Book of the Dead of Ani, Sheet 35, Egypt, 19th Dynasty © The Trustees of the British Museum.

More commonly, however, realism in the visual arts refers to the image that depicts something as would be seen by the eye. In the case of Pollock, the painting is neither representing nor symbolizing anything. Instead it is a direct recording of an action in paint. If it is a representation, it is of an artist's process and materials rather than how one sees or depicts the world. Nevertheless, as Sturken and Cartwright point out, '[t]he function of visual art . . . has not always been to reproduce objects, people, and events in the real world as the eye of the observer would see them'. They note specific examples, including early Christian art in which '[v]ariations in scale and mixing of graphic and decorative elements with representational ones in a single scene suggest that concern with symbolism overshadowed any possible concern about making things look as they would to the eye' (2009, p.142). Ancient Egyptian art is another example. In reference to a funerary papyrus (Figure 6.3), they argue how the apparent aerial view 'serves as a space in which text and image are organized sequentially, like a contemporary comic book'. Thus, they explain:

> 'Spatial logic does not reflect the scene as it would be seen by eye. But this does not mean that the representation is primitive or that spatial logic is undeveloped. Rather, other epistemic systems of logic are at work here than those to which we are accustomed, and more than one way of using space is being invoked at once.'
>
> (Sturken and Cartwright, 2009, pp.149–150)

The term 'epistemic' is used in reference to the work of the philosopher and historian of ideas Michel Foucault. In *The Order of Things* (1974), Foucault uses the term **episteme** (derived from the word epistemology, the science of understanding) to describe dominant systems of meaning and knowledge, or world-views, as they develop in a given period in history. With the example of the funerary papyrus, symbolism and varying spatial logics are *systems* of depiction, or 'ways of seeing', which remain dominant throughout the medieval period. Yet, during the European Renaissance (between the fourteenth and seventeenth centuries) this changes altogether with the rise of **perspective** as a newly dominant system of representation. Perspective refers to how objects are seen, or plotted spatially from the position of a single, fixed vantage point. When a photographer holds a camera up to a scene, or when an artist holds up their pencil, they are framing the scene before them from a single point of view and seeking to measure everything from that one position.

FIGURE 6.4

Ascent of the Prophet Muhammad © The British Library Board. A sixteenth century Persian miniature painting celebrating Muhammad's ascent into the Heavens, a journey known as the Miraj.

Perspective is not a sudden discovery or invention of the Renaissance period. It is referred to in earlier periods, but it is not a favoured system of representation. Plato, for example, 'regarded techniques for rendering depth as a kind of deception' (Sturken and Cartwright, 2009, p.150). The Ottoman miniaturists of the sixteenth century similarly held a distrust for mimesis. The view taken was that the appearance of worldly things was not permanent and worth devotion, so ruling out a realistic mode of representation. Orhan Pamuk's novel *My Name is Red* (2001) offers a dramatic narrative of the threat to the Ottoman world-view due to the introduction of European Renaissance styles. The novel is a murder-mystery set in sixteenth-century Istanbul, skilfully told through the visual narratives of **Ottoman miniature painting**. The novel enables the tradition of miniature painting to be 'interpreted as a way of dealing with the iconoclastic tradition of Islam. In this context, images are not seen as things-in-themselves but they are treated as "footnotes" even when the image seems to dominate the written word on the page' (Çiçekoglu, 2003, p.1). Ottoman miniature painting conjured a very different world-view to that of the European Renaissance painting tradition. Where the Renaissance painters sought to depict the human form (particularly the face) in a realistic manner, the Ottoman artists adopted a more stylized and abstract aesthetic with the aim to evoke an infinite and transcendent reality. Thus the difference felt between the Ottoman and Renaissance styles is not simply a technical difference, but relates to the values attached to them; making for a deep-set epistemic clash with respect to ways of understanding and upholding the social order.

The scientific revolution of the 1400s through to the 1600s, with advancements of knowledge in astronomy, navigation and physiology, was in accord with the mathematical precision of perspective. In the Latin, *perspicere* means to 'see clearly', to 'inspect', and also to 'look through'. One of the earliest, and most widely known treatises on linear perspective was by the scholar of law and theologian Leone Battista Alberti. In *De Pictura* (1435), he famously describes the rectangular picture frame as an open window through which one looks to make a study of an object. Albrecht Dürer's *Draftsman Drawing a Nude*, published in *The Painter's Manual* in 1525, is one of the best-known illustrations of this idea. By the mid-1600s onwards, perspective

FIGURE 6.5
Illustration from Dürer's *Four Books on Measurement* published in 1525 (woodcut). Courtesy of Bridgeman Art Library.

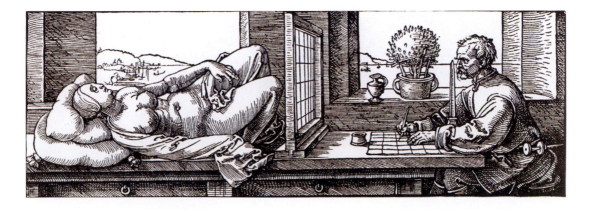

is more deeply associated with the sciences and rationality. This period, referred to as the **Enlightenment**, brings science together with ideas of progress and liberty. One of the key philosophers of the time was the mathematician René Descartes. As a rationalist, Descartes considered representations to be of the 'mind', leading to a new, 'modern' epistemology, or conception of how we understand the world. Jay (1988) refers to Cartesian perspectivalism as a *dominant* 'modern scopic regime': 'The assumption [. . . is] that Cartesian perspectivalism is *the* reigning visual model of modernity . . . often tied to the further contention that it succeeded in becoming so because it best expressed the "natural" experience of sight valorized by the scientific world view' (Jay, 1988, p.5).

What is made apparent by historicizing vision is the nature and unfolding of competing hegemonies of seeing and of being seen (Jay 1988; Crary, 1988). As noted, perspectivalism is premised upon a mode of sight from a single point of view. The **camera obscura** – an enclosed interior with light entering through a single hole to allow for an inverted image to appear on an opposite wall – is a technology with a long history, strongly associated with perspectivalism. As Crary notes, 'the

FIGURE 6.7 Giotto di Bondone, *Scenes from the Life of Saint Francis: Death of the Knight of Celano* (detail). Assisi, Church of San Francisco © 2012 Photo Scala, Florence.

FIGURE 6.8 *Rudolf IV Emperor of Austria and Tyrol* (detail), c.1365. Courtesy of Bridgeman Art Library.

camera obscura was not simply an inert and neutral piece of equipment', but in fact came to represent 'a model . . . for how observation leads to truthful inferences about an external world' (1988, p. 30–31). However, during the nineteenth century greater emphasis is placed upon our own physiology, leading to 'a model of subjective vision in which . . . we find an image of a newly productive observer whose body has a range of capacities to generate visual experience; it is a question of visual experience that does not refer or correspond to anything external to the observing subject' (p. 34). In the writings of Goethe published at this time, and with the work of numerous scientists, we find evidence of a growing interest in phenomena such as the retinal afterimage. The British artist, Turner, provides visual expression of these interests:

> '. . . in the late paintings of Turner, in which there is that piercing confrontation of eye and sun, paintings in which the strictures that previously had mediated and regulated vision are abandoned. Nothing now protects or distances the observer from the seductive and sensual brilliance of the sun. The symbolic confines of the camera obscura have crumbled.'

> (Crary, 1988, p. 35)

FIGURE 6.9 Masolino, *Healing of the Lame Man and Raising of Tabitha* (detail), Florence Santa Maria del Carmine. Photo © Scala, Florence 2012.

FIGURE 6.10 Robert Campin, *A Man* (detail), c.1430. © National Gallery, London

It is important to note, Crary warns against placing too much emphasis on the visual arts as a means to elucidate our 'visual' history. 'We've been trained to assume', he writes, 'that an observer will always leave visual tracks, that is, will be identifiable in terms of images'. Whereas in fact visuality 'takes shape in other, grayer practices and discourses, and whose immense legacy will be all the industries of the image and the spectacle in the twentieth century' (Crary, 1988, p.43). The metaphor of truth associated with the camera obscura subtly shifts in the nineteenth century to a metaphor of concealment and inversion. Notably for the philosopher and economist, Karl Marx, 'the way that the light comes into the camera obscura and is then inverted was a metaphor for how bourgeois ideology inverts the actual relations of labor and capital and substitutes appearance for reality' (Sturken and Cartwright, 2009, p.163). Today, the mathematical precision of perspectivalism and physics of the camera obscura continue to inform a common understanding of vision. Digital photography software, for example, is most adept at dealing with geometric forms. In Photoshop, for example, the sharpen tool (which appears to give sharper focus to an image) is much more effective when dealing with an architectural form than the human body.

Nonetheless, optical devices have long conjoined with our desire to accurately render visual representations of the human form. The artist David Hockney (2001)

put forward a controversial thesis about the widespread use of optical devices, going back as far as the 1400s. He suggests the camera lucida, which is a prism used to cast an image of one's surroundings upon a surface, was used by a range of artists to capture a greater likeness than is otherwise achievable. He points out, however, the camera lucida is very difficult to use:

> '. . . optics do not make marks, only the artist's hand can do that, and it requires great skill. And optics don't make drawing any easier either, far from it – I know, I've used them. But to an artist six hundred years ago optical projections would have demonstrated a new vivid way of looking at and representing the material world.'

> (Hockney, 2001 p.14)

It should be stressed, Hockney's findings are not conclusive, yet he offers some fascinating observations. For example, four paintings painted 130 years apart vividly bring into focus a new way of seeing. The first two images (Figures 6.7 and 6.8), dating back to the 1300s, offer interesting expression, but are 'awkwardly' rendered. Nevertheless:

> 'By 1425, in Italy, Masolino [Figure 6.9] has more order in the face; the turban seems to follow the form of the head and looks as though it fits properly. But just five years later, in Flanders, something happens. Robert Campin's face [Figure 6.10] looks startlingly "modern"; it could be someone from today. There is clear lighting . . . suggesting a strong source of light; the folds in the turban aren't awkward; the man's small double chin is seen clearly; and the mouth and eyes are far more related, giving an intensity to his appearance. This painting has a totally different "look".'

> (Hockney, 2001, p.66)

Overall, the two most significant (and inter-related) implications that follow from the concept of visuality are the way in which it makes vision historical and the emphasis it places upon a visual *subject* (rather than object) – both having the effect of opening up the field of visual culture to novel attempts at cultural analysis and interpretation. The concept gives rise to a fluid genealogy of visual culture, of multiple sites of meaning and perspective, each depending on the current social and cultural matrix surrounding the viewer and viewed.

Spectatorship and visual subjects

In *Ways of Seeing* (1972), John Berger makes the following distinction between 'seeing' and 'looking': 'We only *see* what we *look at*. To look is an act of choice' (p.8, emphasis added). Furthermore, our ability to see equally makes us aware that we can also be seen. These are fundamental principles at the heart of theories of the visual subject. Sturken and Cartwright (2009, pp.93–139) provide a useful overview of differing theories and accounts of the visual subject in modernity. We can begin, for example, with the ideas of René Descartes, who evokes a mind/body split: 'For Descartes, the world becomes known when we accurately represent it in thought, not when we experience it through the senses and not when we imagine it in our mind's eye' (Sturken and Cartwright, 2009, p.95). Descartes' rationalist philosophy relates to a modern, liberal discourse, situating the individual as a self-knowing, unified and autonomous entity. However, the technological and social changes associated with the period of modernity – and in particular with respect to the rise of capitalism – reveal significant social inequities. Karl Marx offered an important critique of the individual as self-determining. When his ideas are brought together with ideas of the visual subject, we begin to consider 'seeing' and 'being seen' in terms of power relations, ownership and control. The historian and philosopher Jacques Rancière, for example, defines our political status in terms of who has the right to see and to be seen. He coins the phrase the 'division of the sensible' to describe 'the cutting up of the perceptual world . . . And this redistribution itself presupposes a cutting up of what is visible and what is not, of what can be heard and what cannot, or what is noise and what is speech' (Rancière, 2004, p.225; see also Mirzoeff, 2009, pp.17–20).

Another important critique of the rational, autonomous individual comes from psychoanalysis, which emerges at the turn of the twentieth century. Through the analysis of dreams and adopting therapeutic practices, Sigmund Freud famously revealed how we are guided by our unconscious as much as conscious mind. The French psychoanalyst, Jacques Lacan, later develops Freud's ideas to argue for the notion of a split subject. Lacan describes how, during the first 6–18 months of our infant life, we go through what he calls the 'mirror stage'. Referring both literally to seeing oneself in a mirror and/or seeing others around us as mirrors of ourselves, Lacan describes a scene of *méconnaissance* – whereby we misrecognise or misconstrue (1977, pp.1–7). As the infant begins to establish motor skills and to distinguish themselves from the parental body, the 'ego' begins to form. The child begins to consider himself or herself an independent, unitary subject. Yet, of course the child is still highly dependent and looking in a mirror they see only clumsy, disjointed actions. What they see, in fact, is 'an Ideal-I, an ego ideal, and this encounter is traumatic, as the subject is constituted in a fundamental split between self and image, me and not-me' (Sturken and Cartwright, 2009, p.101). Whilst the mirror stage refers explicitly to early childhood development, it can also be read metaphorically to describe an ongoing experience we have of ourselves as being divided. Without being able to step outside of ourselves, we can never truly witness our own unitary form. We project a sense of Self, but we can never be sure how we are received by others. Thus, like the infant in the mirror-stage, we constantly look for signs of ourselves in others, but in turn this perpetuates our subject-hood as fundamentally split between Self and image. Thus, in addition to Berger's distinction between 'seeing' and 'being seen', which evokes the potential for power relations *between* subjects, Lacan's psychoanalytic account adds the dilemma of our own self-misrecognition.

The concept of the divided subject has been highly influential in visual studies, particularly in relation to debates of spectatorship, surveillance and the 'gaze'. As Sturken and Cartwright point out, '[t]heories of the gaze and spectatorship are theories of address, rather than reception . . . When we study address, we consider the ways that an image or visual text invites certain responses from a particular category of viewer, such as male or female viewer' (p.102). The fact that looking is always a relational activity – and one of 'addressing' another – raises questions of power, identity and control. In *Discipline and Punish* (1977), Michel Foucault describes the designs of a prison structure known as the **panopticon** (designed by utilitarian social reformer Jeremy Bentham (in 1791), but never actually built). Prison cells are arranged in a circular building, in the middle of which a central tower commands the view of each and every one of these cells. It is a highly efficient architectural structure, since one prison guard can immediately survey the entire inhabitants of the prison from the safety of the autonomous observation tower. Furthermore, the inmates are unable to see if the guard is actually present, making it virtually unnecessary to place a guard in the tower at all.

> 'What mattered was the imagined spectator fixed in the mind of each inmate. Unlike the dungeon, which removed prisoners from sight yet afforded them some protection from scrutiny, the panopticon subjected prisoners to a relentless gaze. Imagining being watched thereby kept them in line.'
>
> (Sturken and Cartwright, 2009, p.107)

The term 'panopticon' is widely adopted as a term to describe practices of self-regulation. In a literal sense, CCTV creates a similarly unmanned system of surveillance, which leads people to internalize or imagine being watched. However, various forms of photo-ID, biometrics and all kinds of social-media tagging continually expand ways in which we are watched, we watch ourselves and/or imagine we are being watched.

A schematic account of the visual subject can be given with a still from the film *Mullholland Drive* (Figure 6.11); a film which portrays a fluid and confusing set of identities and plotlines, typical of its director, David Lynch. In this still we see one of the principle characters, who is literally searching for her identity due to suffering amnesia. She assumes the name 'Rita' after seeing a poster for the 1946 film *Gilda*, staring Rita Hayworth. You can see a fragment of the poster in the smaller mirror, on the left-hand side of the image. Rita 'presents' herself in front of the mirror – she lets herself be seen. We literally see the fact the mirror reflects Rita and everything that surrounds her. But we might think of it metaphorically too, with the mirror suggesting any optical or representational device used to capture the image. Everything it 'draws' into its lens becomes a representation – as part of which, Rita becomes an *object* to be seen. But where is Rita looking? We know from the narrative she is searching for herself, and temporally associates with the *Gilda* film poster. Again, both literally and metaphorically, she looks outside of herself for her own meaning and this matches with her gaze in the still, which casts about into the

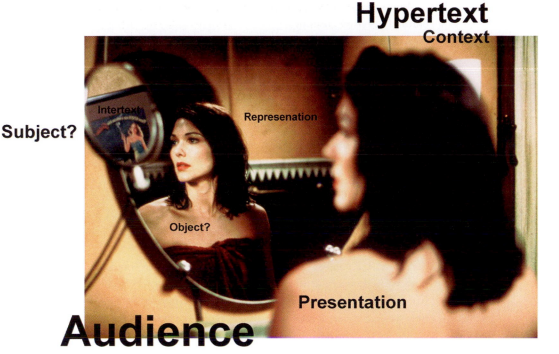

Hypertext
Context
Intertext
Subject?
Represenation
Object?
Presentation
Audience

FIGURE 6.11
Annotated film still
from *Mullholland Drive*
(Dir. David Lynch,
2001).

distance and crucially outside of the frame. Her own *subject* would appear – albeit unstably – to exist somewhere beyond herself. As mentioned, psychoanalytical readings provide an account of a divided self, both situated within one's bounded body, yet constantly searching beyond for recognition and differentiation from others. Looking at this one still, we might say Rita exists somewhere outside of the frame and is really only imaginary; a projection of an identity. It is an identity both external and internal (or internalized). We become labelled by codes of meaning outside of ourselves. When we are born we have no conception of the symbolic order into which we arrive, yet we are immediately prescribed as either male or female and we are given a name, and so on. In this film still, the name Rita exists in a nested set of codes: the actress Rita Hayworth in the film *Gilda* appears on a poster, which 'Rita' assumes as her own.

What about the frame itself? In this annotated film still are the words 'Audience' and 'Context'. Any moment of looking evokes the possibility of audience. Does Rita have an audience within the film diegesis? Is she imagining one? Or is she simply an actress working upon the notion of a cinematic audience, which might include us? Audience, then, can exist both outside and within the frame – it bears its own weight upon the scene (we behave in certain ways when we know, or suspect we are being watched); yet equally the scene impresses itself upon the audience, giving them something to reflect upon. We can understand 'context' in a similar way. There is literally a surrounding scene – or in film language the *mise-en-scène* – within which Rita is placed. Yet, equally, we place Rita in the film, and the film in our own culture, in ways specific to how we contextualize or match it against a set of socially and culturally shared meanings.

Also included is the term 'Hypertext'. The word perhaps most immediately evokes ideas about the World Wide Web, since it has become jargon for the networked set of links that we click as we surf the Net. An Internet search for the film *Mullholland Drive* reveals a wide range of such hyperlinks, from plot outlines to fanclubs and much more besides (even the film still itself can be 'searched' using an image-based search engine – see Supplement II, Image Research). However, we can also think of a more conceptual notion of the 'Text', as discussed in post-structuralist writings. The best-known account is given in Roland Barthes' essay 'From Work to Text' (1977, pp.155–164), in which he states, 'the work can be held in the hand, the text is held in language, only exists in the movement of a discourse' (p.157). This brings us back to an idea noted at the start of this chapter for a fluid notion of the visual 'object' and opens up many different ways in which we can map and construct the visual subject.

The 'visual subject' and the term 'gaze' refer us to forms of looking in which power relations are at stake, typically with more power attributed to the person who is looking, than the person looked at. Important questions can be raised about how we come to look at or be looked at with regards to race, class, gender, sexuality and so forth. Laura Mulvey's (1989) notion of the '**male gaze**', for example, first developed in her ground-breaking essay 'Visual Pleasure and Narrative Cinema' in 1975, is perhaps the best-known and debated theory of the gaze. More recently, the relationship between gender and viewing relations has taken to be less polarized. It is argued for example '[v]iewers readily deploy fantasy to occupy the "wrong" gender position in their spectatorial relationships to films. Women can identify with the male position of mastery or exercise voyeuristic tendencies in looking at men or women. Men can be looked on with pleasure and desire by men or women' (Sturken and Cartwright, 2009, p.130). Susan Bordo (1997, p.124) makes a further claim that 'we never respond *only* to particular body parts or their configuration but *always* to the meanings they carry for us'. Her argument is that we all have idiosyncratic and deeply engrained associations with the human body that come before we see them dressed or edited in certain ways on the screen. In recognizing this, she suggests, 'the old feminist charge of "objectification" seems inadequate to describe what is going on when women's bodies are depicted in sexualized or aestheticized ways. The notion of women-as-objects suggests the reduction of women to 'mere' bodies, when actually what's going on is often far more disturbing' (p.124).

Similar debates range over questions of race and ethnicity. A common classroom example is a party political poster, which the UK's Conservative Party used to reach out to ethnic minority groups during a campaign in the 1980s. The poster (Figure 6.12) shows a young black man dressed in a suit, with the main caption 'Labour say he is black. Tories say he is British'. The advertisement is reproduced in Paul Gilroy's *There Ain't No Black in the Union Jack* (2002). Gilroy is highly critical of how the man is made to stand-out alone in an ill-fitting suit, bearing no genuine trace of his own identity. Black people, Gilroy suggests, 'are being invited to forsake all that marks

With the Conservatives, there are no 'blacks', no 'whites', just people.

Conservatives believe that treating minorities as equals encourages the majority to treat them as equals.

Yet the Labour Party aim to treat you as a 'special case', as a group all on your own.

Is setting you apart from the rest of society a sensible way to overcome racial prejudice and social inequality?

The question is, should we really divide the British people instead of uniting them?

WHOSE PROMISES ARE YOU TO BELIEVE?

When Labour were in government, they promised to repeal Immigration Acts passed in 1962 and 1971. Both promises were broken.

This time, they are promising to throw out the British Nationality Act, which gives full and equal citizenship to everyone permanently settled in Britain.

But how do the Conservatives' promises compare?

We said that we'd abolish the 'SUS' law.

We kept our promise.

We said we'd recruit more coloured policemen, get the police back into the community, and train them for a better understanding of your needs.

We kept our promise.

PUTTING THE ECONOMY BACK ON ITS FEET.

The Conservatives have always said that the only long term answer to our economic problems was to conquer inflation.

Inflation is now lower than it's been for over a decade, keeping all prices stable, with the price of food now hardly rising at all.

Meanwhile, many businesses throughout Britain are recovering, leading to thousands of new jobs.

Firstly, in our traditional industries, but just as importantly in new technology areas such as microelectronics.

In other words, the medicine is working.

Yet Labour want to change everything, and put us back to square one.

They intend to increase taxation. They intend to increase the National Debt.

They promise import and export controls.

Cast your mind back to the last Labour government. Labour's methods didn't work then.

They won't work now.

A BETTER BRITAIN FOR ALL OF US.

The Conservatives believe that everyone wants to work hard and be rewarded for it.

Those rewards will only come about by creating a mood of equal opportunity for everyone in Britain, regardless of their race, creed or colour.

The difference you're voting for is this:

To the Labour Party, you're a black person.

To the Conservatives, you're a British Citizen.

Vote Conservative, and you vote for a more equal, more prosperous Britain.

LABOUR SAYS HE'S BLACK.
TORIES SAY HE'S BRITISH.

CONSERVATIVE ☒

FIGURE 6.12
Conservative Party election poster, 1978/1979. © Getty/Hulton Archive. Courtesy of The Conservative Party Archive.

them out as culturally distinct before real Britishness can be guaranteed' (2002, p.65). Figure 6.13 shows an almost identical advertisement used in the same political campaign, but in this case showing a young Indian man. The fact this man is again seemingly addressed as an individual and yet placed within the exact same template appears to compound Gilroy's fierce critique. However, given that the specific advertisement used by Gilroy (Figure 6.12) has retained far more currency (in teaching materials and in reproductions in books, etc.), helps remind us of the significance not just of visibility, but also invisibility (in this case the relative invisibility of the Indian man).

The same 'visual' logic of the election posters can also been seen in the more contemporary imagery of Benetton advertisements, where the attempt to look beyond colour is even more startling. Adopting a globalized slogan, 'The United Colors of Benetton', the clothing retailer brought together their signature use of colour in garments with explicit multi-racial representation in their advertisements. Given the frequently provocative nature of Benetton's advertising during the 1990s, it is tempting to argue about whether racial archetypes are used for positive effect

FIGURE 6.13

Conservative Party election poster, 1978/1979. © Getty/Hulton Archive. Courtesy of The Conservative Party Archive.

or unnecessarily appropriated in order to sell clothes. This, however, according to Celia Lury, is to miss a more profound cultural shift:

> '"Race", in this imagery, is not a matter of skin colour, of physical characteristics as the expression of a biological or natural essence, but rather of style, of the colour of skin, of colour itself as the medium of what might be called a second nature or, more provocatively, a *cultural essentialism.*'
>
> (Lury, 2000, p.148)

The arguments made regarding the visual subject – with reference here to gender and race – alert to the importance of cultural critique attuned to how we are trained to see and what choices we make in looking. However, it is worth keeping in mind, as Elkins (2003, p.83) argues, '[v]isual images might not always be the optimal place to look for signs of gender, identity, politics, and the other questions that are of interest to scholars'. One example Elkins gives are the analyses of the media treatment of the death of Princess Diana, which often sought to demonstrate the media's complicity in the creation of a global media network. The question he raises is whether or not these kinds of pictures are really in *themselves* important in our understanding of globalism, or simply instances of this phenomenon, otherwise equally (if not better) handled by non-visual theories of globalization. Similar doubts could be raised for the examples given above. Are they really in *themselves* important in understanding social and cultural trends? Image studies needs to question just what 'work' is being done by images themselves and by the analysis given to them. On occasion, we need to acknowledge 'the images are there just because the writers are invested in them, not because images are needed to make the arguments work' (Elkins, 2003, pp.82–83).

Metapictures

A recurrent problem for the study of visual culture is the tension that ensues when *writing* about the visual. The idea of a 'pictorial turn' (and a shifting semiotic landscape), as discussed in Chapter 3, brings to the fore the need to move away from models of analysis based solely upon notions of textuality. Yet, equally, the prospect of a 'picture theory' remains always a moving target. The following extract describes a seemingly simple classroom exercise, 'Showing Seeing', which potentially disarms and/or acts to destabilize the divide between theory and practice, text and image. In turn it leads to consideration of what we might term 'metapictures'.

SHOWING SEEING

W.J.T. MITCHELL

(from *What Do Pictures Want? The Lives and Loves of Images*, 2005, pp.336–356)

[T]he object of the show and tell performance is the process of seeing itself, and the exercise could be called showing seeing. I ask [participants] to frame their presentations by assuming that they are ethnographers who come from, and are reporting back to, a society that has no concept of visual culture. They cannot take for granted that their audience has any familiarity with everyday notions such as color, line, eye contact, cosmetics, clothing, facial expressions, mirrors, glasses, or voyeurism, much less with photography, painting, sculpture or other so-called visual media. Visual culture is thus made to seem strange, exotic, and in need of explanation.

The assignment is thoroughly paradoxical, of course. The audience does in fact live in a visible world, and yet has to accept the fiction that it does not, and that everything which seems transparent and self-evident is in need of explanation. I leave it to the students to construct an enabling fiction. Some choose to ask the audience to close their eyes and to take in the presentation solely with their ears and other senses. They work primarily by description and evocation of the visual through language and sound, telling *as*, rather than telling *and* showing. Another strategy is to pretend that the audience has just been provided with prosthetic visual organs, but does not yet know how to see with them. This is the favored strategy, since it allows for a visual presentation of objects and images. The audience has to pretend ignorance, and the presenter has to lead them toward the understanding of things they would ordinarily take for granted.

The range of examples and objects that students bring to class is quite broad and unpredictable. Some things routinely appear: eye-glasses are favorite objects of explanation, and someone almost always brings in a pair of mirror shades to illustrate the situation of seeing without being seen, and the masking of the eyes as a common strategy in a visual culture. Masks and disguises more generally are popular props. Windows, binoculars, kaleidoscopes, microscopes, and other pieces of optical apparatus are commonly adduced. Mirrors are frequently brought in, generally with no hint of an awareness of Lacan's mirror stage, but often with learned expositions of the optical laws of reflection, or discourses on vanity, narcissism, and self-fashioning. Cameras are often exhibited, not just to explain their workings, but to talk about the rituals and superstitions that accompany their use. One student elicited the familiar reflex of camera shyness by aggressively taking snapshots of other members of the class. [. . .] Perhaps the simplest gadget-free performance I have ever witnessed was by a student who led the class through an introduction to the experience of eye contact which culminated in that old first-grade game, the stare-down contest (the first to blink is the loser).

[. . .]

The simplest lesson of showing seeing is a kind of de-disciplinary exercise. We learn to get away from the notion that visual culture is covered by the materials or methods of art history, aesthetics, and media studies. Visual culture starts out in an area beneath the notice of these disciplines – the realm of non-artistic, non-aesthetic, and unmediated or 'immediate' visual images and experiences. It comprises a larger field of what I would call vernacular visuality or everyday seeing that is bracketed out by the disciplines addressed to visual arts and media. [. . .] In particular, it helps us to see that even something as broad as the image does not exhaust the field of visuality; that visual studies is not the same thing as image studies, and that the study of the visual image is just one component of the larger field.

As Mitchell describes here, the exercise in 'Showing Seeing' provides a de-disciplinary effect. In other words, the exercise reveals the various framings and assumed knowledge of different perspectives on the visual. It alludes to the fact that different fields of study have their own preconceived ideas and will place their own specific emphasis upon an analysis of the visual. Thus:

> 'A more ambitious aim of showing seeing is its potential as a reflection on theory and method in themselves. As should be evident, the approach is informed by a kind of pragmatism, but not (one hopes) of a kind that is closed off to speculation, experiment, and even metaphysics. At the most fundamental level, it is an invitation to rethink what theorizing is, to picture theory and perform theory as a visible, embodied, communal practice, not as the solitary intro- spection of a disembodied intelligence.'
>
> (Mitchell, 2005, p.355)

In effect, the exercise gives 'theory a body and visible shape that it often wants to deny, to reveal theory as representation'. As such, we are asked to understand repre- sentation not as a particular object, but rather 'as relationship, as process, as the relay mechanism in exchanges of power, value, and publicity' (Mitchell, 1994, p.420).

TASK

Showing Seeing

Devise your own 'Showing Seeing' presentation. Re-read the extract here to help you get started. You might also find it useful to look back over earlier parts of this chapter to think about a particular aspect of visual culture and/or visuality that you wish to explore. Remember: the 'object' of the performance is the process of seeing itself and you need to imagine your audience has no prior knowledge to draw upon. It is as if you are reporting to a society with no concept of visual culture.

The exercise in Showing Seeing can be understood in terms of the concept of the 'metapicture' (Mitchell, 1994, pp.35–82). Mitchell defines metapictures as 'pictures that refer to themselves or to other pictures', which is to say they are 'pictures that are used to show what a picture is' (Mitchell, 1994, p.35). The idea behind the metapicture is to consider what it would mean to 'think' about pictures without having to resort to a second-order discourse of any kind. Of course, trying to write about metapictures inevitably evokes the problem of a second-order discourse. Instead, then, let us look at some examples:

Mitchell (1994, p.39) reproduces a drawing by Saul Steinberg, *The Spiral* (1964). In it we see a man drawing a picture. However, '[h]e is close to the end; the available space is almost filled, and the drawing has nowhere to go but into the draughtsman's own body, for the man is in his own picture, standing in the centre of the spiral he

has drawn' (Mitchell, 1994, pp. 39–40). There are different ways of interpreting the image, and if only depending on which direction we think the line of the spiral is heading. If read as going ever inward, the drawing would seem to be the entire product of the man in the picture, to the point that eventually he has nowhere left to go. Read the other way, however, we might begin to think about the activity of the 'real' artist drawing a man in the middle of a sheet of paper and then continuing outwards. Alternatively, the picture might be said to show a changing history of art representation. So, for example, read clockwise, 'the drawing could be taken as an allegory of a familiar history of modern painting, one which begins with representation of the external world and moves toward pure abstraction' (p.40). Such interpretations begin to suggest how a picture can offer an analysis or 'picturing' of another picture. Essentially, this is a metapicture 'in a strict or formal sense, a picture about itself, a picture that refers to its own making, yet one that dissolves the boundary between inside and outside, first- and second-order representation, on which the metapictorial structure depends' (Mitchell, 1994, p.42).

The metapicture need not only refer to the making of pictures, but can also relate to images as a collection, or in terms of their genre. The cartoon in Figure 6.15, 'Egyptian Life Class' (1955), is by Alain. In the picture the nude model is posed precisely in the flat, stiff perspective we associate with ancient Egyptian paintings. Yet, the members of the class are each practising a Western technique of perspective

I   DRAWING BY ALAIN © 1955 THE NEW YORKER MAGAZINE, INC.

drawing. This illustration is what Mitchell terms a metapicture of '*other* pictures'. It is a metapicture that refers 'not to itself, but to a class of pictures that are generally understood to be different in kind from itself' (Mitchell, 1994, p.42). Alain's 'Egyptian Life Class' cartoon was cited by Gombrich (2000 [1960], pp.2–4) as a means to provide 'a key to the "riddle of style" in the history of art, the puzzling fact that ways of picturing the world are different in different times and places' (Mitchell, 1994, p.43). Gombrich chooses to make only a 'serious', analytic point about Egyptians somehow perceiving nature in a different way. In so doing, he would appear to overlook the fact that 'the whole point of the cartoon is that the Egyptian art students are not shown as "different" at all, but behave just as modern, Western art students do in a traditional life-class' (Mitchell, 1994, p.44). Mitchell does not mean to suggest one reading is more appropriate than the other, but rather that both are necessary in order for the joke to work. Thus, the two readings stand in a dialectical relationship, by which Mitchell explains, 'they contradict one another, oppose one another, and yet they also require, give life to, one another'. As a metapicture this drawing 'is not reducible to one reading or the other but is constituted in the argument or dialogue between them' (p.45).

At the heart of the concept of the metapicture is the idea of a dialectical or multi-stable image. In other words, a 'meta' analysis requires a picture to present more than one point of view at the same time. Mitchell *illustrates* the concept with

FIGURE 6.15

Alain, *Egyptian Life Class*. Courtesy of the Brustlein Estate.

183

FIGURE 6.16
Joesph Jastrow, *The Duck-Rabbit.*

reference to various well-known drawings of optical illusions, with the key example being the 'Duck-Rabbit' illustration – which, as he notes, has an ecology or 'habitat' all of its own (Mitchell, 1994b, pp. 53–56). The crucial point about the Duck-Rabbit is its paradox: we can see there is both a depiction of a duck and rabbit within the same drawing, though we cannot see them both at the same time. Yet, it is the way we can relate the one image to the other that makes the drawing unique and revelatory. The same playful effect can be said to operate – on various levels – in Magritte's painting of a 'pipe', *Les trahison des images* (1928–1929), discussed in Chapter 3. A further, subtler example of the metapicture is Velázquez's *Las Meninas* (1656) – a rich composition that immediately raises questions of reality and illusion, with its uncertain relationship between the viewer and the figures depicted:

> 'From a formal standpoint, *Las Meninas* equivocates between the strict self-reference of Steinberg's "New World" and the generic self-reference of Alain's cartoon. It represents Velázquez painting a picture, but we will never know whether it is *this* picture or some other, since he shows us only its back. The formal structure of *Las Meninas* is an encyclopaedic labyrinth of pictorial self-reference, representing the interplay between the beholder, the producer, and the object or model of representation as a complex cycle of exchanges and substitutions.'
>
> (Mitchell, 1994b, p. 58)

The complexities of *Las Meninas* as a metapicture have led it to be one of the most widely discussed artworks within the Western canon. Svetlana Alpers (1983) remarks upon two main lines of argument about the painting. Firstly, given the painting's realism, much is made of the fact that 'we are looked at by those at whom we are looking' (Alpers, 1983, p. 31). Indeed, the picture is not simply intended for

FIGURE 6.17

Diego Velázquez, *Las Meninas or The Family of Philip IV* (c.1656). Courtesy of Bridgeman Art Library.

the viewer's eyes. It is a large painting, close to three-square metres, making it 'intended also for the viewer's body. The size of the figures is a match for our own. This appeal at once to eye and to body is a remarkable pictorial performance which contradictorily presents powerful human figures by means of illusionary surfaces' (p.31). It is tempting to describe the painting as an exercise in Showing Seeing, par excellence!

A second, dominant line of argument, however, reveals a disciplinary weakness of art historical writing. Alpers argues, art history has tended to place too much emphasis upon questions of plot, making 'the question of the nature of the pictorial representation' unthinkable. Or, as Mitchell suggests: 'The problem with art historical writing about *Las Meninas* was like the problem with the psychological literature on the Duck-Rabbit: it made the picture far too *thinkable*' (1994b, p.60). Writing outside of the field of art history, Michel Foucault offers a more profound reading, arguing Velázquez's painting to depict 'Classical representation' itself. Alpers tempers Foucault's argument by suggesting '*Las Meninas* is produced not out of a single, classical notion of representation . . . but rather out of specific pictorial traditions of representation' (Alpers, 1983, p.39). Nonetheless, Foucault's analysis draws our attention to the painting for its enduring quality as a metapicture. As much as the painting hails us, whereby we position ourselves as the intended addressee of the scene, we are as much aware of (and unsettled by) the fact the painting does not include us. We stand marooned, in no-man's land. As such 'representation, freed finally from the relation that was impeding it, can offer itself as representation in its pure form' (Foucault, 1974, p.16).

TASK

Metapicture Hunt

Having considered W.J.T. Mitchell's account, search for your own examples of metapictures. These might appear in advertisements, films, magazines, novels, artworks, and various ephemeral materials. Some examples may be pictures that show picturing, or a genre of pictures. Others – like the duck-rabbit illustration – might oscillate in terms of what they show, or present a more elaborate and subtle consideration of pictures (as we find with Velázquez's *Las Meninas*). Collect as many examples as you can and attempt to arrange them in order of how effective you think they are as metapictures. Make some notes to explain your reasoning.

Summary

Unlike the two preceding chapters, and those which follow, the topic of visual culture does not refer to a specific set of image-making practices, but rather introduces critical concepts for understanding images and visual culture(s) in all their breadth. Thus key terms have been introduced, including: 'visual culture', 'visuality', 'reproduction', 'remediation', 'scopic regime', 'the gaze' and 'metapicture'. Hopefully these terms can help to inform how you articulate your thoughts about images and visual culture in all their variety. Underpinning this chapter has been a reflexive approach to visual culture, to encourage engagement with the visual on its own terms, but equally to offer critique. The exercise in 'Showing Seeing' is emblematic of this approach, which helps us to reflect on the perennial problem of analyzing the visual through interpretive and semiotic frameworks, as examined in the opening three chapters of this book.

Further reading

Benjamin, Walter (1992) 'The Work of Art in the Age of Mechanical Reproduction' in *Illuminations,* trans. by Harry Zohn. London: Fontana Press, pp.211–244.

Berger, John (1972) *Ways of Seeing*. London: Penguin Books.

Bordo, Susan (1997) *Twilight Zones: The Hidden Life of Cultural Images from Plato to O.J.* California: University of California Press.

Bryson, Norman, Holly, Michael Ann and Moxey, Keith (eds) (1994) *Visual Culture: Images and Interpretations*. Hannover: Wesleyan University Press.

Davis, Whitney (2011) *A General Theory of Visual Culture*. Princeton: Princeton University Press.

Elkins, James (2003) *Visual Studies: A Skeptical Introduction*. New York: Routledge.

Evans, Jessica and Hall, Stuart (eds) (1999) *Visual Culture: The Reader*. London: Sage.

Foster, Hal (ed.) (1988) *Vision and Visuality*. Seattle: Bay Press.

Fuery, Patrick and Fuery, Kelli (2003) *Visual Cultures and Critical Theory*. London: Arnold.

Howells, Richard and Negreiros, Joaquim (2011) *Visual Culture*. Second Edition. Cambridge: Polity.

Mirzoeff, Nicholas (ed.) (2002) *The Visual Culture Reader*. Second Edition. London: Routledge.

Mirzoeff, Nicholas (2009) *An Introduction to Visual Culture*. Second Edition. London: Routledge.

Mitchell, W.J.T. (2005) *What Do Pictures Want? The Lives and Loves of Images*. Chicago: University of Chicago Press.

Rogoff, Irit (2002) 'Studying Visual Culture' in Nicholas Mirzoeff (ed.) *Visual Culture Reader*. Second Edition. London: Routledge, pp.24–36.

Rose, Gillian (2012) *Visual Methodologies: An Introduction to the Interpretation of Visual Materials*. Third Edition. London: Sage.

Sturken, Marita and Cartwright, Lisa (2009) *Practices of Looking: An Introduction to Visual Culture*. Second Edition. Oxford: Oxford University Press.

7 Scientific imaging

As with each of the topics covered in Part 2 of this book, scientific imaging is a vast and complex subject. Yet, it is perhaps doubly difficult to explore, since it often relates to expert knowledge and highly specialized and technical imaging equipment and processes. Nevertheless, this chapter aims to draw out some key themes and problematics. It begins by considering both images *in* science and the dilemma of 'reading' science from a humanities perspective. Attention is then given to 'ways of seeing', starting with the naked eye and progressing to consider how vision functions in the brain. A common theme in scientific imaging is the idea of 'seeing the unseen'. Commentaries from scientists provide insights into the role images play in science, including an entry on how MRI scans are constructed and the significance of images to quantum physics. The chapter concludes with thoughts on how we can categorize science images according to the 'object' of enquiry, with a spectrum that runs from the material, physical entity to the invisible though nonetheless real entity, and finally the purely conceptual, theoretical idea.

Images in science

There are many depictions of science, whether in classical paintings, literature and popular culture. A well-known painting is Rembrandt's *The Anatomy Lesson of Dr. Nicolaes Tulp* (1632). The scene portrayed is that of the dissection of a human corpse. The strong contrast in the lighting is suggestive of ideas about the Enlightenment, the age in which reason is seen to both reform society and advance knowledge. Thus, despite the dramatic lighting, the main focal point is not the corpse, but the audience that surrounds. As Sturken and Cartwright (2009, p.352) put it: 'Such a painting is . . . not simply a document of the practice of science in its time, it is also a portrait

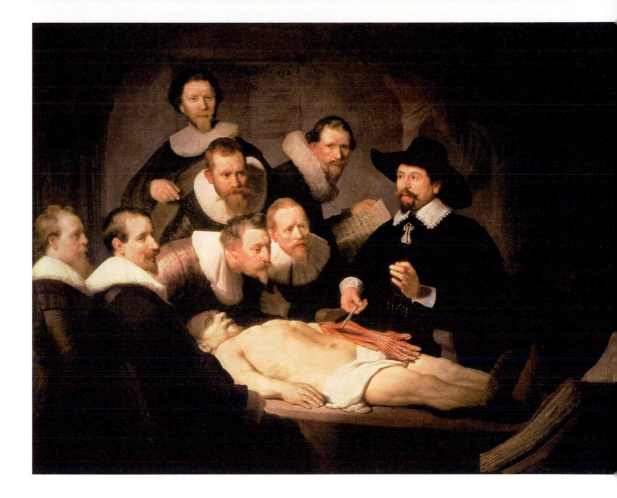

FIGURE 7.1

Rembrandt van Rijn,
*The Anatomy Lesson
of Dr. Nicolaes Tulp*,
1632. Courtesy of
Bridgeman Art
Library.

of the social relations around that practice'. Rembrandt's painting is emblematic of a wider desire to represent the realms of science – even to stage a theatre of science, whether as a means to promote its cause or to offer a critique. In their chapter, 'Scientific Looking, Looking at Science', Sturken and Cartwright (2009, pp. 347–387) offer an explicit visual culture critique of science, reminding us that 'scientific images and looking practices are as dependent on cultural context and culturally informed interpretation as images from popular culture, art, and the news' (p. 347).

However, the domain of science is itself replete with images that reveal fascinating insights, especially if we begin to treat them precisely on scientific terms. Phylis Morrison's (2002, pp. 13–23) brief history of images *in* science (as opposed to being about science) begins as early as 30,000 years ago with cave paintings. While these are not scientific images in any modern sense, she suggests they reveal how 'the painter had observed and could reproduce telling details of the anatomy of familiar animals' (p. 14). A later example is the thousand-year old Dunhuang star map from China, described as 'one of the oldest star-charts in any civilization'. It includes constellations of the Great Bear and Sagittarius among others, and its 'use of white, black and yellow . . . correspond with the three ancient schools of astronomy (those of Shih Shen, Kan Tê and Wu Hsien)' (Ford, 1992, p.150). A further, well-known example, is **Copernicus**' drawing from the start of the sixteenth century of the world system, showing the earth moving around the sun. 'Not only was this concept a revolution in thought, but it was also the harbinger of a new way of doing science' (Morrison, 2002, p.15). These images are not necessarily *the* science itself, but they are examples of the early importance of visualizing and communicating science. Galileo's moon drawings, which first appeared in print in 1610, are an example of where imaging and science start to become more intrinsically connected.

The telescope, or 'perspective tube' as it was referred to, was invented in Holland, c.1608. The Englishman, Thomas Hariot, used it to make drawings of the lunar surface, yet interestingly he did not offer any explanation of its markings; 'Europeans of his time still had no reason to doubt Aristotle's ancient definition of

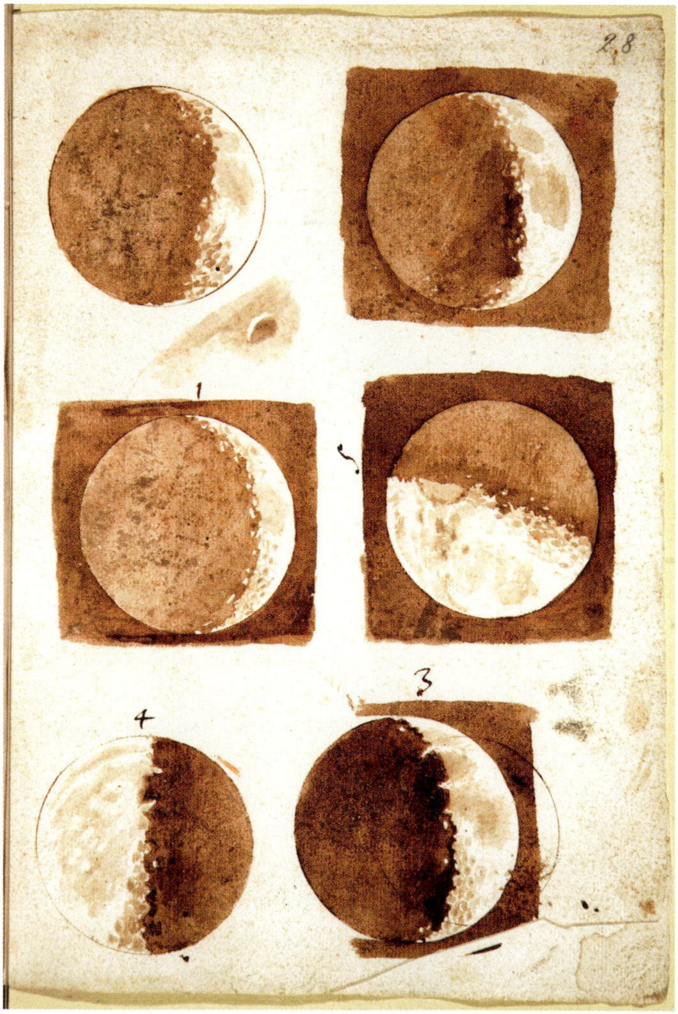

FIGURE 7.2a [Left] Galileo, wash drawings of the moon, 1609 © Getty/Gammo-Rapho. Photograph: Eric Vandeville.

FIGURE 7.2b [Right] Galileo, map of the moon, illustration from *Sidereus Nuncius*, 1610. Courtesy of Bridgeman Art Library. As Samuel Edgerton (2009, p.162) explains: 'Galileo's original wash drawings reveal a much more "painterly" lunar surface than do the published engravings. Most modern historians have talked about only the latter, which by virtue of their metallic, linear technique, make Galileo's moon look like the arid and lifeless body our modern astronauts discovered it to be. His wash renderings, on the other hand, show that he still regarded the moon somewhat in the old medieval "watery" spirit. With the deft brushstrokes of a practiced watercolorist, he laid on a half dozen different grades of washes, imparting his images an attractive soft and luminescent quality.'

the moon as a perfect sphere, the prototypical form of all planets and stars in the cosmos' (Edgerton, 2009, p.156). A year later, however, Galileo formed a very different opinion. In his illustrated book, *Sidereus nuncius* [Messenger from the Stars], in 1610, Galileo notes how the surface of the moon is not in fact smooth and even. Quite the contrary, he writes how it is 'like the face of the Earth itself, which is marked here and there with chains of mountains and depths of valleys' (Galileo cited in Edgteron, 2009, p.161). His sketches of the moon (and the later engravings which appeared in print) were based on his direct observations. As visual evidence they had a profound effect. The moon could no longer be regarded a 'heavenly' body, but something much more tangible and 'earthly'. The universe becomes a place of physics that can be measured and explored, with Galileo's images being part of the 'line of evidence that finally led to the consensus that Copernicus' ideas about the solar system's geometry had been right' (Morrison, 2002, p.16).

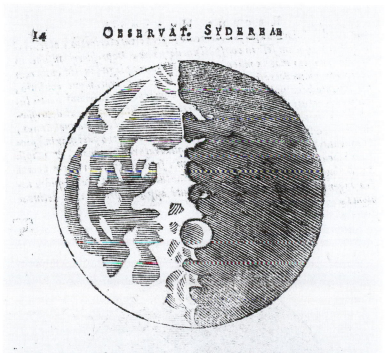

14   OBSERVAT. SYDEREAE

Hæc eadem macula ante secundam quadraturam nigrioribus quibusdam terminis circumuallata conspicitur; qui tamquam altissima montium iuga ex parte Soli auersa obscuriores apparent, quà verò Solem respiciunt lucidiores extant; cuius oppositum in cauitatibus accidit, quarum pars Soli auersa splendens apparet, obscura verò, ac vmbrosa, quæ ex parte Solis sita est. Imminuta deinde luminosa superficie, cum primum tota fermè dicta macula tenebris est obducta, clariora montium dorsa eminenter tenebras scandunt. Hanc duplicem apparentiam frequentes figuræ commonstrant.

Optics has been central to the developments of scientific imaging, with the invention of the telescope and microscope for example enabling us to go far beyond what we can see with the naked eye. In addition, photography has been vital in *recording* reality, enabling us to freeze time, take in aerial views, and – certainly with x-rays – to see what is otherwise invisible to us. However, over the twentieth century a range of non-lens based visualization technologies have become central to scientific and medical work. **Sonography**, particularly ultrasound, whilst initially developed for military purposes, was used experimentally in medicine in the 1960s and by the 1980s had become a standard diagnostic tool. In astronomy, radio telescopes are used to detect and collect data based on the emission of radiation at set radio wavelengths. This technology has meant we can 'image' astronomical objects that remain unobservable in visible light, such as distant galaxies and nebulae, as well as radio emissions from planets. Of course where astronomy looks out over great distances, microscopy looks the other way. Our bid to look deeper and deeper into the structure of things has led to developments such as the scanning probe microscope, which can measure electron density. The images produced can appear to show solid objects, yet electrons are not even part of the **electromagnetic spectrum**; in fact at this quantum level we can even begin to question what we mean by an image. The field of particle physics has moved our attention away from pictures of resemblance and representation, towards images that in essence are mathematical. As Elkins suggests, complexity of these images is not what they show, but 'the complexity of *leaving* the image and finding meanings that the image can no longer contain. Never since the inception of Western images has the subject matter of the image been so far beyond the reach of the image itself' (Elkins, 2008, p.190). We will return to the subject of particle physics later in the chapter, as well as consider a variety of technologies that enable us to see the unseen.

The historian of science, Peter Galison, draws attention to an underlying tension of the image across all of the sciences. On the one hand it appears '[w]e *must* have scientific images because only images can teach us. Only pictures can develop within us the intuition needed to proceed further towards abstraction'. The retort, however, is that 'we *cannot* have images because images deceive' (Galison, 2002, p.300). The 'problem' of images as described by Galison echoes the commentary on iconoclasm relayed in Chapter 3. In this case, rather than specifically a tension between image and text, the tension is one of image and data; image and logic or abstraction. Don Ihde (1998) refers to the frequently suggested idea that 'scientific "seeing" is highly visualistic' (p.159). He refers to 'analytic depiction' in Leonardo da Vinci's technical drawings and the analytic drawings in astronomy that begin with Galileo's observations (noted above). Ihde's claim is that visualization has an advantage over other modes of engagement. It is not that it is necessarily the 'clearest' of senses, since 'hearing delivers within its dimension distinctions and clarities which equal and in some cases exceed those of visual acuity' (1998, p.161). Yet, visualization provides us with a way of looking repeatedly at a whole form to make analytical distinctions. Galison describes a dialectical process, a 'back and forth between visualizable evidence and statistical analysis', whereby 'new data [can mean] new possibilities for rendering the information visually striking, and at the same time [make] possible the computation of new kinds of statistical, non-visualizable, correlations' (2002, p.316).

Despite the obvious importance of the image and image practices to science throughout history, it is actually only recently – from the late 1970s – that historians and philosophers of science have paid particular attention (Lynch, 2006). Today, of course, there is 'widespread acclaim to the idea that science [is] overwhelmingly about the visual' (Galison, 2002, p.300). This has given rise to the interests and concerns Sturken and Cartwright (2009, pp.347–387) describe, to place science within a cultural context. Anthropological and sociological studies of science, such as Latour and Woolgar's (1986) *Laboratory Life* and Lynch's (1985) *Art and Artifact in Laboratory Science*, have examined both the 'social construction' of science and an underlying interest in the visualization of scientific knowledge (Trumbo, 2006, p.275). A semiotic perspective emerges from these studies, whereby it is under-stood, despite the central premise of objectivity in science, '[w]hat is known and passed on as *science* is the result of a series of representational practices' (Pauwels, 2006, p.vii). Dispelling the myth of the hard sciences, as operating in some way distinct from culture, has led the way for greater interaction between scientists, artists, scholars and critics.

Elkins, however, remains sceptical of the value of the current exchange between the humanities and the sciences. He cites two significant obstacles. Firstly, he argues, we need to find a way to 'welcome science into the discourse of the humanities without introducing it or framing it as a social construction'. Secondly, science needs to be considered 'without undue popularization' (Elkins, 2003, p.93). C.P. Snow, in a lecture given in 1959 titled 'The Two Cultures and the Scientific Revolution' (Snow, 1998), recognized the problem of both the humanities and the sciences only really knowing a popularized version of each other. Elkins notes of the continued pertinence of the lecture and in particular Snow's 'rude question' which reveals the gulf between the humanities and the sciences: '[Snow] liked to ask people in the humanities what the Second Law of Thermodynamics is, and when they couldn't answer, he said their ignorance was comparable to not knowing what *Hamlet* is' (Elkins, 2003, p.159). Today, it remains the case that 'virtually no one outside of the sciences reads unpopularized science, and hardly anyone in the sciences reads the professional literature of the humanities' (Elkins, 2008, p.2). Thus, even with greater crossover appearing to take place, it is has been very difficult to overcome a divide. Felice Frankel's work in science photography is one example of significant engage-ment in science by a non-scientist. Importantly, Frankel does not take her guide from artistic criteria or values, but considers her work to be technical, scientific photography. A point of debate emerges, since Elkins argues '[art] history is pertinent because it guides her choices of compositions, colors, symmetries, and textures' (2007, p.10). On the other side of the coin, in interviews conducted for *American Scientist* magazine, scientists have referred to the concept of 'beauty' as a way of appreciating the science itself, which Elkins argues does not take us far enough in the direction of either a discourse of aesthetics, nor the physical sciences (Elkins, 2007, pp.10–13).

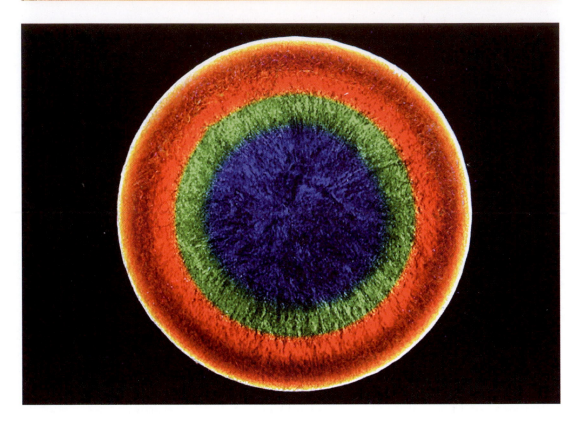

FIGURE 7.3 Felice Frankel, *Block copolymer 2, detail of time series.* With kind permission of Felice Frankel. Frankel's science imagery has been widely exhibited and reproduced in print. Frankel's *On the Surface of Things* (2007), for example, is a high-quality print volume of her work. Elkins notes 'it can be read by scientists and artists; both will recognize meanings that are not spelled out, but neither will know how to make a bridge between the two domains. What is needed', he suggests, 'is an inch-by-inch analysis of her photographs, to bring out the individual artistic decisions and their histories, together with . . . an inch-by-inch account of the scientific meaning of each form' (Elkins, 2007, p.10). In her book *Envisioning Science* (2002), a detailed handbook of the design and craft of scientific images, Frankel does offer just such an inch-by-inch account of her work.

Trying to account for the differences between 'the humanities' and 'the sciences' can lead us to an unnecessary polarized view of either domain. It is too easy to think of 'science' as a single, homogenous enterprise – whereas in fact the different branches of science are as different to each other as they are to subjects within the humanities. Furthermore, separating the humanities and the sciences in overly stark ways can lead us to forget the nuanced and creative thinking and 'play' that goes on in the sciences, in and around a purported quest for objectivity. Jay Lemke, for example, writes of science discourse in terms of hybridity and multimedia:

'The "concepts" of science are not solely verbal concepts, though they have verbal components. They are semiotic *hybrids*, simultaneously and essentially verbal, mathematical, visual-graphical, and actional-operational. The actional, conversational, and written textual genres of science are historically and presently, fundamentally and irreducibly, *multimedia genres*. To do science, to talk science, to read and write science it is necessary to juggle and combine in various canonical ways verbal discourse, mathematical expression, graphical-visual representation, and motor operations in the world.'

(Lemke, 1998, p.87)

The complexity of the 'scientific text' that Lemke describes inevitably gives rises to concerns about levels of information and visual literacy. In order to understand science we need a critical awareness of the representation of science and scientific findings (Hoffmann, 1995; Priest, 1998; Trumbo, 2006). However, it is not only the literacy of those outside of science that we must consider. Science communication undoubtedly 'relies on visual representation to clarify data, to illustrate concepts, and to engage a public informed through an ever-increasing arsenal of computer graphics and new media tools', yet significantly, 'relatively little attention has been directed toward the challenge of building visual literacy among scientists, communicators, and the public' (Trumbo, 2006, p.280). Roth *et al.* (2002), for example, find a lack of uniformity even in the way scientists read graphs. Pauwels (2006, p.x) similarly notes how the 'complexity and hybridity and the lack of formal training in the visual cultures of science' leads to young researchers being 'ill-prepared to perform scientific representational practices thoughtfully and skillfully'. Nevertheless, despite these difficulties – or indeed because of them – the subject of science and image is both fascinating and vital. In fact, as Elkins might suggest, the subject leads us into a whole new realm and understanding of what we even mean by the image.

The naked eye

Before turning to technologies that enhance our vision and visualization of the world, it is pertinent we consider the very receptacle through which we see. We tend to place a great deal of faith in what we can see with the naked eye; the aphorism 'Seeing is Believing' being a common refrain. For Plato, 'truth was embodied in the **Eidos** or Idea, which was like a visible form blanched of its color. The human eye, he contended, is able to perceive light because it shares a like quality with the source of light, the sun' (Jay, 1994, p.26). Human beings all 'see' identically. Which is to say, we all have the same mechanically structured eyes, which we can understand in terms of the universal scientific laws of optical geometry first devised by the ancient Greek philosopher, Euclid (fl. 300 BC). However, an appreciation of vision in these terms still does not really elucidate *how* and *why* we see as we do (and of course does not account for idiosyncratic discrepancies and deterioration in eyesight). We might still ask, what do we really know about our *own* eyes?

Figure 7.4 shows a digital image, or ophthalmogram of the back of the eye. It is a common enough image, recorded at a high-street optician during a routine eye appointment by an ophthalmologist using a specialist microscope. Apparently this particular image shows the eye is healthy, yet, without expert knowledge it is not easy to know that fact. Indeed, whilst the truth is staring us in the face, we cannot

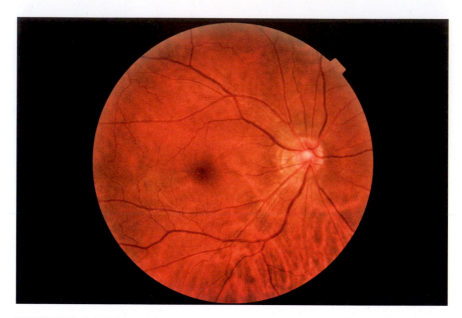

FIGURE 7.4 Ophthalmogram. Showing the optic disc as a bright area on the right where blood vessels converge, the dark spot to the left of the centre is the macula, which includes the fovea, a small pit high in the concentration of cone cells responsible for high-resolution vision. As part of a routine eye examination, ophthalmoscopy can help to detect and evaluate symptoms of retinal detachment or eye diseases such as glaucoma. However, the eyes also exhibit symptoms of other aspects of our health. In patients with headaches, for example, the finding of swollen optic discs is a sign of raised intracranial pressure, which could indicate a number of serious conditions.

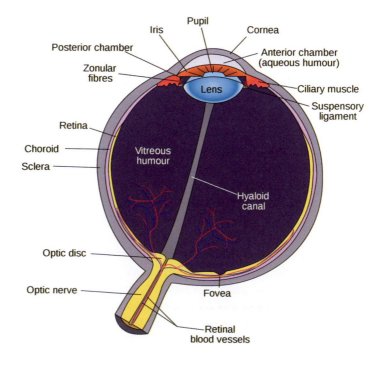

FIGURE 7.5
Schematic of the human eye.

see it unless we know what we are looking for. Of course, instead of looking at the image as medical evidence we might find ourselves simply marvelling at the colours, the lines and shapes. How we look at the image potentially changes its status from being a 'scientific image' to an 'art image', but its *production* is undoubtedly based upon the scientific practice of ophthalmoscopy; enabling health professionals to see the interior surface of the eye, which includes the retina, optic disc, macula and fovea, and posterior pole (see Figure 7.5).

TASK

Eye-test

Read the extract which follows by art historian James Elkins, in which he explains how to look at your own eye. Attempt the process yourself and in doing so reflect on what it feels like to become aware of your eyes as biological entities. What does it accomplish (if anything) for your understanding of vision? Does Elkins' account help you better comprehend how your eye works, and/or do you gain a more intuitive understanding of your eye as a biological entity?

HOW TO LOOK AT THE INSIDE OF YOUR EYE

JAMES ELKINS

(from *How to Use Your Eyes*, 2000, pp.232–237)

The easiest way to become aware of what's inside your eye is to look at a broad expanse of unclouded sky or a bright smooth wall. Don't move your eyes. If you stare intently, after a minute you'll probably become aware of cloudy or wormy forms drifting slowly around. The blurry shapes are called 'floaters' . . . They are actually red blood cells deep inside your eye, suspended between the retina, in the back of the eye, and the transparent ball of jelly – the 'vitreous body' – that fills the eyeball. There is a very thin layer of watery fluid around the vitreous body, which lubricates it so that it doesn't stick to the inside walls of the eye; floaters are blood cells that have hemorrhaged from the retina and escaped into the watery layer. [. . .] Since blood cells are sticky, they tend to link together into clumps and chains; if you look closely, you'll notice that the chains are really made up of little balls.

    [. . .]

    You may notice that your floaters have three or four little rings around them – those are the diffraction pattern caused by light bending around them on its way to the retina. Physicists have measured them and found that the smallest, outermost rings are only 4 or 5 microns across – that's four thousandths of a millimeter, a thousand times smaller than the smallest speck that you could see in everyday life. Four microns is only ten times the wavelength of the light that makes the floaters visible.

[. . .]

Floaters are easy enough to see, and with a little ingenuity you can see even deeper into your eye. You need a very intense light source such as a strong projector lamp or a high-wattage bulb. Small bulbs are best; if you have only a large one, put it as far away from you as possible. In a dark room, use a magnifying glass or a strong lens to focus the light from the bulb onto a sheet of aluminum foil. Put a tiny pinprick into the aluminum foil, as small and as perfectly round as you can make it. The idea is to have the light focused so exactly that it converges just on the pinhole and not on the rest of the sheet. Then go around to the other side of the sheet, look through the pinhole, and you'll see a burst of light. Almost everything you see around the light itself is actually on the inside of the eye: you're looking at shadows in your eye, cast on your own retina.

[. . .]

There is even a way to have a look at the very back of the eye, at the blood vessels that spread out over your retina. Even though the vessels lie on top of the retina, we aren't normally aware of them because the photoreceptors underneath them have gotten used to living in the shade. But if you can shine a very bright light on the retina from an unusual angle, the shadows will shift and the blood vessels will suddenly become visible. I have done this using the same apparatus, but without the aluminum foil sheet. Just take away the foil and focus the light source right into your eye. Don't look at the bulb itself, but look away, toward a dark corner of the room. At first you might not see anything, but if you move your eye slightly to one side, and then back, you'll see a sudden flash of thick, undulating veins. [. . .]

It's an uncanny sensation suddenly seeing your own retinal blood vessels 'projected' onto the walls of the room. It happens because you have shifted the normal angle of incoming light and cast skewed shadows of the vessels onto the retina. But how odd to think that every day, wherever you look, you're looking *through* a net of curving blood vessels. It is as if we are all seeing the world from behind a dense spiderweb.

Inner vision

Apart from the brain itself, our eyes are the most complex organs, composed of more than two million working parts and capable of processing 36,000 bits of information every hour. Not surprisingly, perhaps, a long-held view was that the visual world was 'impressed' upon the retina and then received by the brain for decoding. In this way, seeing was generally considered a passive process. It is only in the last thirty years or so that we have come to learn a great deal more. Vision is understood now to be an active process, with around half our brain involved. What we see is not the retinal image, but our *construction* of perceived shapes, textures, motion, colour and forms. Donald Hoffman (1998, p.13) describes the 'fundamental problem of vision' to be the fact that the retinal image actually has 'countless possible interpretations'. We make specific readings in order to see as we do, though this does not mean we necessarily control exactly what we see. There is a difference, for example, between a *phenomenal* and *relational* sense of vision. The former refers to our physiological ability to see (which can include delirious visions) and the latter how we interact with 'things' prompting vision (Hoffman, 1998, pp.6–7). Hoffman provides a useful example, with a simple figure of a ripple.

SEEING THINGS

DONALD HOFFMAN

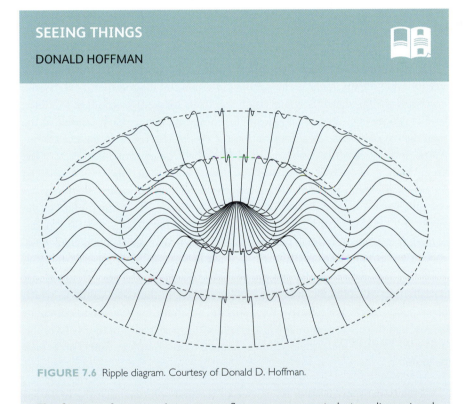

FIGURE 7.6 Ripple diagram. Courtesy of Donald D. Hoffman.

This figure is of course a drawing on a flat – or, more precisely, two-dimensional (2D) – surface. You can check this, should you wish to, by touching it. But the figure also appears to be, as the name 'ripple' suggests, a surface that is far from flat, and that undulates in space like waves on a pond. You can check this by viewing the figure. Indeed, *try* to see the ripple as flat; I have never succeeded.

Logic dictates that the ripple cannot be at once flat and not flat, so either the hand or the eye (or both) must be in error. [. . .] But for now, look again at the ripple and note that it has three parts: a bump in the center, a circular wave around the bump, and another circular wave on the outside. As an aid to discuss the figure, I drew dashed curves along the boundaries of these parts.

[. . .] Your visual system not only fabricates the ripple, it then endows it with parts. But could it be that the dashed curves – and not your visual system – are the real culprits here, and that without the dashed curves you would see no parts? You can check that this is not so. Simply turn the figure, or your head, upside down. You now see an inverted ripple with new parts: the dashed curves now lie on crests of waves and not, as before, in the troughs between waves.

(Hoffman, 1998, pp.2–3)

The neurobiologist, Semir Zeki, offers some of the most accessible accounts of recent developments in our understanding of vision and neuroesthetics. His book, *Inner Vision* (1999), details how our vision is actually formed as a result of modular, parallel processing, rather than as a single, composite image. Early studies of the brain discovered the cerebral localization for vision. The retina of the eye is connected to the back of the brain, referred to as the primary visual cortex, V1. The direct mapping of the retina in V1 was first taken to compound the view that seeing is a passive process. The retina itself is not evenly formed. Its centre, the fovea, for example, has the highest density of receptors. Similarly, 'the "retinal map" in the cortex of V1, unlike an ordinary photographic plate, is not a straightforward, unde-formed, translation. It is a map that emphasises a particular part of the field of view' (Zeki, 1999, p.17). However, later research has shown how many areas of the brain around V1 are involved in the process of vision, leading to the idea of 'functional specialization'. Cells in the brain are highly selective in the visual signal to which they respond. Cells are selective for a specific attribute, such as form, colour or motion, and these concentrate in a 'geographically separate part of the visual brain' (p.61). We begin to understand vision as a much more complex, 'inner' process of the brain:

'Functional specialization is . . . one of the first solutions that the brain has evolved to tackle the problem of acquiring knowledge about the world . . . The kind of information that the brain has to discard or sacrifice in getting at the essence of one attribute, say colour, is very different from the kind of infor-mation that it has to discard to get to the essence of another attribute, say size . . . The brain has evidently found it operationally more efficient to discount these different kinds of signals in different areas, ones whose entire anatomy and physiology are specifically tailored to the needs for getting to the essentials

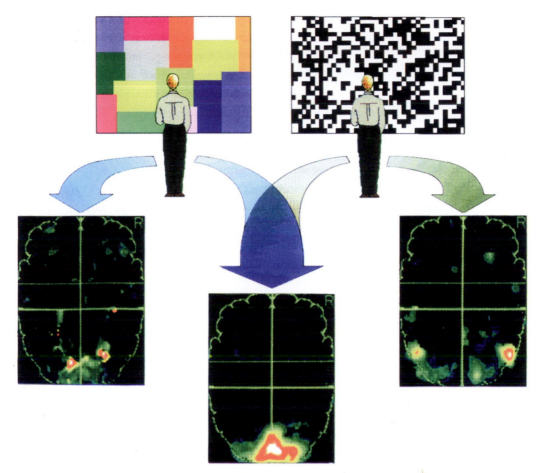

FIGURE 7.7 Reproduced with permission from Semir Zeki. The route from the retina to the brain is known as the optic pathway. Signals are carried to a relatively large portion of the cerebral hemispheres, at the back of the brain, known as the primary visual cortex, or V1 (centre). However: 'A simple experiment demonstrates functional specialization in the human brain. Whilst viewing a coloured scene, area V4 is activated (lower left). Whilst viewing a moving scene area V5 shows activation (lower right)' (Zeki, 1999, p.64).

of particular attributes. It has, in brief, adopted the solution of parallel processing, or processing different attributes of the visual scene simultaneously and in parallel.'

(Zeki, 1999, p.62)

The idea of parallel processing becomes more nuanced when it is revealed that the brain actually processes different attributes at different speeds. From one second to the next we see the world around us as a single integrated visual image, with all attributes temporally coordinated. But in neural terms a second is a very long time. It takes less than 1 millisecond for an impulse to cross a synaptic barrier. If we examine a briefer window of time, we see attributes – colour, motion and form – are not integrated:

'. . . colour is perceived before form which is perceived before motion, the lead time of colour over motion being about 60–80 milliseconds. This suggests that the perceptual systems themselves are functionally specialised and that there is a temporal hierarchy in vision, superimposed upon the spatially distributed parallel processing systems.'

(Zeki, 1999, p.67)

It is hard to comprehend milliseconds, nonetheless, Zeki argues parallel processing points to the fact that our perception is made up of different consciousnesses, and furthermore, 'these different consciousnesses are also asynchronous' (p.67). We still have a lot to learn about how an image is finally assembled in the brain, but functional specialization has shown us that 'the process of "seeing" is far from complete at the level of V1', and, 'has raised the question of whether "seeing" and "understanding" are indeed two separate processes, with separate seats in the cortex' (p.68).

The developing sciences of the mind are overturning many of the traditional assumptions made (by those in the humanities) about consciousness, inference and emotion (Stafford, 2008; 2009). As Stafford argues, 'certain "general" morphological structures of aesthetic experience, namely, the fact that much higher thinking can be done without language, are evident in the way that perception, physiology, and thought are inextricably mixed' (Stafford, 2008, p.32). Zeki is himself attuned to the philosophical quandaries of our 'inner vision'. In *The Republic*, Plato spoke of ideal, universal forms and their exisiting, empirical manifestation. He writes: 'Does a couch differ from itself according as you view it from the side or the front or any other way? Or does it differ not at all in fact though it appears different, and so of other things?' (cited in Zeki, 1999, p.37). Plato asks the question in relation to mimetic art, such as painting. He holds the view that a single image, in this case the depiction of a couch, is not representative of all couches; it could not be a *universal* representation. From Zeki's point of view:

'Plato was really comparing the "phantasm" of painting to the reality of perception, a function of the brain, where there is no problem with a particular facet or view, because the brain usually has been exposed to many views of the same object and has been able to combine them in such a way that a subsequent single view of one facet is sufficient to allow it to obtain a knowledge of it and to categorise it.'

(Zeki, 1999, pp.38–39)

Plato's theory of the ideal form is an abstraction, apparently beyond our empirical engagement with things in the world. He argued for a distinction between the ideal and non-ideal realm. (Look back at the references to Plato in Chapter 3, and the extracts by Mitchell on the 'Family of Images' in Chapter 2, and 'Image as Likeness' in Chapter 3. See also Mitchell's diagram of mental images (Figure 2.6), as discussed in Chapter 2.) From a neurological perspective, the Platonic Ideal is the brain's stored representations of essential features, which is to suggest 'there are no ideal forms that have an existence in the outside world without reference to the brain' (Zeki, 1999, p.40). Zeki's account equates more readily to Plato's student and colleague, Aristotle, who explored the idea that 'universals' depend upon repetitive exposure.

Artists, of course, have long engaged with these quandaries as to whether art presents essential 'truth' or whether it is merely a means to represent an idea of truth through ephemeral sense data. The Surrealists are an interesting case. Drawing on principles of automatic writing, dreams and spontaneity, they generally espoused 'the artist can find the models that he depicts in his mind, his inner vision, not the external world'. Yet, as Zeki points out, 'this naturally ignores the fact that the models in the internal world of the brain . . . are themselves heavily derived from what the brain observes and categorises in what it sees in the external world' (1999, pp.47–48). Zeki makes a particular case of René Magritte, whose painting *Les trahison des images* (1928–1929) we considered in Chapter 3 (see Figure 3.6). For Zeki, Magritte very precisely entertains a 'neurological enterprise' with his strange images, which reveal how 'a picture cannot represent an object; only the brain can do that, having viewed an object from many different angles and having categorized it as belonging to a particular class' (Zeki, 1999, p.47). In the end, at a fundamental level, we are faced with the fact of our own biological construct, making it 'neurologically impossible to conceive visually of ideal forms without a brain that has been exposed to the visual world from birth. This is why the only viable definition of the Platonic Ideal is in terms of the functions and functioning of the brain' (Zeki, 1999, p.40). With this caveat in mind, we can perhaps proceed to consider ways in which we have sought to enhance vision.

Seeing the unseen

As previously mentioned, photographic technologies had a profound impact on the sciences. 'The mechanical eye of the camera not only augmented those of the telescope and microscope in its role as recorder but also possessed an important potential to act in its own right as a direct agent for the extension of human vision' (Kemp, 2006, p.301). Photographic techniques that involve frequencies invisible to the unaided eye have been of particular significance. Wilhelm Röntgen's discovery of the **x-ray** in 1895 was the first of an array of visualizing techniques to be invented. Of all the various ways we have now of imaging the body James Elkins suggests the 'old-fashioned x-rays are still among the most beautiful' (2000, p.34); due he argues to the fact the x-ray is not a digital image and as such has 'a much higher resolution than the pixellated computer-generated images used in more "advanced" techniques' (p.34). Yet, despite the ubiquity of the x-ray and its clarity of detail, it remains a difficult image to 'read'; furthermore it lacks spatial detail (Elkins, 2000, pp.34–37; Pasveer, 2006).

Many newer imaging technologies enable us to reconstruct the body in three dimensions; 'they slice it and reassemble it electronically, providing vivid images of the depths and thicknesses of the body's insides' (Elkins, 2000, p. 36). Thus, for an internal topography of the human body we now use **computed tomography** (CT) or computerized axial tomography (CAT) scans, whereby x-ray beams are received by a series of detectors and then digitized to a produce sectional images. **Magnetic resonance imaging** (MRI) produces sectional 'slices' by using a strong magnetic field and radio frequency to detect hydrogen protons in fat and water. A similarly powerful imaging technique is **positron emission tomography** (PET), which involves injecting short-lived isotopes into the blood stream. **Ultrasound** is another important technique, which perhaps we find 'easier to grasp, since it resides within our normal sensory compass, albeit heard rather than seen' (Kemp, 2006, p. 317). Ultrasound is used most frequently in obstetrics to track the development of the fetal body. Arguably, there is very little evidence to show significant benefits to prenatal care, yet ultrasound is a routine and popular imaging technique. Surveying a number of cultural and narrative references to ultrasound in popular culture, Sturken and Cartwright (2009, pp. 364–369) suggest 'the fetal sonogram serves a purpose beyond medicine . . . [It is] an image with deep cultural, emotional, and even, for some, religious meaning' (p. 365).

Outside of medicine there are of course many other scientific imaging techniques, which have similarly extended our capability to see. In astronomy, the optical telescope has been superseded by a number of sophisticated and vastly more powerful imaging devices. The radio telescope, mentioned at the beginning of this chapter, is one example, which differs from optical telescopes in that they operate in the radio frequency portion of the electromagnetic spectrum. The **Hubble Space Telescope** is another, high-profile technology, which has led to breakthroughs in astrophysics, such as accurately determining the rate of expansion of the universe. The Hubble telescope – with an aperture of 2.4 meters – orbits the Earth and has various instruments on-board to observe a range of electro-magnetic frequencies. Crucially, by orbiting outside Earth's atmosphere, the Hubble telescope can take sharp images with almost no background light. Deep Field images give the most detailed visible-light image ever made of the universe's most distant objects. In this case, '[t]he idea was to point the Hubble Space telescope at a part of the sky far from any bright star and see what it would record if its cameras were left open for a maximal amount of time. For over 100 hours the telescope peered into space, and it brought back an astonishing image, full of galaxies fainter than any that had ever been seen' (Elkins, 2008, p. 100).

Our ability to look far into the distance is matched by developments in **microscopy**, in particular the invention of the electron microscope. There are a variety of electron microscopes, but essentially they use a beam of electrons to create an image. Electron microscopes have a greater resolving power than a light-powered optical microscope because the wavelength of an electron is much shorter than visible light. When transmitted through a specimen the electrons are scattered, in so doing the electron beam reveals information about the structure of the specimen, which is then magnified by the objective lens system of the microscope. The scanning probe microscope – which we will return to in detail in this chapter – is of further significance, not least because it operates without the use of an optical lens. An important advantage of using a probe tip is that the resolution of an image is no longer limited by wavelengths, whereas lens-based microscopes will always reach an absolute limit when looking at objects that are as small as light photons themselves.

The range of new imaging technologies available, from ultrasound to the scanning probe microscope, brings us to the very limits of our perception. Elkins details the distinctions we need to make between comprehension and intuition with the following account:

COMPREHENSION AND INTUITION

JAMES ELKINS

What matters in perception is the boundary between the magnitudes that can be grasped and those that can only be written in symbols. There are, in fact, practical limits to each person's intuition, and practical ways of extending that intuition. The wonderful book *Powers of Ten* demonstrates this by providing a series of pictures that zoom inward from a person's hand down toward subatomic particles, and then another series that zoom up and out to encompass the universe. The picture on each page is ten times smaller or larger than the one before. If the picture that represents one square meter is taken as a starting point, then the imagination can follow at least three orders of magnitude in either direction (that is from 10^0 to 10^{-3} or 10^3). [. . .] The first image depicts a man asleep on a picnic blanket. I can easily follow as the scale increases, zooming up into the air . . . The pictures make intuitive sense – I can imagine making the trip in a helicopter – up to about 10^5, where the view is really from space. I can follow the downward sequence as well, zooming onto the man's hand, until the pictures reach the scale labeled 10^{-3} (one square millimeter), which is about the limit of my vision.

Of course I can *read* the book and interpret what I am seeing, but . . . my comprehension . . . gives out long before my apprehension . . . I can keep reading about powers of ten, and powers of those powers, but I quickly have to abandon any hope of bringing it all together in intuition. The first few pages of *Powers of Ten* are easy to assimilate, and then when I try to picture the next leap into outer space, or the next jump down toward the molecules in the man's hand, my thought slows down . . . I can't comprehend the picture of the earth from space. I know how it looks from television and magazines, but I don't quite see how it is connected with the aerial views I know from first-hand experience. In Kant's terms, if the change of magnitude takes too long to interpret, it cannot be used to help comprehension.

(Elkins, 2008, pp.92–93)

Elkins reminds us that at certain magnitudes we rely solely on visual representations of things for which we can have no first-hand experience. Of course an astronaut will have the experience of seeing the earth from space, and a scientist peering down a microscope can witness a molecular level. But eventually, the magnitudes become so small or large that they extend way beyond any human intuition. Thus, we come to a paradox of scientific imaging that we 'see' well beyond anything within the domain of the visual. This in turn has significant implications for what we even mean by imaging. Added to which, the various 'visualization' processes have changed 'not only how scientists pursue knowledge but also what scientists seek to know. In other words, knowledge – its objects and its processes – has changed with this shift toward the visual in ways of knowing the world' (Sturken and Cartwright, 2009, p. 349).

Picture control

Nicolas Rasmussen's *Picture Control* (1997), an historical account of the electron microscope as it was developed for use in biological research in America from the 1940s to the 1960s, tells a political as much as scientific story. As Rasmussen puts it: 'Control of who could make pictures with the electron microscope, how pictures should be made, what pictures would be printed, and how those pictures ought to

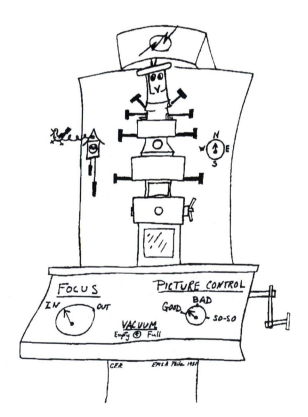

FIGURE 7.8

Cartoon of an electron microscope, signed by Cecil Hall ('CEH') and inscribed 'EMSA Phila. 1951'. Courtesy of the Microscopy Society of America.

be used in establishing biological facts were the dominant issues when the new instrument was introduced to biologists at the outset of the Second World War' (Rasmussen, 1997, p.1). Rasmussen's account offers important insights into the social construction of science, yet the title of the book is a play on the phrase 'picture control' as it appears in a cartoon of an electron microscope drawn in 1951 by one of its pioneers, the molecular biologist Cecil Hall. Reproduced at the beginning of Rasmussen's book, the cartoon depicts the crude control panel of the Radio Corporation of America EMU microscope (see Figure 7.8). On the front of the console we see 'a picture control . . . as one of the three relevant readouts and, along with focus, one of the two open to intervention' (Rasmussen, 1997, p.1). While a social critique of science is undoubtedly important, if we are to properly understand scientific image-making we also need to consider some practicalities. In the following extract, Alain Pitiot – whose expertise lies in image processing and computational neuroscience – presents an account of the contemporary use of magnetic resonance imaging (MRI). We soon see the continued significance of 'picture control', particularly with respect to how computer algorithms combine or are in tension with how human operators use the equipment.

MAGNETIC RESONANCE IMAGING

ALAIN PITIOT

Our understanding of the structural and functional organization of the human body has benefited considerably from the fast paced development of modern medical imaging technologies such as ultrasound, positron emission tomography, or magnetic resonance imaging (MRI), to name but a few. These enable not only the precise analysis of dead tissues but also the non-invasive exploration of living ones, which makes it possible to both elucidate the anatomical characteristics of organs and to observe the way they function and interact with each other. Chief amongst them, MRI is an astonishingly versatile imaging technique. The combination of high spatial resolution, minimal invasiveness and the remarkably large pool of tissue contrast mechanisms afforded by MRI have made it a particularly useful tool both in biomedical research and in clinical diagnosis.

Increasingly, automated image analysis procedures are replacing manual assessment of MRI scans as the latter often suffers from operator dependence and from the resource constraints associated with such a time-consuming, laborious process. Amongst other applications, image analysis can provide quantitative measurements of structural characteristics (e.g. cortical thickness), it helps monitor the progression of a disease process or enables the statistical analysis of anatomic variability across groups such as controls and patients with neurological diseases. Regrettably, all too often analysis only follows acquisition, in that the parameters of the MR scanner are optimized before the analysis of the acquired images, following criteria best suited for human observers, not machines. For instance, a radiographer in charge of an MR scanner will often strive to achieve the best *visual* compromise between contrast and noise *independently* of the image analysis tools that will be used to process the acquired images (and may care more about contrast than noise). Such a sub-optimal approach betrays the true nature of the digital pictures produced by MR scanners and other medical imaging devices: they are essentially incomplete representations. Indeed, while they do contain descriptive information about the entities they represent (in this case, the protons within human tissues), they are in fact only an abstraction of them. The characteristics of the produced pictures are then inextricably linked to the difficult choice of the abstracted characteristics.

In this respect, MR images can be seen as organized collections of values linked via a chain of treatments and sensors to some underlying physical measures. Consequently, they are fundamentally a means to analyze measurements: once the values are mapped to a palette of colours or to shades of grey, the human eye can better decipher the otherwise cryptic nature of a raw list of numbers. The necessity to understand these values then becomes that of extracting meaningful information from the associated visual representations. This image analysis task is shared between the machine which collects (MR scanner) and processes (computer program) inputting data and the human operator who, in addition to guiding the machine in these tasks, post-processes and more importantly interprets the produced information.

As an illustration, Figure 7.9 shows a slice of the brain of a single volunteer acquired in an MR scanner using four different settings for a parameter called the inversion time (TI). While a rapid glance suffices to convince that all four images come from the same brain, it is evident that their visual characteristics are vastly different. For instance, in the second scan from the left (TI=300ms) white matter appears in a light shade of gray and gray matter is almost black, whereas in the next scan along (TI=500ms), both gray and white matter are rendered in the same shade with a thin black line separating them. Some of these

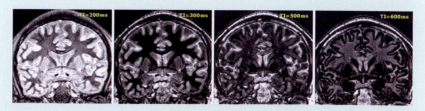

FIGURE 7.9 Magnetic Resonance Imaging read-out. Courtesy of Alain Pitiot.

images are also more noisy than others. One may ask: 'Which is the most appropriate image?' The answer depends on the application at hand, and is often informed by experience and habit. Rationalizing this decision process will be key to making the most of the immense potential of MRI.

All visualization technologies inevitably have their own constraints and limitations. Telescopes, for example, 'are limited by a number of factors, including their size, the coating and design of the optics, the atmosphere they have to look through', but also 'the software used for image analysis' (Elkins, 2008, p.119). Problems of resolution differ for microscopy, which as noted is limited by the wavelength of light itself. Similarly, however, the emphasis in microscopy is increasingly on image-analysis software; which includes 'deconvolution, image simulation, and image combination – all techniques of image altering that are largely unknown in the humanities' (Elkins, 2008, p.128). A standard computer program, known as NIH Image, has built-in options, which is one reason why imaging in journals such as *Nature* and *Cell* can often look similar. As Elkins points out, there are two potential problems: firstly, 'the changes are made without being documented in the publication'; and secondly, as with Pitiot's account of the MRI, 'changes are made by scientists who do not fully understand the mathematical routines involved' (Elkins, 2008, pp.128–129).

Image and logic

The power of computing can have a detrimental effect on our engagement with images as much as an enhancing one – depending on the kind of values we attach to images and the uses to which we wish to put them. Peter Galison (1997) provides an account of two traditions of imaging, an *image-tradition* and a *logic-tradition* (NB. Galison writes his account in reference to images in particle physics, but his general schema is useful for thinking across a range of science imaging techniques). Elkins provides a useful précis of Galison's thesis:

> 'Image-tradition pictures are what art historians call naturalistic or illusionistic, and what literary critics call mimetic: in Galison's words, they "preseve the form of things as they occur in the world". Often, they have "fine-grained, . . . persuasive detail" [. . .] Like photographs of historical events, they can be taken as proof that an event took place. The logic tradition . . . produces images that abandon the "sharp focus" of the image tradition in favor of statistical and digital data. Logic-tradition images often rely on "aggregate masses of data" instead of single pictures, and they entail "counting" instead of naturalistic picturing. Image-tradition pictures resemble what they depict, whereas logic-tradition images may not, and they tend to be statistical or pixellated.'
>
> (Elkins, 2008, p.157)

Galison's account of the image- and logic-tradition of scientific imaging provides a useful way to differentiate between the significance and quality of images as they occur across different image practices in the sciences. The extract that follows, for example, which discusses the use of a scanning probe microscope, can certainly be considered in terms of *both* the image- and logic-traditions of imaging.

RIPPLES IN AN ELECTRON POND

PHILIP MORIARTY

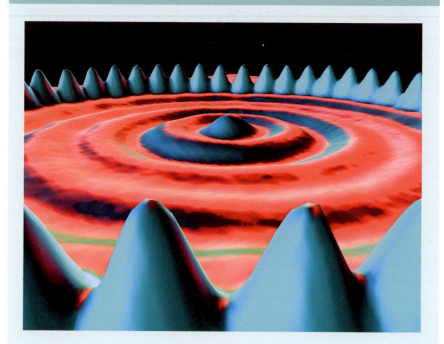

FIGURE 7.10 Quantum Corral Wave. Image originally created by IBM Corporation.

To the casual observer, the image shown here (Figure 7.10) may not be the most inspiring – its stand-out feature may well be the far-from-subtle colour palette. For many scientists, however, the image provokes an almost visceral response, representing, as it does, an iconic and thrilling advance in our ability to manipulate matter. So, what is this image and how was it made? Why is the structure we see called a quantum corral? To help answer these questions, it is essential to understand how the structure was created. Each individual 'blob' comprising the circular corral is an individual iron atom, carefully moved into position and imaged using an instrument known as a scanning probe microscope (SPM). The SPM thus acts both as an imaging device *and* as a tool for the manipulation of matter at the single atom level.

An SPM is a microscope like no other. It can resolve single atoms, even – with the state-of-the-art equipment – achieving individual *chemical bond* ('sub-atomic') resolution. Yet, unlike traditional microscopes it doesn't use lenses, or mirrors, or, indeed, optics of any type to form an image. Some have claimed that because SPMs do not image in the same way as a conventional microscope – i.e. they don't exploit the bending of light waves – the pictures they produce somehow are not an accurate representation of the microscopic/nanoscopic world. Yet, at these very close separations, a number of different physical and chemical interactions between the tip and the underlying surface come into play (including, for example, the formation of a chemical bond between the atom at the end of the tip and that directly below on the surface of interest). Crucially, with an atomically sharp tip many of these interactions will vary on an atomic scale. By moving the tip back and forth across the surface (using very precise piezoelectric motors) and measuring the variation in the strength of the interaction, an atomically resolved image can be built up.

The particular tip-surface interaction exploited to generate the image of the corral is a rather counter-intuitive quantum physics effect known as electron tunnelling. Although the tip and sample are never brought into contact, for sufficiently small separations (less than about one nanometre) a current can still flow. This is completely contrary to our experience in the everyday world. A gap between two wires, for example, does not permit a current to flow – we have an open circuit situation. At the quantum level, however, electrons can 'tunnel' through the gap and produce a measureable, but rather small (nanoamps) current. The key point is that this current is exquisitely sensitive to the separation of the tip and the sample. It is *so* sensitive that being located directly above an atom or in the 'gaps' between atoms makes all the difference.

In many experiments the aim is to image the surface without disturbing it too much – we want to capture it in its 'native' state. If, however, we move the tip closer to the surface than is the norm for imaging, we can interact much more strongly with the underlying atoms. This is the strategy that Crommie and his co-workers at IBM Almaden used to create and image the corral. With the tip held relatively far from the sample, the surface atoms are not disturbed and an image of their positions can be generated. Moving the tip closer to the sample produces a much stronger interaction and enables single atoms to be dragged around to produce pre-defined structures such as the corral.

While the fabrication of the forty-eight atom corral itself using an SPM is a remarkable feat of atomic scale engineering, this is not the most important aspect of the image. What lies inside the corral is even more striking. It is as if a stone had been dropped into a pond – we see ripples, just like waves on water. The ripples inside the corral are the signature of confined electrons. Quantum mechanics tells us that entities such as electrons, protons, atoms, and molecules

FIGURE 7.11a Silicon atoms. Courtesy of the Nanoscience Group, University of Nottingham.

FIGURE 7.11b Data pertaining to silicon atoms. Courtesy of the Nanoscience Group, University of Nottingham.

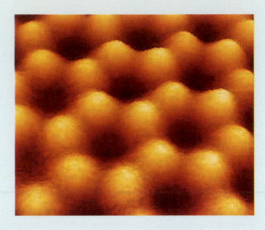

```
.  .   Enable = 1 --
.  .   Enable_Storing = 1 --
.  .   Auto_Oversampling = 1 --
.  .   Oversampling_Factor = 1280 --
.  .   Initial_Delay = 0 Seconds

# Start of Data:
0.00103767  0.000992844 0.00291736  0.00311572  0.00232894  0.00250919
       0.00230224  0.00233276  0.00510413  0.00315387  0.00340564
       0.00415332  0.00210578  0.00225360  0.00297649  0.00191695
       0.00193126  0.00207240  0.00200469  0.000635216 0.000469277 -
0.000135353 0.00108821  0.000684807 0.000874589 0.000896523 0.000655243
      -0.000103881         0.000625680 -0.000245979          1.97655e-006
      -0.000826766        -0.00314229 -0.00417607 -0.00482552 -0.00634568
      -0.00639432 -0.00708001 -0.00834649 -0.0104121  -0.00957577 -
0.0105695    -0.0117177  -0.0107803  -0.0109529  -0.0114307  -0.0106715
      -0.0120410  -0.0105047  -0.00864594 -0.00806229 -0.00833600 -
0.00652497  -0.00506299 -0.00387662 -0.00375836 -0.00358575  2.39111e-
005   0.00110156  0.00322730  0.00562293  0.00666530  0.00799567
       0.0103303   0.0103665   0.0123559   0.0124799   0.0129157
       0.0139771   0.0139676   0.0130950   0.0111533   0.0106774
       0.0104533   0.00902183  0.00822265  0.00662143  0.00549133
       0.00331313  0.00229175  0.00402934  0.00168712  0.00142104
       0.00268085  0.00247104  0.00384528  0.00438316  0.00513561
       0.00517947  0.00708015  0.00762565  0.0113393   0.0125256
       0.0119401   0.0150452   0.0144074   0.0155287   0.0196248
       0.0185528   0.0228644   0.0204249   0.0163584   0.0119582
       0.00964172  0.00627334  0.00626571  0.00459010  0.00355251
       0.00199897  0.00288779  0.00269229  0.00164706  0.00151641
       0.000741074 0.00118453  0.000508378 -0.000256469          -
0.000186851 -0.00183194 -0.00125115 -0.00203984 -0.00239938 -0.00286286
      -0.00273602 -0.00464814 -0.00424950 -0.00276177 -0.00229542 -
0.00156682  -7.56020e-006         0.000521729 0.00242049  0.00320251
       0.00379855  0.00503547  0.00713546  0.00829704  0.00969131
       0.00884921  0.00961120  0.00963123  0.00807197  0.00840957
       0.00788219  0.00656612  0.00544174  0.00415809  0.00195033
       0.00112827  0.000567505 -0.00257390 -0.00377934 -0.00493520 -
0.00776952  -0.00809090 -0.00992100 -0.0123128  -0.0137252  -0.0141801
      -0.0145835  -0.0165996  -0.0157651  -0.0175714  -0.0170001  -
0.0185365   -0.0185146  -0.0165853  -0.0176067  -0.0176467  -0.0162267
      -0.0169782  -0.0163430  -0.0151834  -0.0154390  -0.0134849  -
0.0135154   -0.0136680  -0.0107650  -0.0106992  -0.0101709  -0.00716489
```

are not really just simple particles, but have a wave-like character. Sometimes that wave-like character is rather elusive and difficult to pin down; not so for the quantum corral. Electrons on the copper substrate chosen for the experiment ordinarily spread out like a 'sea' or a gas across the surface. When these electrons encounter objects at the surface, they are reflected just like waves on a pond.

The corral reflects electron waves, setting up resonances akin to those formed by a vibrating guitar string or, better, a vibrating drum head. The analogy with the drumhead is particularly appropriate as there are very strong similarities between the mathematics used to describe the resonances excited by a drummer and the equations that predict the shapes of the electron waves within the corral.

But any SPM-generated picture, like any other digital image, is just a series of numbers. The beauty in the measurement – Nature's 'signature', if you will – is embedded in that number stream; the visualization in the form of an image just helps scientists to interpret the data. Trying to visualize the contents of a 2D or 3D matrix of numbers and extract the salient features is, to put it mildly, far from easy – either for a human or computer algorithm. A comparison between a 3D rendered atomic force microscope image of silicon atoms and its corresponding raw data makes this abundantly clear (see Figure 7.11). This is why scientists plot graphs, generate histograms, or produce images – in each case pattern recognition and analysis is made very much easier.

Philip Moriarty's account of the quantum corral image not only illustrates Galison's two traditions of physics imaging, the image-tradition and the logic-tradition, but also reveals how they seemingly co-exist. The production of a picture of the corral wave is not strictly necessary to determine the underlying physics and mathematics, yet, as Moriarty suggests, it has the power to excite the imagination (and connect intuitively) in a way that is not possible from only a raw data matrix. The quantum corral is undoubtedly part of the iconography of modern science, partly because of its visual eloquence. Yet, equally, it can only be an illustration of what is an important, and eloquent finding in physics. In other words the mathematics is key to this image, but as long as one is aware of this fact – as long as one can properly read off the data – quantum physics need not be bereft of imagery.

As suggested earlier in the chapter, problems arise where science is not treated seriously *as* science. A final example can be taken again from particle physics. Figure 7.12 shows a bubble-chamber image. It was produced in a large chamber, set with a series of cameras. The forming of bubbles allows for the tracing of particles and the images are made using 'ordinary 35mm film, and tens or hundreds of thousands would be taken in the course of a typical experiment' (Elkins, 2008, p.160). It is then possible to reconstruct the tracks of particles in three dimensions; the cameras are set as such to 'image individual bubbles as point sources, exactly as if they were stars in an astronomical image' (p.161). On first viewing, the seemingly complex bubble-chamber image can lead the uninitiated to shut down what Elkins calls the 'viewer's intuitive understanding of images of particles' (2008, p.175). From a humanities perspective, for example, the problem arises from a habit to read *complexity* in the way we might a figurative painting, as if deriving from a representational form.

The image in Figure 7.12 'has all the characteristics of a painting or fine-art photograph: lovely soft stains, atmospheric depth, mysterious dark clouds, intricate calligraphic traces, hidden lights, and a landscape-and-cloud composition, all playing against a distorted and dysfunctional grid' (Elkins, 2008, p.175). Indeed, the image could easily be looked at as we might a painting by Cy Twombly (discussed in Chapter 4), to the point where we seek to 'zoom in on parts of the image and find new levels of seductive detail. The image seems prefabricated for modernist art criticism'

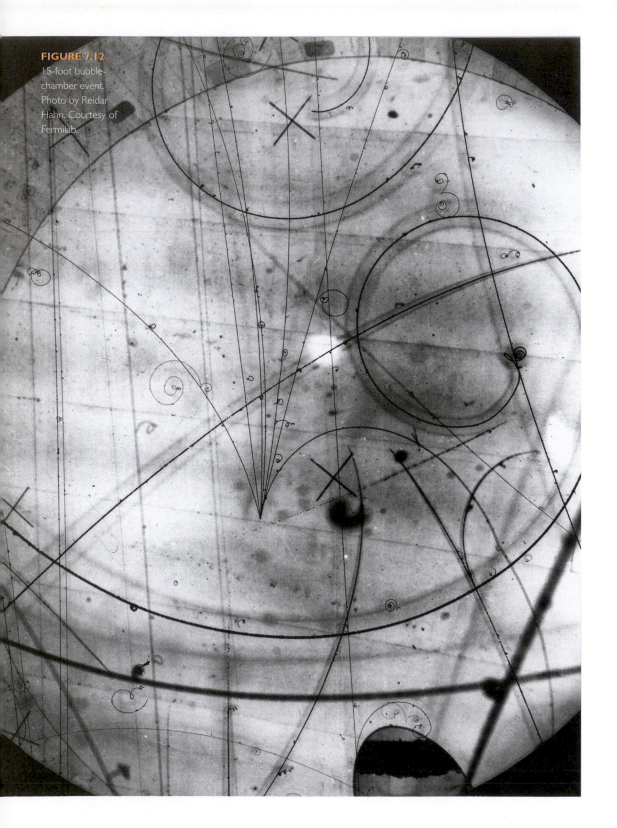

(p.175). Yet the picture turns out – in purely scientific terms – to be relatively simple. In fact: 'Nothing is as it appears in bubble- and cloud-chamber images – even complexity itself. The half-art images . . . are actually simple by physics standards. Their bewildering lines are traces of just a few kinds of stable particles, and . . . their lovely atmospheric effects are unwanted artifacts' (Elkins, 2008, p.177). For the physicist, then, the image is relatively straightforward, even repetitive. Significantly, bubble-chamber photographs would rarely be viewed in isolation, but rather examined with other kinds of supporting images used for plotting pathways and making calculations (see Figure 7.13).

Despite vast heterogeneity in science imaging (with this chapter only scratching the surface), we can begin to see some common themes. Images in science are produced under very specific conditions. They require dedicated knowledge for their production and interpretation. As with the bubble-chamber images, science images are typically a means to an end, not an end in themselves. Indeed, they are rarely exhibited as standalone objects. The value of an image for scientific understanding varies widely. Galison's account of an image-tradition and a logic-tradition in science is one way to begin categorizing differences. Further to which, Pauwels offers a useful schema (Figure 7.14), plotting a broader continuum from the material to the conceptual. He notes: 'Visual representation in science may *refer* to objects that are believed to have some kind of material or physical existence, but equally may refer to purely mental, conceptual, abstract constructs and/or immaterial *entities*' (Pauwels, 2006, p.2). All of the examples of science visualizations given in this chapter refer to objects of material, physical existence – which we can place on the left-hand side of Pauwels diagram. However, as these 'objects' begin to recede as

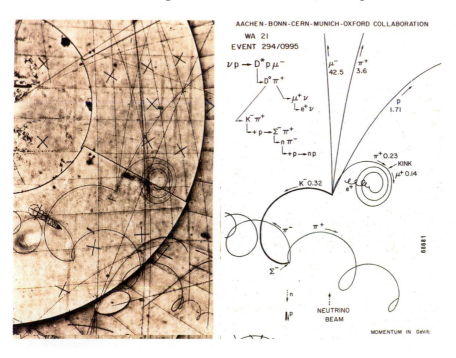

FIGURE 7.13

Bubble chamber image: D meson production and decay. © 1978 CERN. Bubble-chamber image and supporting documentation. This event shows real particle tracks from the Big European Bubble Chamber, which was used to observe neutrino and hadron beams between 1973 and 1984.

visual phenomena, or are even 'invisible' (to the human eye), they are placed in increments, shown from the left to right, on a spectrum from 'material/physical' to 'mental/conceptual'. In many cases phenomena are initially postulated as theoretical entities, such as the 'quark' in quantum physics, long before technologies are available to picture them and prove their existence. It is worth drawing a parallel between Pauwels' diagram and W. J. T. Mitchell's diagram of a family tree of images (Figure 2.6) in Chapter 2 of this book. Mitchell similarly places the material, tangible image-forms on the left-hand side of his diagram, such as graphic and optical images. As we move across to the right-hand side, images become less tangible and more conceptual, from the perceptual (which sits in the middle) to the mental and verbal. It is worth pondering how Mitchell's and Pauwels' diagrams relate to each other, both in terms of how they categorize the image and what they suggest about how we articulate ideas through images.

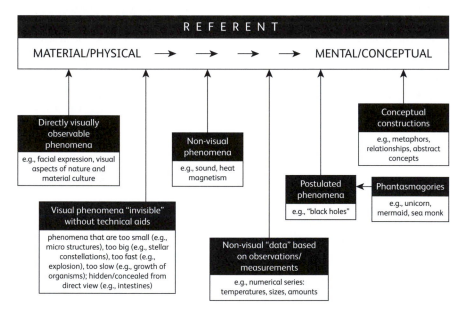

FIGURE 7.14 Diagram: 'The divergent nature of the referent, from material existence to mental construction'. Courtesy of Luc Pauwels. The diagram offers a spectrum of what science typically refers to as 'objects' of study. Going from left to right, objects move further away from what can be directly observable by the human eye. On the far left the diagram plots material, physical referents that can be easily observed. It moves then to objects and phenomena that only become visible with imaging tools and processes, such as high-speed photography, telescopes, microscopes and medical imaging tools. Further to the right, objects or phenomena appear which may not have visual characteristics as such (e.g. sound waves, thermal radiation), but can still be translated into visual representations. Of course, the sciences are not simply concerned with visually reproducing visual or non-visual phenomena, but with providing *data*. Moving over from the centre of the diagram, to the right, we come to the visualizing of data, which often involves much more abstract, arbitrary and conventional representations, though these can be *motivated* and even iconic (more on this topic in Chapter 8). On the far right of the diagram we find 'postulated phenomena' and 'conceptual constructions', which can include the representations of abstract concepts, hypothetical relationships and postulated phenomena (e.g. black holes). Here, the referents can become purely mental constructs with no prior physical or historical basis.

TASK

Science Scrapbook

In a media-rich environment, we are saturated with scientific images. New discoveries and/or theoretical possibilities are reported in the news media. Documentaries are made based on astronomical data and imaging. Advertisers use x-rays, CAT scans, and molecular modelling to lend authority to products. TV drama series provide elaborate insights into medicine and forensic science, and so it goes on. How do we make sense of all these images?

Collect as many articles of science-related images you can find, whether in newspapers, magazines, or on television and online. Alternatively, you may have access to your own set of images, if working in a lab for example, or from appointments with medical practitioners (e.g. an ophthalmologist or radiographer). Make brief notes and annotations about the images you collect and try to build up a reading of the images based on increasing levels of understanding. What do you already know about the images and what they show? Categorize them in terms of: (1) what you intuitively understand; (2) what you can comprehend through further research; and (3) what goes beyond your understanding. How would you find out more information? Would you consider the images you have found to be within the image-tradition or the logic-tradition of science, as described by Galison? Finally, where would you place the images on Pauwels diagram showing the changing nature of the referent from material existence to mental construction?

Summary

In this chapter we have considered a variety of scientific imaging and aspects of the history of images in science. Reference was made to C.P. Snow's lecture of 1959 titled 'The Two Cultures and the Scientific Revolution', in which he notes the divide between the humanities and the sciences. Elkins argues the divide remains to this day, with only popularized accounts of both sides being widely read. As a result, scientists tend to press on with their work without much regard for a wider context in which they produce images, and those working in the humanities tend to draw on simplified accounts of science and overemphasize a social critique of the sciences. This chapter has tried to make a point of considering scientific imaging as much from a practical point of view – including two extracts from scientists explaining how imaging works within their fields. Whilst there are undoubtedly issues at stake about how as a society we organize and control the production of science and scientific images, there is also a need to acknowledge the complexities of devising and handling the formation of images that are pertinent to both scientific research and the wider communication of science. Questions remain about levels of data and visual literacy – though as noted, concerns are not just about levels of literacy amongst the wider public, but equally the literacy required of scientists to think with images, learn from images and to communicate with them.

This chapter also considered human vision. Commentary began with the eye itself, but progressed to the functioning – and indeed 'functional specialization' – of the brain. Drawing on the work of Semir Zeki, who presents one of the most accessible accounts of recent research, an important epistemological point was reached. There is a constant inside/outside process to our vision – we have to be exposed to the visual world from birth in order to gain visual competence, yet equally vision is not a passive process whereby the image is impressed upon the brain. Through an elaborate system of parallel processing the brain is active in constructing the images we see. If anything, images in science begin to test the boundaries of what we mean by 'seeing' and the very concept of the 'image' itself. Pauwels' diagram of the varied nature of the referent in science imaging offers a useful schematic for contemplating the vast repertoire of imaging and the status we afford both images and ideas.

Further reading

Chen, Chaomei (2003) *Mapping Scientific Frontiers: The Quest for Knowledge Visualization*. London: Springer.

Elkins, James (ed.) (2007) *Visual Practices Across the University*. München: Wilhelm Fink Verlag.

Elkins, James (2008) *Six Stories from the End of Representation: Images in Painting, Photography, Astronomy, Microscopy, Particle Physics, and Quantum Mechanics, 1980–2000*. Stanford: Stanford University Press.

Ford, Brian (1992) *Images of Science: A History of Scientific Illustration*. London: The British Library.

Frankel, Felice (2002) *Envisioning Science: The Design and Craft of the Science Image*. Cambridge, Mass.: MIT Press.

Galison, Peter (1997) *Image and Logic: A Material Culture of Microphysics*. Chicago: University of Chicago Press.

Galison, Peter (2002) 'Images Scatter into Data, Data Gather into Images' in Bruno Latour and Peter Weibel (eds) *Iconoclash: Beyond the Image Wars in Science, Religion and Art*. Cambridge, Mass.: MIT Press, pp. 300–323.

Kemp, Martin (2006) *Seen/Unseen: Art, Science, and Intuition from Leonardo to the Hubble Telescope*. Oxford: Oxford University Press.

Pauwels, Luc (ed.) (2006) *Visual Cultures of Science: Rethinking Representational Practices in Knowledge Building and Science Communication*. Hanover, NH: Dartmouth College Press.

Snow, C.P. (1998) *The Two Cultures*. Cambridge: Cambridge University Press.

Sturken, Marita and Cartwright, Lisa (2009) 'Scientific Looking, Looking at Science' in *Practices of Looking: An Introduction to Visual Culture*. Second Edition. Oxford: Oxford University Press, pp. 347–387.

Zeki, Semir (1999) *Inner Vision*. Oxford: Oxford University Press.

8 Image and information

FIGURE 8.1
Ensō, Zero and 'O'.

This chapter turns attention to images as information, or at least as a means to communicate information and ideas. At the close of Chapter 3, on images and text, reference was made to a theory of **notation**. The philosopher Nelson Goodman distinguishes notation as a nonlinguistic symbol system able to possess certain functional and systematic qualities. A primary example he gives is the music score, which is the transcription of music we can hear into a visual script using an established, sharable system of notation. Notation is not a picture, nor is it text – it is something in between. Figure 8.1 illustrates the principle. On the left we see a circular swirl of ink which we might recognize as a Japanese calligraphic circle, or *ensō*, which for Zen Buddhists carries a variety of meanings such as the universe, void, the moon and so forth. In the middle is the numerical figure for zero, and on the right the letter 'o'. At a glance we see three circular figures, which we might even argue to be interchangeable. All three figures could be used as a number zero or a letter 'o' – yet, if we were to frame the illustration and place it upon the wall it would immediately be seen as a picture. We also see the differences, accustomed as we are by both distinctive features and different contexts of use.

Goodman (1968, pp.127–173) offers a logical, philosophical account of notation, as it differs from text and image. At the core of his argument is a distinction between 'replete' and 'attenuated' density of symbol systems. He gives an example of an electrocardiogram (a graphic image of the electrical activity of the heart, as detected by electrodes), which just happens to suggest the familiar shape of Mount Fuji as drawn by the artist Hokusai (famous for his wood-block paintings from the 1800s):

'The black wiggly lines on white backgrounds may be exactly the same in the two cases. Yet one is a diagram and the other a picture. What makes the difference? [. . .] The difference does not lie in what is symbolized. [. . .] The only relevant features of the diagram are the . . . points the center of the line passes through. The thickness of the line, its color and intensity, the absolute size of the diagram, etc., do not matter . . . For the sketch, this is not true. Any thickening or thinning of the line, its color, its contrast with the background, its size, even the qualities of the paper – none of these is ruled out, none can be ignored.'

(Goodman, 1968, p.229)

In Goodman's account, the drawing of Mount Fuji is 'replete' since all aspects are part of what it presents. By contrast, the electrocardiogram is 'attenuated' because much of what we see is not essential to the 'information' we need to take from it – in other words, many features can be altered, as long as the information we need to 'read-off' remains accurate. Goodman's argumentation is not always easy to follow and also potentially 'leads to odd conclusions, as it compels him to say that things such as ungraduated thermometers "depict" temperature' (Elkins, 1999, p.70). This chapter does not seek to unpack and develop further the philosophical debates around image, text and notation (see Elkins, 1999, pp.68–81; 82–91). Nonetheless, it takes a practical look at how images combine with both text and notation as means to communicate information and ideas.

The semiotic landscape

When introducing the notion of the 'Pictorial Turn' in Chapter 3, reference was made to a changing 'semiotic landscape'. To recap, Kress and van Leeuwen (2006b) have shown language displaced from its 'unchallenged role as *the* medium of communication, to the role as *one* medium of communication' (p.36). They also distinguish between images as a medium of information and language as a medium of commentary, suggesting that images as much carry an argument. In the domain of education, for example, Kress and van Leeuwen note how in the early years, school children are encouraged to create both visual and written work. Yet, by the time children enter secondary education, illustrations largely disappear from work (and/or become specialized and technical), while writing increases in importance. The situation remains much the same today, except that now *all* school subjects make much more use of visual materials and yet still there remains little or no 'teaching or "instruction" in the (new) role of images' (p.16). In summary, 'materials provided *for* children make intense representational use of images; in materials demanded *from* children – in various forms of assessment particularly – writing remains the expected and dominant mode' (p.16). Even where children are encouraged to include illustrations, these materials tend to function more as decoration to the main written text – and it is only the latter that is properly assessed.

Images have of course become ever more abundant in their use across all sorts of domains and situations. The educational context is hardly unique in having adopted an increasing use of images and, increasingly, to have paid attention to **visual literacy**. Yet, the lack of critical consideration of both the reading and *making* of images within school education is suggestive of what Kress and van Leeuwen describe as 'old visual literacy' – whereby 'visual communication has been made subservient to language and in which images have come to be regarded as unstructured replicas of reality' (2006b, p.23). By contrast, they describe 'new visual literacy' in terms of a mixed economy of language and images, or even '**multimodality**' (Kress, 2010) – whereby there are more open structures of meaning that come through the combination and/or independence of different modalities. These so-called 'old' and 'new' visual literacies can certainly co-exist, and there is the suggestion we are 'in the middle of a shift in valuation and uses from the one mode to the other' (Kress and van Leeuwen, 2006b, p.23).

Kress and van Leeuwen trace a shift from an old to a new visual literacy through a series of specific examples. They describe two children's picture books for instance. The first is a classic Ladybird book, *Baby's First Book*, which uses naturalistic pictures on one page and short sentences on the other to anchor the meaning. The second is Dick Bruna's *On My Walk*, which consists of eight pages of illustrations without any text. The illustrations are much more stylized, using simple graphic lines and flat, single-toned colours. The two books present contrasting 'semiotic landscapes'. In the Ladybird book language provides an authoritative 'reading' of the image. Despite the fact the illustrations are rich in detail they could easily be replaced, since the text provides the overriding meaning. By contrast, in Dick Bruna's *On My Walk* the image carries the meaning:

> 'Parents who read [Bruna's] book with their children could all tell a different story, could even use different languages . . . The world of "one image, many different verbal texts" ("commentaries") imposes a new mode of control over meaning, and turns the image, formerly a record of nature . . . into a more powerful, but also more rigorously controlled and codified public language, while it gives language, formally closely policed in many social institutions, a more private and less controlled, but also less powerful, status. The "readings" parents produce when they read *On My Walk* with their children may all be different, yet these different readings will necessarily have common elements, deriving from their common basis – the elements included in the image, and the way these elements are compositionally brought together.'
>
> (Kress and van Leeuwen, 2006b, pp.26–27)

An important consideration here is how an image gets placed in relation to other elements of an overall design. Whether we think of the multimodality of Kress and van Leeuwen's 'semiotic landscape' or the 'ecology of images' described in this book (see Chapter 2), a recurring theme is the ongoing complexity and alterations of the *context* of any given image. There is seemingly no such thing as a 'pure' image.

MULTIMODALITY

GUNTHER KRESS

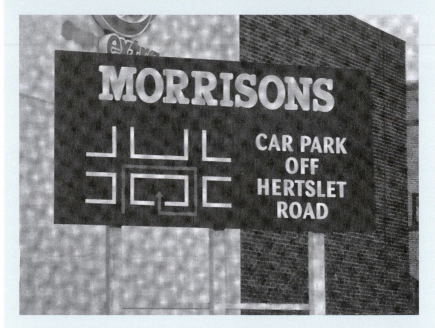

FIGURE 8.2 Morrison's car park sign. Courtesy of Gunther Kress.

If writing alone had been used, would this sign work? I don't think it could: there is too little time to take it in. [. . . I]f shoppers tried to *read* the sign . . . [whilst driving] . . . the intersection would clog up. With writing alone, the message would, quite simply, be too complex. Using three modes in the one sign – *writing* and *image* and *colour* as well – has real benefits. Each mode does a specific thing: image *shows* what takes too long to *read*, and writing *names* what would be difficult to *show*. Colour is used to *highlight* specific aspects of the overall message. Without that division of semiotic labour, the sign, quite simply, would not work. Writing *names* and image *shows*, while colour *frames* and *highlights*; each to maximum effect and benefit.

If writing by itself would not work, could the sign work with image alone? Well, just possibly, maybe. *Writing* and *image* and *colour* lend themselves to doing different kinds of semiotic work; each has its distinct potentials for meaning –

and, in this case, image may just have the edge over writing, and that, in a nutshell . . . is the argument for taking 'multimodality' as the normal state of human communication.

Except that, just across the road . . . there is another supermarket. It too has a sign . . . just as high up; it shows *its* customers how to get into *its* car park. . . . The sign is different: not different in modes used but in *how* the modes are used. Colour is different, lines are differently drawn; the sign has a distinctly different *aesthetic*. Multimodality can tell us what modes are used; it cannot tell us about this difference in *style*; it has no means to tell us what that difference might *mean*. What is the difference in colour about or the difference in drawing style? What identity is each of the two signs projecting? What are the supermarkets 'saying' about themselves? What are they telling their customers about themselves? Are these differences accidental, arbitrary? Would the *style* of one sign serve equally well for the other supermarket? (Kress, 2010, pp.1–2)

Kress and van Leeuwen (2006b) note other examples of a shift in visual literacy. In documentary film, the trend away from the authoritative 'voice of god' narration of classic documentaries towards 'direct cinema' plays out a similar shift away from a dominance of language to a more multimodal representational style. Similarly, the changing style noted from the two children's books, 'from "uncoded" naturalistic representations to stylized, conceptual images' (2006b, p.30), can be found with the covers of contemporary news magazines. Previously, magazine covers would be produced using predominately documentary photographs (and as is often still the case), yet increasingly 'the photographs on magazine covers are contrived and posed, using conventional symbols to illustrate the essence of an *issue*, rather than documenting newsworthy *events* . . .' (2006b, p.30).

The seemingly innocuous differences between the designs of two children's book, or the use of an illustration on a magazine cover, are potentially symptomatic of a much more fundamental trend in how we make, share and comprehend knowledge and ideas. One suggestion Kress and van Leeuwen make regarding the children's book by Dick Bruna is that it came to be popular at a specific time in Holland (its country of origin) as the country began to experience an increasingly divided and fragmented sense of culture, due to a broadening demographic. Thus, '[f]or a message to reach . . . the whole population, it had to be adaptable to a variety of cultural and ideological constructions and, as we have seen, the Bruna books use the visual medium to achieve exactly that' (Kress and van Leeuwen, 2006b, p.29). These are not particularly contentious hypotheses, particularly if taken in isolation. Yet, for Kress and van Leeuwen, the real interest comes in their combination; indeed this is the 'crucial feature of the new semiotic landscape' (p.41). More broadly, then, the semiotic landscape brings to light important social, political and cultural questions.

TASK

Semiotic Safari

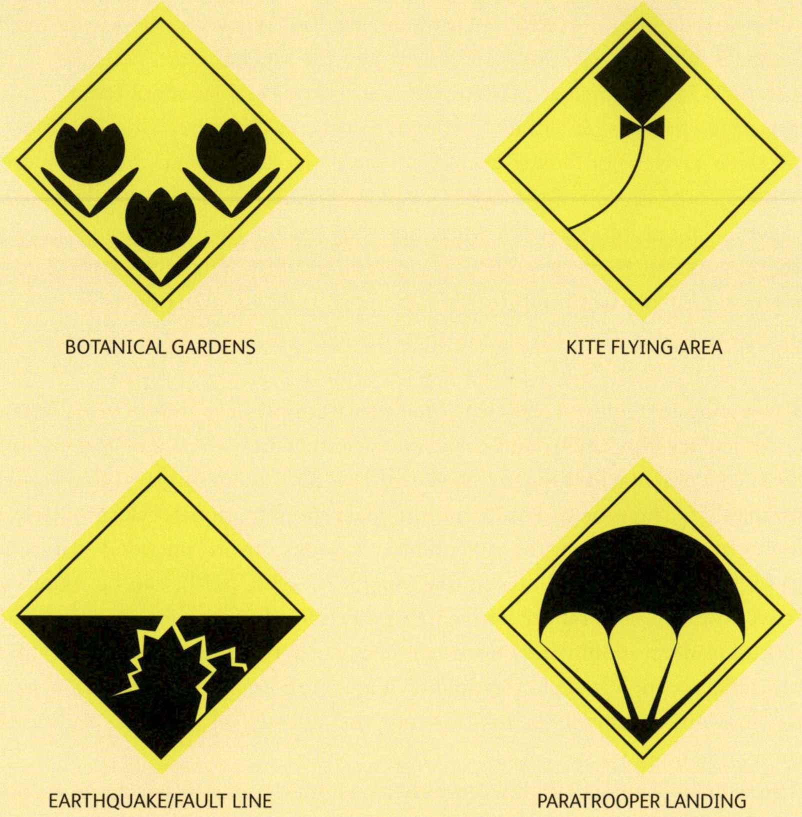

BOTANICAL GARDENS

KITE FLYING AREA

EARTHQUAKE/FAULT LINE

PARATROOPER LANDING

FIGURE 8.3 Imaginary Road Signs, from Judith Wilde and Richard Wilde's *Visual Literacy* (1991, p.100)

Keeping in mind changes in semiotic styles and a purported shift from old to new visual literacy, set off on a 'semiotic safari'. Hunt and capture (on camera) examples of multimodal signs and create your own 'semiotic zoo'. How do all the signs you've gathered work, how do they express meaning and how do they each compare?

Having gathered evidence of existing signs, design some signs of your own for situations which you think are in need of instructions. How and why might you extend the range of messages we experience in our everyday landscapes? Perhaps you might want to account for more complex social problems or cultural interests. Alternatively, devise road and informational signs for bizarre, imaginary situations. Some examples from Judith Wilde and Richard Wilde's *Visual Literacy* (1991, pp.98–109) might offer inspiration (see Figure 8.3). Using the familiar idiom of the road sign, they set a task of designing functional signs for unusual, idiosyncratic topics such as an ant farm, target range, kite flying area and paratrooper landing. Finally, consider how the landscape might look without informational signs. How would the removal of signs alter a busy social space?

Image and environment

The 'semiotic landscape' is obviously a metaphor, which seeks to describe public communication within a given social context. Drawing on its etymology, Kress and van Leeuwen make the point that the 'features of a landscape . . . only make sense in the context of their whole environment and of the history of its development'; thus the metaphor has clear parallels with how an 'ecology of images' is described in this book (see Chapter 2). Mindful of pushing the metaphor too far, Kress and van Leeuwen nonetheless wish to draw attention to social implications. We can think of their semiotic analyses as offering both a micro- and macro-reading. They engage in close analysis of specific designs, yet equally they try to extrapolate to describe broader social phenomena.

The statistician, Edward Tufte (1990, pp.37–38), refers to various axonometric city map projections and high-resolution aerial photographs as achieving micro/macro readings. Louis Bretez and Michel Etienne Turgot's famous *Plan de Paris* (Figure 8.4) is one good example. Its 'fine texture of exquisite detail leads to personal micro-readings, individual stories about the data . . . [Yet, detail] cumulates into larger coherent structures' (Tufte, 1990, p.37). This in turn leads to a somewhat unusual outcome, as Tufte explains: 'Simplicity of reading derives from the context of detailed and complex information, properly arranged. A most unconventional design strategy is revealed: *to clarify, add detail*' (p.37). The urban planner, Kevin Lynch, also finds complexity in the built environment, where again '[n]othing is experienced by itself, but always in relation to its surroundings, the sequences of events leading up to it, the memory of past experiences' (Lynch, 1960, p.1). In his classic study, *The Image of the City* (1960), Lynch provides a schematic account of cityscapes, and what he calls the 'environmental image', leading to a definition of *imageability*:

> '. . . that quality in a physical object which gives it a high probability of evoking a strong image in any given observer. It is that shape, color, or arrangement which facilitates the making of vividly identified, powerfully structured, highly useful mental images of the environment. It might also be called *legibility,* or perhaps *visibility* in a heightened sense, where objects are not only able to be seen, but are presented sharply and intensely to the senses.'
>
> (Lynch, 1960, pp.9–10)

FIGURE 8.4 Michel Etienne Turgot and Louis Bretez, *Plan de Paris* (Paris, 1739).

In Lynch's account, it is only 'powerful civilizations' that could begin to 'act on their total environment at a significant scale. The conscious remolding of the large-scale physical environment has been possible only recently, and so the problem of environmental imageability is a new one' (p.13).

Of course, the 'semiotic landscape' does not refer to a physical landscape, yet there are interesting parallels in how Kress and van Leeuwen describe its growing complexity and expansion. They suggest, for example, that '[g]lobal flows of capital and information of all kinds, of commodities, and of people, dissolve not only cultural and political boundaries but also semiotic boundaries' (2006b, p.36). One result, as mentioned previously, is a shift in the previously unchallenged role of language 'as *the* mode of communication, to a role as one mode among others, to the function, for instance, of being a mode for comment, for ratification, or for labelling . . . ' (p.36). With respect to issues of environment, one particular area in which language arguably fails to grasp the full meaning of a situation is in relation to global, or even planetary matters.

Figure 8.5 shows man-made space debris as it orbits the Earth. As an image it is particularly effective in communicating an enormous amount of 'data'. The estimated tens of millions of pieces of space debris are mainly only small particles, less than a centimetre in diameter. However, there are many thousands of pieces of space debris over 10 centimetres in diameter that are tracked by computers at space stations and military compounds in order to differentiate the debris from missile attacks. In 2011, NASA announced 22,000 different objects were being tracked. In the same year, a report by the National Research Council in the USA warned the amount of debris orbiting the Earth was at a critical level. Picked up by mainstream news outlets, such as the UK's BBC, the report brought to wider attention the potential of a 'tipping point', whereby it is thought enough debris is in orbit to continually collide with itself so creating even more debris. The news report included an artist's impression of the debris, which was striking in itself, yet lacked the precision of a diagram (as shown here). It is important to note, however, the dots representing the objects in Figure 8.5 are not to scale with that of the Earth. If they were you would not be able to see them. The creator of the image, Nicholas L. Johnson (working at NASA), made the size of the space objects slightly bigger than the typical dots that would appear on photocopies of the time (in the mid-1980s). Such illustrations cannot be used to calculate collision risks (the enlarged size of the objects suggest a greater risk than actually exists), but the distributions and the growth patterns make for valuable information. As Tufte explains, micro/macro designs such as this are required to portray large quantities of data at high densities:

'. . . up to thousands of bits per square centimeter and 20 million bits per page, pushing the limits of printing technology. Such quantities are thoroughly familiar, although hardly noticed: the human eye registers 150 million bits, the 35mm slide some 25 million bits, conventional large-scale topographic maps up to 150 million bits, the color screen of a small personal computer 8 million bits.'

(Tufte, 1990, p.49)

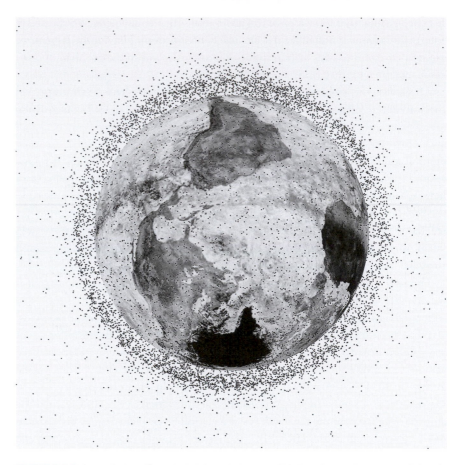

FIGURE 8.5 Space Debris. © NASA/Nicholas L. Johnson, Teledyne Brown Engineering, Colorado Springs, Colorado. This illustration is one of many depicting the population of man-made objects in orbit around the Earth since the mid-1980s. It was used to identify the exact location at a given point in time of approximately 16,000 objects, as tracked by the U.S. Space Surveillance Network. The smallest objects are approximately 10cm in size. The number of objects 1cm or larger is approximately 500,000. Most of the debris is relatively close to Earth. Not shown on this illustration are the 10 billion to 100 billion paint chips that orbit the Earth.

Despite the advances of new visual technologies and visualization techniques, the limitations of our abilities to comprehend macro concerns and complicated computational data are all too frequently revealed. Climate change makes for a very good example. Generally-speaking we do not have direct experience of anything we can conclusively link to a changing climate. The science can be very complicated and differing political, economic and moral concerns add to the complexity. News reporting in this area involves the difficult task of making sense of difficult and/or conflicting information, as well as needing to present a newsworthy story. The timeframe of climate change, which occurs over many years, is certainly at odds with the pace of news production and consumption. Images are particularly powerful in bringing a story to life and – in keeping with Kress and van Leeuwen's account of a shifting semiotic landscape – an argument can be made they play a part in social 'interactions', aiding our understanding of climate change. The question, then, is whether the way we 'see' climate change influences the way we come to 'know' or understand it. The following account, based on the content analysis of Canadian national print media (DiFrancesco and Young, 2011) actually reveals a number of problems in the way in which images relate to language in the reporting of climate change.

IMAGES OF CLIMATE CHANGE

DARRYN ANNE DIFRANCESCO

A study of Canada's two national newspapers, *The National Post* and *The Globe and Mail*, over a period of six months offers some interesting insights into how images are used to represent climate change in the media. Looking carefully at both the images and text used as well as their interrelations, the study (DiFrancesco and Young, 2011) found that images used to represent climate change were inconsistent and varied, and lacked a recurrent motif or symbol. The most significant thematic finding was that rather than displaying images of the environment, as was expected, the majority of articles in fact featured images of people, predominantly politicians. Subsequent analyses of the images as well as the text revealed that images were more likely to be included with articles that were more emotional or moral in tone. This, however, does not mean that the articles without images were less detailed or complex. On the contrary, articles without images were just as thematically complex as those with visuals, suggesting that images – at least in this context – do not 'add' anything to texts analytically. The most striking finding from this study was the fact that the images accompanying articles about climate change were often dissociated from the language or text of the articles. In a few cases the images suited the text, while in others they appeared disconnected. In a number of cases, images and texts pulled the narrative in different directions. This 'narrative disjuncture' presents a new task for readers, who are faced with the extra challenge of decoding conflicting messages in addition to interpreting them.

One particular case shows how images and language can present both complementary and conflicting narratives about climate change. An article entitled 'National carbon market faces opposition' (*The Globe and Mail*, 12 March 2008, p.B.3) featured an image of Canada's 2008 Environment Minister. The image was a photograph taken at a press event and featured the minister as well as a number of journalists who stand across from him. It presented a clear narrative of opposition, with the politician facing the journalists in what appeared to be a position of confrontation. In the photograph the minister's facial expression is tense and determined, and he displays body language that could be described as standoffish, stonewalling, or perhaps as hiding something. The journalists standing across from him thrust their microphones towards him expectantly, as if seeking to expose him. The image supports the title of the story as an illustration of the kind of 'opposition' thought to be faced by the government in its carbon market initiative. The linguistic prompt of the article's subtitle further reinforces the reading of the image, which read: 'As [the federal government] moves to establish an emissions trading system, some provinces are already going their own way.'

However, the main text of the article presents quite a different story than is anticipated based on the image of the politician and the linguistic prompts. While the latter emphasize a narrative of 'conflict' (both between the minister and the journalists, as well as the federal government and the Canadian provinces), the article text allocates almost no space to this discussion. Instead, it reviews the potential to earn revenue through climate change mitigation practices, specifically through the establishment of a national market for carbon emissions. Thus, the only common thread is the mention of the carbon market. While the image and subtitles are framing devices, they do not add anything to the text of the article, and instead offer a new and different reading of the scenario. On the one hand, climate change is viewed as inciting political conflict, while on the other it is a means for government revenue. This example illustrates a case of narrative disjuncture, where images and language tell different stories about climate change. Notably, climate change as an *environmental issue* is left untouched by *both* image and text.

DiFrancesco and Young's study (2011) can help us understand the role of images and text in the reporting of climate change in a number of ways. Firstly, it appears climate change is still awaiting its iconic image. The relative inconsistencies in images used to represent climate change and the environment more generally suggests the difficulty of linking abstract language claims with complicated, long-term environmental changes. Journalists and editors may find it challenging to select images as adequate visual representations of climate change, and instead resort to more images of people, which are not only easier to interpret, but are also more 'concrete'. The widespread use of images of politicians in articles about climate change demonstrate how journalists and editors make a shift towards an understanding of climate change as more of a political issue than an environmental one. Furthermore, while images sometimes help to frame and contextualize the text content of articles, there is often a disjuncture between what is pictured and what is discussed. Overall, there is a lack of consistent images used to represent climate change, as well as the problem of dissociation even in a single article between what is presented by both image and text.

Informational images

The difficulty of using visual representation in the news reporting of issues such as climate change raises questions about how images convey information, data and knowledge. The particular case of the Canadian print news journalism highlights how images can exist within a wider 'ecology' of editorial and compositional decisions. DiFrancesco and Young's (2011) study reveals interesting dynamics in the composition and juxtaposition of text and image *across* a page-layout of a newspaper. (For more on the 'meaning of composition', see Kress and van Leeuwen, 2006b, pp.175–214.) However, we can also consider how images as entities in themselves can be used to present information – to be, as it were, informational images.

The history of informational images goes back millennia, arguably to cave paintings and certainly later with the first discernible maps made on clay tablets. In addition, early historical records show the widespread use of icons and notations to record items, such as cattle and stock. However, the use of abstract, non-representational pictures to record statistical information is a much more recent invention. It was not until the mid-1700s through to the 1800s that statistical graphics were properly invented, coming long after 'such triumphs of mathematical ingenuity as logarithms, Cartesian coordinates, the calculus, and the basics of probability theory' (Tufte, 2004, p.9). There is, then, a period of some 5,000 years between the first recorded geographic maps and 'data maps' which combine statistical information. Tufte cites the Yü Chi Thu (Map of the Tracks of Yü the Great) made in the eleventh century AD China as an example of a highly advanced map of its day, and in Europe, Petrus Apianus' *Cosmographia* of 1546 as demonstrating something close to 'statistical graphicacy' (p.22). Yet, he argues, 'no one had yet made the quantitative abstraction of placing a measured quantity on the map's surface . . . let alone the more difficult abstraction of replacing latitude and longitude with some other dimensions, such as time and money' (Tufte, 2004, p.22).

Today, statistical graphics such as bar charts, data maps and time-series (one of the more frequently used forms of graphic design, showing data over a period of time) are commonplace and part of any child's schooling. Their invention dates back to the late 1700s and in particular to the work of William Playfair. In 1786, he published the first data graphs in *The Commercial and Political Atlas*. Filled with statistical graphs, bar charts, line graphs and histograms, the book provides detailed economic records. Later, Playfair introduced the first area chart and pie chart in his *Statistical Breviary* (1801). At the heart of Playfair's work is an enduring fundamental principle: 'Graphics *reveal* data. Indeed graphics can be more precise and revealing than conventional statistical computations' (Tufte, 2004, 13). Writing in *The Commercial and Political Atlas*, Playfair contrasts his graphical charts with tabular presentation of data in the following way:

> '. . . a man who has carefully investigated a printed table, finds, when done, that he has only a very faint and partial idea of what he has read; and that like a figure imprinted on sand, is soon totally erased and defaced. The amount of

mercantile transactions in money, and of profit or loss, are capable of being as easily represented in drawing, as any part of space, or as the face of a country; though, till now, it has not been attempted. Upon these principles these Charts were made; and, while they give a simple and distinct idea, they are as near perfect accuracy as is any way useful. On inspecting any one of these Charts attentively, a sufficiently distinct impression will be made, to remain unimpaired for a considerable time, and the idea which does remain will be simple and complete, at once including the duration and the amount.'

(Playfair, cited in Tufte, 2004, p.32)

Playfair is credited with inventing the humble bar chart, which he did because he needed the means to represent a data set of which he held only one year's worth of data. He was himself sceptical of the chart due to its lack of comparative data – and it is certainly true that 'noncomparative, highly labeled data sets usually belong in tables' (Tufte, 2004, p.33). Playfair's real contribution to statistical graphics is the 'time-series' – which make up all but one of the 44 charts in his first publication. Crucially for Playfair, 'graphics were preferable to tables because graphics showed the shape of data in a comparative perspective' (Tufte, 2004, p.32). Figure 8.6 – taken from Playfair's last book, which examines the increase in the price of wheat relative to wages – demonstrates his technique, here plotting three parallel time-series: prices, wages and the reigns of the British monarchy (Figure 8.6).

One problem with the time-series is that time itself is not necessarily an explanatory variable, i.e. time does not equate to causal explanation. One technique for enhancing the time-series is to include spatial features, which can add narrative value. A seminal example is Charles Joseph Minard's information graphic of Napoleon's invasion of Russia in 1812 (Figure 8.7). In a single two-dimensional image, the graphic presents four key variables as they contributed to the downfall of Napoleon's army: (1) the army's direction; (2) the location the troops passed through; (3) the size of the army as troops died from hunger and wounds; and (4) the freezing temperatures. As a composite image, 'Minard's graphic tells a rich, coherent story with its multivariate data, far more enlightening than just a single number bouncing over time' (Tufte, 2004, p.40).

The development of more complex data graphics required a shift away from the latitude-longitude coordinates of a map. The step from maps to statistical graphics took thousands of years and then even with the work of Playfair and others in the eighteenth century analogies to the physical world continued to inform the conceptual basis of time-series diagrams. However, gradually more abstract, relational graphics began to appear. The mathematician and astronomer, Johann Heinrich Lambert, offered key theoretical statements on relational graphics as early as 1765. In respect of a graph he drew showing the evaporation rate of water as a function of temperature, Lambert argues how observational readings are not necessarily accurate, and so the graph needs to be drawn as close as possible to a 'true' reading. In effect, he begins to shift – or at least combine – the practice of graphic representation from the plotting of actual results to the modelling of theoretical

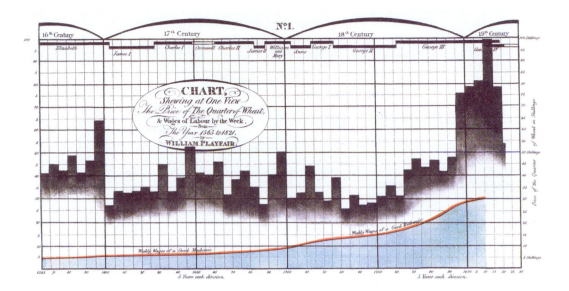

FIGURE 8.6 William Playfair, *Chart Showing at One View The Price of the Quarter of Wheat and Wages of Labour by the Week,* *1565–1821. From the Commercial and Political Atlas and Statistical Breviary.*

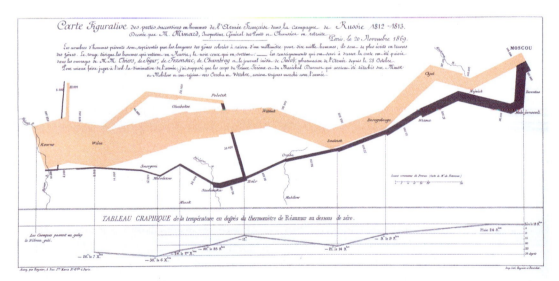

FIGURE 8.7 Charles Jospeh Minard, *Tableaux Graphiques et Cartes Figuratives de M. Minard, 1845–1869,* Bibliothèque de L'École Nationale des Ponts et Chaussées, Paris, item 28 (62 × 25 cm).

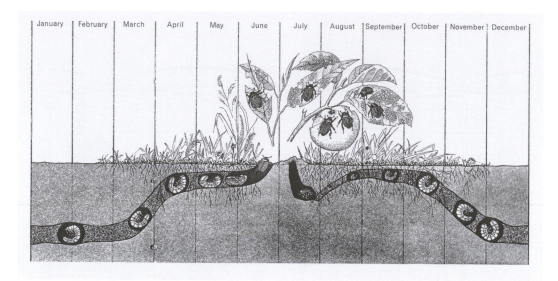

FIGURE 8.8 Life Cycle of Japanese beetle (L. Hugh Newman, *Man and Insects*, 1965, pp.104–105). The time-series in its more expanded sense, incorporating spatial, narrative elements, is commonly found in books and articles to help bring to 'life' complex ideas and processes. In this case 'a space-time-story graphic ingeniously mixes space and time on the horizontal axis. This design moves well beyond the conventional time-series because of its clever plotting field, with location relative to the ground surface on the vertical axis and time/space on the horizontal' (Tufte, 2004, p.43).

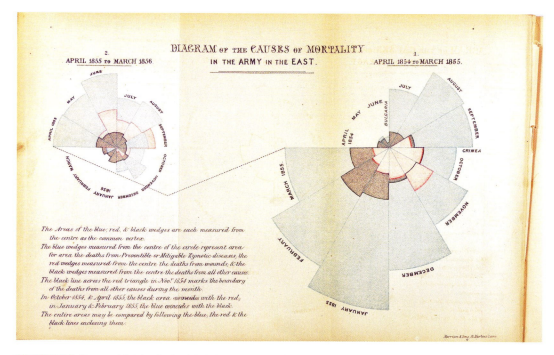

FIGURE 8.9 Florence Nightingale, Statistical chart invented by Florence Nightingale to show the predominance of disease as a cause of mortality in the British army during the Crimean War, April 1854 to March 1855 and April 1855 to March 1856 (1858). Courtesy of Bridgeman Art Library.

234

constructions. Similarly, in *The Statistical Breviary* (1801), Playfair 'broke free of analogies to the physical world and drew graphics as designs-in-themsleves' (Tufte, 2004, p.44).

Florence Nightingale used similar kinds of information graphics to help persuade Queen Victoria to improve conditions in military hospitals. Adapting Playfair's pie chart, Nightingale is credited with developing a form of diagram combining both bar charts and pie charts known as a polar area diagram, or otherwise known as the Nightingale rose or coxcomb diagram. Equivalent to a modern circular histogram, Nightingale's diagrams provide the visual recording of various statistics, pertinent to the conditions of medical care during the Crimean War (see Figure 8.9). Nightingale is described a true 'pioneer in the uses of social statistics and in their graphical representation' (Cohen 1984, p.128); indeed she was elected the first female member of the Royal Statistical Society (and later as honorary member of the American Statistical Association). Her work can be understood within the context of broader developments in statistical analysis during the nineteenth century, which saw the advance of new social sciences such as experimental psychology and sociology; along with more sophisticated and extensive state record-keeping; and the use of statistical reasoning and probability in the physical sciences.

Today, the widespread use of spreadsheets and statistical software has made the creation of statistical graphics straightforward and indeed has enabled more complex modelling. In many cases now the process of visual statistical representation is automatic with a computer able to generate a variety of graphical styles and modes. One domain in which this is very evident is corporate business, where it is apparent the mathematics of statistical design is increasingly less of a concern than the 'creative' (and even seductive) use of graphics and informational templates. The following entry on the use of images by corporate managers describes a shift from images used to convey information, to images used to *express* ideas.

IMAGE MANAGEMENT

MIMEI ITO

Corporate managers invest a lot of time and resources into creating visual images. Typically, these images are used in presentation slides or printed materials for their customers, business partners, and internally for communications amongst staff. Visual representations used in business presentations typically take the form of graphs, charts, tables, and diagrams. Business images are 'designed' to represent data and information in a clear and concise manner. Handbooks of the 1950s and 1960s offered advice to managers in how to make best use of graphics to represent information in an unbiased, precise and clear manner. Today, computer software provide ready-made templates and contemporary guidebooks focus on how to create 'powerful' and effective visual presentations.

Arguably, what is visualized today is less quantitative data or information, but rather ideas. The notion of 'ideas' in this context implies a body of powerful narratives that solicit empathy and excitement among business professionals. Drawing on Daniel Pink's (2006) account of left-brain and right-brain thinking within the field of management, Garr Reynolds' *Presentation Zen* (2008), a popular guidebook on business presentation, argues that 'the best presentations of our generation will be created by professionals – engineers as well as CEOs and "creatives" – who have strong "whole mind" aptitudes and talents' (Reynolds, 2008, p.19). Drawing on these quasi-scientific narratives, managers today are under pressure to create presentation materials which are not only logically consistent and accurate (left-brain thinking), but also creative and affective (right-brain thinking).

The trend is for business presentations to focus on abstract drawings and diagrams rather than quantitative data graphs and charts. A good example is a 2×2 matrix for product marketing analysis invented by the Boston Consulting Group (BCG) in the late 1960s (Figure 8.10). The diagram classifies products or businesses into four quadrants according to each product's/business's current market share and future growth possibility, so that managers can analyze the business value of products and business units from the perspective of an investment portfolio. The BCG diagram has been so popular that numerous different versions appear in business literature, corporate brochures, and management textbooks (Lowy and Hood, 2004). The 2×2 matrix is now one of the most widely used forms of diagram in contemporary business practice.

Another well-known example is a diagram created in the late 1970s by Michael Porter, an influential professor of business at Harvard, which he used to explain a model of corporate strategy. The diagram was originally printed in *Harvard Business Review* (Porter, 1979), and later revised to appear in Porter's highly influential book *Competitive Strategy* (1980). This revised version has gained wide currency in management literature and business presentations (and its template is available in well-known slide presentation software). These diagrams – along with many such illustrations used in business – are designed to explain specific ideas and processes within management. Yet, arguably, they are not mere diagrammatic illustrations, but in fact 'icons' of specific management models and techniques. A student of image studies might be interested to explore why a particular design of a management diagram is considered to be more powerful and influential compared to other designs. For example, we could ask why Porter's diagram was revised for his 1980 book, and further, we could consider the reasons why it has been the revised version that gained currency in wider management discourse. In part, this may be due to the wider circulation

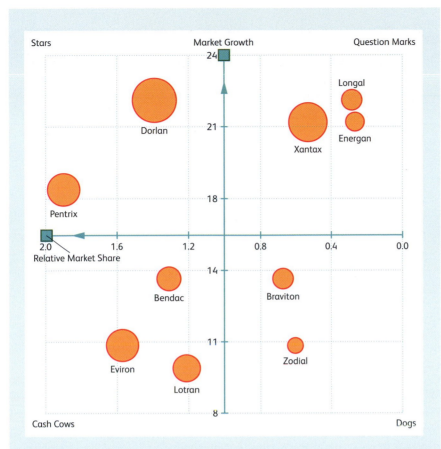

FIGURE 8.10 The Boston Consulting Group Matrix. The 2 × 2 matrix is based on a Carroll diagram, or Lewis Carroll Square (named after the author of the *Alice* stories, who was also a scholar of mathematics). Carroll diagrams are taught in schools, and are used extensively outside the field of education, since they are a neat way of categorizing and comparing between information. They appear in a range of forms, but typically compare between two sets of variables to make a four-way grid. The BCG matrix is used to rank business units (or products) on the basis of the two variables of relative market share and growth rate. Four terms are used: Cash Cows (high market share, slow growth); Dogs (low market share, slow growth); Question Marks (low market share, rapid growth); and Stars (high market share, rapid growth). It is common to find versions of the diagram with icons for these terms, but what is significant about the BCG Matrix is its inclusion of scale and the visualization of scale. As the example shows, the matrix visualizes the relative market share of a portfolio of products versus the growth of their market. Measurements are visualized with squares of equal scaling. The items placed on the grid use relative distances to indicate placement relative to market share/growth and are visualized with circles that differ in size by their sales volume. Criticisms are made of the matrix for the way it compartmentalizes the market and its processes. Also, in this case, it could be argued we attribute more importance to one element over another due to the inclusion of the visualization of sales volume (with the use of different sized circles).

of his book, but equally we could consider how its graphic representation lends itself to wider dissemination and appropriation.

The recent obsession to visualize ideas in management and to demonstrate creativity reflects one aspect of the emergence of a new form of corporate capitalism. Nigel Thrift (2005, p.44) refers to 'the rise of soft capitalism', in which 'management is no longer seen as a science' but as an 'art form'. Similarly, Boltanski and Chiapello's (2005) analysis of the 'new spirit of capitalism' points out how managers must now possess and demonstrate '*intuition* and *talent* (in the sense in which we speak of an artist's talent)' (p.113). Thus, we can critique a shift from presenting information to that of presenting ideas (in an infor-mational style), as a shift toward a specific form of intellectual and/or creative labour. As such, visualization within management discourse and practices can be understood not so much as the visualizing of information, but the bringing to the fore (even the extraction) of ideas 'located' in the brain of the manager. The myth constructed within the modern corporate context is that the 'art' of presentational graphics is to communicate an inner reservoir of 'tacit knowledge'.

Infographics

Whilst informational graphics have a history dating back at least to the work of Playfair and others in the late 1700s, the combined phenomena today of networked computing, high-quality print processes and access to vast amounts of data has given rise to a popular trend in creating and disseminating information graphics or **infographics**. Infographics are defined as graphic visual representations of infor-mation, data or knowledge. Elements of the aforementioned business graphics fit under this label. Similar techniques in visualizing and scaling information as found in the BCG matrix, for example, are frequently adopted in contemporary info-graphics.

The infographic is essentially what Playfair called a statistical graphic or informa-tional image, however, there are some distinctive features. Infographics have entered into mainstream culture. They appear regularly in newspapers and magazines, but also they proliferate on the Internet as both an amateur and professional pursuit. Various websites exist solely dedicated to the design, dissemination and critique of infographics. Significant connection can be made with the ideas underpinning social media and freedom of information. Various data sets are now available in raw form on official government statistical websites, as well as corporate and third sector homepages. Media outlets also provide access to data; newspapers such as the *Guardian* release raw data for people to scrutinize for themselves, and the term 'data journalism' has gained real currency. Simon Rogers, editor of the *Guardian* Datastore and Datablog remarks how data was once the preserve of books, of 'very expensive books where graphics are referred to as "figures"', whereas now, he goes on to say, 'we have spreadsheets and files formatted for computers. Which means we can make the computers ask the questions' (Rogers, 2011). There are bigger datasets available on more specific issues, opening up whole new dimensions for journalism.

Where previously data journalism might have required painstaking work with a single dataset, and/or weeks of investigative data management, there has arisen 'a new short-form of data journalism, which is about swiftly finding the key data, analysing it and guiding readers through it while the story is still in the news' (Rogers, 2011). Of course, along with open access to data, there is also greater access to the means of production, with various free tools available for making infographics, such as Google's 'Fusion Tables' and 'Charts Tool', IBM's 'Many Eyes' and the Timetric Network for open access datasets. The social media wesbite visual.ly claims to be 'the world's largest community for sharing infographics and data visualizations'. Just as blog platforms have made it possible for anyone to establish their own website without any prior knowledge of web design, online tool developers such as visual.ly enable individuals to create professional quality designs with their own data.

However, while open access remains an important facet of infographics, 'good design' is of central importance. A principle that frequently unites the design of infographics is the idea that information can be 'beautiful'. In his book *Information is Beautiful* (2009), David McCandless describes us as 'all visual now' as we look for and absorb information from a wide range of sources: 'We're steeped in [information]', he writes, 'Maybe even lost in it. So perhaps what we need are well-designed, colourful and – hopefully – useful charts to help us navigate' (2009, p.6). *Beautiful Data* (Segaran and Hammerbacher, 2009) – written by data practitioners – refers throughout to the idea of 'elegance' in data collection and visualizations. Yet what is meant here by 'beauty' and 'elegance'? As noted in the preceding chapter, beauty is often evoked in the context of science imaging, which can be problematic in equating aesthetic judgements with scientific data. Design practices which surround the production, distribution and use of infographics reveals a lot more behind the rhetoric of 'information is beautiful' then simply beauty. Noah Iliinsky (2010, p.1) suggests with infographics 'beauty can be considered to have four key elements, of which aesthetic judgment is only one. For a visual to qualify as beautiful, it must be aesthetically pleasing, yes, but it must also be *novel*, *informative*, and *efficient*.'

Infographics seek to offer novel ways of presenting information. There is seemingly always room for 'a fresh look at the data or a format that gives readers a spark of excitement and results in a new level of understanding' (Iliinsky, 2010, p.1). Yet, even in seeking to be novel and open up information in new ways, accuracy and clarity of information itself lies at the heart of any 'good' design; which in turn relates to the importance of efficiency:

> 'A beautiful visualization has a clear goal, a message, or a particular perspective on the information that it is designed to convey. Access to this information should be as straightforward as possible, without sacrificing any necessary, relevant complexity. [. . .] Irrelevant data is the same thing as noise.'
>
> (Iliinsky, 2010, p.2)

Tufte uses the term 'chartjunk' to refer to unnecessary elements, or noise, of an infographic. There are varieties of chartjunk, but he cites three as being widespread. *Unintentional optical art* occurs where statistical graphics are drawn with unnecessary patterns, which can interact with the 'physiological tremor of the eye to produce the distracting appearance of vibration and movement' (Tufte, 2004, p.107). The use of dark *grid lines* is also described as chartjunk. Whilst important for the initial plotting of data, 'the grid should usually be muted or completely suppressed so that its presence is only implicit – lest it compete with the data' (Tufte, 2004, p.112). Finally, Tufte refers to *self-promoting graphics*, which occurs, he suggests, '[w]hen a graphic is taken over by decorative forms or computer debris, when the data measures and structures become Design Elements, when the overall design purveys Graphical Style rather than quantitative information' (p.116). In this vein, many contemporary infographics could be criticized for being overly inventive with 'graphics'.

Tufte (2004, pp.53–77) refers to the idea of 'graphic integrity', whereby a graphic does not distort if the visual representation of the data is consistent with the numerical representation. One of the difficulties is pinning down what accuracy means in this context – can we, for example, simply measure the physical surface of a graphic and check against the source data? Or do we also need to take into account 'perceived visual effect'? As we saw with Hoffman's example of two-dimensional rendering of a ripple in the previous chapter, optical effects can lead us to 'see' what is not in fact presented before us. The problem is well observed in cartography. **Tissot's indicatrix** is an important mathematical contrivance demonstrated by French mathematician, Nicolas Auguste Tissot (in the late 1800s), which refers to the distortions that arises from projecting the earth's spherical dimensions upon a single-plane map.

One way to tackle the problem of visualizing information – particularly numerical data – is to provide all source data alongside a graphic (to allow for cross-checking), but this would seem to defeat the purpose. Tufte suggests we at least need to look towards uniformity in methods for deriving graphics from data. As explained in the following extract, for example, Tufte proscribes a set formula to detect what he calls the potential 'Lie Factor' in any given graphic.

LIE FACTOR

EDWARD R. TUFTE

$$\text{Lie Factor} = \frac{\text{size of effect shown in graphic}}{\text{size of effect in data}}$$

If the Lie Factor is equal to one, then the graphic might be doing a reasonable job of accurately representing the underlying numbers. Lie Factors greater than

FIGURE 8.11
Lie Factor formula,
Edward R. Tufte.

FIGURES
8.12–8.14
Lie Factor formula,
Edward R. Tufte.

1.05 or less than .95 indicate substantial distortion, far beyond minor inaccuracies in plotting.

[. . .]

[Tufte provides an extreme example of a graphic used in a *New York Times* article from the 1970s.] [The] newspaper reported that the U.S. Congress and the Department of Transportation had set a series of fuel economy standards to be met by automobile manufacturers, beginning with 18 miles per gallon in 1978 and moving in steps to 27.5 by 1985, an increase of 53 percent:

$$\frac{27.5 - 18.0}{18.0} \times 100 = 53\%$$

These standards and the dates for their attainment were shown [in a seemingly simple diagram that plotted time (by year) against fuel consumption (in miles per gallon). The diagram used the design of a road, in perspective, to give the basic chart more interest. The two outer lines of the road meet at a point on the horizon to suggest perspective. Running horizontally, across the 'road', are a series of lines which indicate on the left the year (from 1978 to 1985), and on the right the miles per gallon in the given year. To complement the sense of perspective, the horizontal lines are shorter and spaced closer together the further they reach into the distance. The effect is that data at the 'front' of the diagram appears bigger and more prominent than the data represented further back in time. Crucially, the line representing 18 miles per gallon in 1978 is only 0.6 inches long, while the line representing 27.5 miles per gallon in 1985 is 5.3 inches long. Although the diagram is relatively small as it appears in the newspaper, in percentage terms the magnitude of the change from 1978 to 1985, as shown by the relative lengths of the two lines, can be calculated as follows:]

$$\frac{5.3 - 0.6}{0.6} \times 100 = 783\%$$

Thus the numerical change of 53 percent is presented by some lines that changed 783 percent, yielding

$$\text{Lie Factor} = \frac{783}{53} = 14.8$$

which is too big.

(Tufte, 2004, pp.57–58)

It is clear, the idea of 'beautiful visualizations' relates strongly to the information itself and an ability to 'reflect the qualities of the data that they represent, explicitly revealing properties and relationships inherent and implicit in the source data. As these properties and relationships become available to the reader, they bring new knowledge, insight, and enjoyment' (Iliinsky, 2010, p.3). One of the best ways to understand the rhetoric around the idea of information being 'beautiful' is to look at well-known informational design 'classics'. Iliinsky refers to two examples. One is Harry Beck's map of the London Underground (as discussed in Chapter 2, with regards to the ecology of images). While today the map has had many additions and has become more complicated, at its core is an important principle: it is not a geographical map. Having been trained in drafting electrical circuit maps (which draw on specific conventions, rather than reflect a true, physical layout), Beck realized a map of an underground transit system was similarly more useful in the form of an abstract visual design. Indeed, 'once you're in the system, what matters most is your logical relationship to the rest of the subway system' (Iliinsky, 2010, p.5). The London Underground map is successful because it strips away irrelevant information. It responds perfectly to two important requirements: the *intended meaning* and the *context of use* (Iliinsky, 2010, p.2); in this case to show how to get from A to B (the intended meaning) whilst travelling underground (context of use).

Another excellent example of visualization is Mendeleev's periodic table, which we might consider as a precursor to infographics. In this case the idea of aesthetic beauty carries very little relevance, yet, as Iliinsky (2010, pp.3–4) argues, the table is novel in that it provided a visual solution to the problem of articulating the relationship between chemical elements. It is also highly informative and generally very efficient as a design. In part, Iliinsky writes, 'the efficacy and success of the periodic table were achieved with the absolute minimum of graphical treatment; in fact, the earliest versions were text-only and could be generated on a typewriter' (p.4). What is powerful about Mendeleev's design is how it *reveals* the 'periodic', repeating properties of the elements. Thus, 'the table allows quick access to an understanding of the properties of a given element at a glance' (p.3). But more important still, and arguably *the* reason it has proved to be such a powerful informational graphic, is that its design also allowed 'very accurate predications of undiscovered elements, based on the gaps it contains' (p.3). In other words, the periodic table is not simply an informational graphic, but a contemplative, exploratory one too.

TASK

D.I.Y. Infographics

Select an existing infographic. Try to deconstruct it. Can you locate the original dataset? What visualization techniques have been used? How would it rate according to Tufte's 'Lie Factor'?

After close analysis of your chosen infographic, try to reconstruct it for yourself, with a view to offering a critique of the original. What story would you like to tell about the data? What imagery would you draw on to construct an infographic and what techniques can you use to help show information? David McCandless' *Information is Beautiful* (2009), Julie Steele and Noah Iliinsky's *Beautiful Visualization* (2010), and Carolyn Knight and Jessica Glaser's *Diagrams* (2009) are useful sourcebooks on data visualization. For a practical guide to constructing an infographic see Matthias Shapiro's (2010) article on the importance of storytelling in informational visualization. In addition, Ben Fry's *Visualizing Data* (2008) and Segaran and Hammerbacher's *Beautiful Data* (2009) offer expert, technical advice on data visualization.

Thinking with images

This chapter has been looking at how images, particularly diagrams, help us to organize and comprehend ideas and information. However, we also consider the *act* of image-making in itself as a means to understanding. The editor of *Current Biology*, Florian Maderspacher, suggests: 'Images may help us think, especially when our imagination fails us. Sometimes an image can stimulate us to think in a new, unanticipated direction' (2006, p.R476). In a richly illustrated study, *Darwins Korallen* (2005), art historian Horst Bredekamp makes a case for how Charles Darwin used images to help devise his theory of evolution. In Darwin's *Origin of the Species* there is just one illustration, a schematic diagram (much like a geological diagram) to show how species change, divide up or remain the same over thousands of years. It is apparent from Bredekamp's account that Darwin considered the diagram central to his theory.

Typically, the diagram is associated with the design of a tree. As Maderspacher points out: 'It has become commonplace to talk about trees and branches when referring to patterns of evolutionary descent; after all, trees have been used for ages to depict the genealogies of families' (2006, p.R476). But a tree has features that are inherently at odds with Darwin's theory. They generally grow in one direction and possess a hierarchical structure. More importantly, as a metaphor, the tree fails to account for dead, fossil species, which Darwin considered important to an overall model of evolution. In his notebooks, Darwin wrote: 'The tree of life should perhaps be called the coral of life' (cited in Maderspracher, 2006, p.R476). Bredekamp traces the importance of coral to Darwin's theories, even linking it to a physical object Darwin owned, 'a brownish, bushy structure which he thought was a coral . . . [though] it is now known to be an alga' (Maderspracher, 2006, p.R477). Darwin's early sketches of evolutionary relationships hold real insights into how Darwin's thinking developed:

'In his initial, rather clumsy sketches of species formation . . . Darwin drew branched, busy structures, which were punctate towards the bottom. As inconspicuous as this may seem, it marks, according to Bredekamp, an important leap in thinking, namely that dead forms – fossils – have to be part of the picture of species formation. Bredekamp ascribes this transition in thinking to the use of the coral as a template, whose calcified dead basal branches could be seen as representing the dead fossils compared to living species. For this, the coral would be better suited than the tree, of which all parts are still alive.'

(Maderspracher, 2006, p.R477)

The importance of image-making for Darwin, in literally developing his thoughts, is encapsulated by one page of his notebooks which famously is headed with the words 'I think', followed by a diagram. The branches of the diagram (going out at all sides) would seem again to suggest the design of a coral rather than a tree. Maderspracher suggests Bredekamp might place too much importance on Darwin's own observations of coral. Instead she suggests Darwin's diagrams 'trace back to

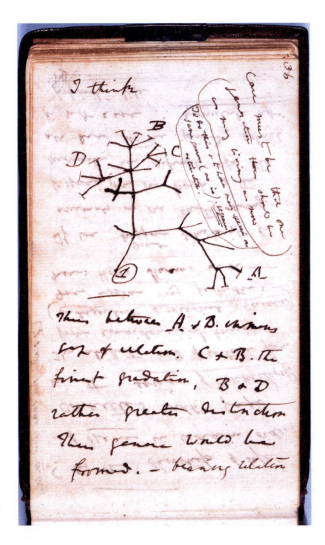

FIGURE 8.15

Charles Darwin, *First Notebook on Transmutation of Species* (1837). Reproduced by kind permission the syndics of Cambridge University Library.

previous visualizations' (2006, p.R477) – in effect noting a wider 'ecology' of illustrative materials. Nonetheless, she praises Bredekamp's book:

> 'The charm of the book lies in its illustrations. It draws attention to these early diagrams, which open a surprising and direct look into the shaping of evolutionary thought in general and of Darwin's idea in particular. Clumsy as his sketches may be, in retrospect, knowing what became of them, they are fascinating. Quite literally, they allow us to watch Darwin think.'
>
> (Maderspracher, 2006, p.R478)

Whilst Darwin's work proved to be of exceptional significance, his notebooks remind us how the simple act of sketching and even 'doodling' can help us think; with the image, as Maderspracher suggests, able to 'stimulate us to think in a new, unanticipated direction'. The benefits of sketching – or 'visual thinking' – has given rise to a new trend in corporate business, whereby artists are employed to attend meetings to produce what are referred to as '**sketchnotes**'. The following entry describes the process in a practical way – which is perhaps the most apt way to properly consider how images enable us to think about ideas and information.

SKETCHNOTES

CRAIGHTON BERMAN

(Adapted from Craighton Berman's 'Sketchnotes 101: Visual Thinking' and 'Sketchnotes 101: The Basics of Visual Note-Taking' for www.core77.com)

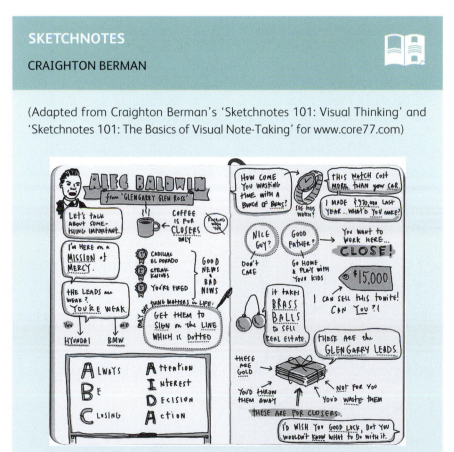

FIGURE 8.16
Sketchnotes ©
Craighton Berman.

Sketchnotes are visual notes that are drawn in real time. [. . .] This form of rapid visualization forces you to listen to a lecture or presentation, synthesize what's being expressed, and visualize a composition that captures the idea – all in real time.

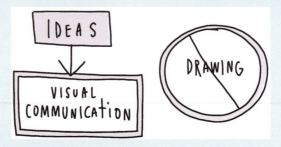

FIGURE 8.17 Ideas to Visual Communication © Craighton Berman.

Instead of recording what's being said verbatim, good sketchnotes capture the meaningful bits as text and drawings. Better sketchnotes use composition and hierarchy to give structure to the content, and bring clarity to the overall narrative of the lecture. The best sketchnotes express a unique personal style and add editorial comments on the content—entertaining and informing all at once.

Before the presentation begins, you may choose to plan a little bit and get the page set up. Take this time to look up the person's name and title, and get it on the page spelled right and in a little more 'designed' manner (typography, a cartooned portrait, etc.). Also worth noting is the time allotted for the lecture. If it's an hour, you can mentally subdivide your sketchbook spread into quarters, and pace your drawing if you want to keep the lecture contained.

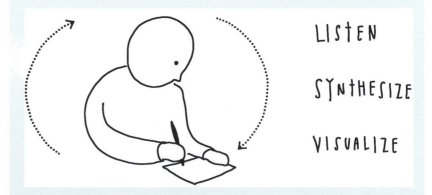

FIGURE 8.18 Listen, Synthesize, Visualize © Craighton Berman.

Once the lecture begins you'll need to begin the process of listening, synthesizing, and visualizing. [. . .] Use the following elements to help build your sketchnotes:

Text: Recording the verbal is quick, direct, and clear and is usually your primary sketchnoting tool. Capture the meaningful quotes and key points, and avoid trying to summarize everything. Typographic treatments can be used to give emphasis to major ideas, and can add interest to large blocks of text. Avoid making lists or outlines and use the spatial properties of the page to your advantage by 'chunking' information. Some ways to force yourself to work spatially might be starting in the middle and working outwards or working in columns for a panel discussion.

Containers: Simply enclosing words in shapes brings emphasis and structure to an otherwise wild page. Some of the more common containers include (but are not limited to): quote bubbles, boxes, circles and thought clouds.

Connectors: Connect ideas and pieces of stories with arrows and lines. A basic chain of thoughts can scintillate around the page and still be clear if they are linked with a simple set of connectors.

Frameworks: Some presenters will have a very obvious structure to their presentation, but often times the insights may benefit from your own synthesis into an understandable underlying structure or model. Common frameworks include 2 × 2s, Venn diagrams, and continuums.

Icons: – Don't forget to put the 'sketch' in sketchnotes. Strive to create 'icons' for objects and concepts: distill reality into a simple drawing that represents the idea as simply as possible and move on.

TASK

Get Sketching!

Following Craighton Berman's 'lesson' in sketchnotes, try to make your own sketchnotes the next time you attend a lecture or talk. You might want to practise before doing the real thing, in which case you can find plenty of lectures on the Internet. Search iTunes U, YouTube or the TED Talks archives, among many other sources. Once you have had a go at making your own sketchnotes, consider what it felt like and whether the process and/or the end result has yielded something different than if you had made regular text-based notes. How would you describe those differences?

Summary

At the very start of this book, in Chapter 1, a critique of semiotics was presented. An important principle was established that images should not be overwritten by a linguistic framework of analysis. This chapter begins with reference to Kress and van Leeuwen's notion of a semiotic landscape, which they suggest presents a multimodal experience. As previously discussed in Chapter 3, with respect to the Pictorial Turn, the semiotic landscape takes account of a shift in culture towards the visual, which opens up ways of thinking about communication, and, in the case of this chapter, the transmission of information. The chapter is also prefaced with a brief account of the philosopher Nelson Goodman's distinction between text and image, along with a third term, notation, which can be said to underline all subsequent reflections on image and information. Thus, consideration is made of what occurs in the reporting of topics such as climate change, which, given the timescales and magnitudes involved, can often go beyond normal levels of intuition, and even comprehension (to use Elkins' terms, discussed in Chapter 7). DiFrancesco's account of reporting on climate change in the Canadian press reveals word and image at odds in how they present information. In this case, word engages in quite complex issues, while the images involved tend to pull a story towards party politics and biography.

The second half of the chapter pays close attention to methods of presenting information and data, highlighting a growing trend for 'expressing' information – this is found for example with contemporary professional presentational styles (as in Ito's account of corporate management) and the development of a new genre of infographics (and sketchnotes), which can be seen to be underpinned by a community of designers passionate about visualizing data. The chapter has not sought to offer an explicit political, ideological critique, but rather give space to consider how images and information come together in conceptual and perceptual ways. After engaging in a more hands-on experience of the relationship between image and information, we can then reflect again on the 'semiotic landscape' as a social, political concern; and so ask what and how information is being presented, for whom, and for what reason.

Further reading

Bergström, Bo (2008) *Essentials of Visual Communication*. London: Laurence King Publishing.

Bertin, Jacques (2011) *Semiology of Graphics: Diagrams, Networks, Maps*, trans. by William J. Berg. Redlands, California: Esri Press.

Cleveland, William S. (1993) *Visualizing Data*. New Jersey: Hobart Press.

Few, Stephen (2009) *Now You See It: Simple Visualization Techniques for Quantitative Analysis*. Oakland: Analytics Press.

Floch, Jean-Marie (2000) *Visual Identities*. London: Continuum.

Fry, Ben (2008) *Visualizing Data*. Sebastopol: O'Reilly.

Knight, Carolyn and Glaser, Jessica (2009) *Diagrams: Innovative Solutions for Graphic Designers*. Mies: RotorVision.

Kress, Gunther (2010) *Multimodality: A Social Semiotic Approach to Contemporary Communication*. London: Routledge.

Kress, Gunther and van Leeuwen, Theo (2006) *Reading Images: The Grammar of Visual Design*. Second Edition. London: Routledge.

Lima, Manuel (2011) *Visual Complexity: Mapping Patterns of Information*. New York: Princeton Architectural Press.

McCandless, David (2009) *Information is Beautiful*. London: Collins.

Meyer, Eric K. (1997) *Designing Infographics: Theory, Creative Techniques and Practical Solutions*. Indianapolis: Hayden Books.

Segaran, Toby and Hammerbacher, Jeff (eds) (2009) *Beautiful Data: The Stories Behind Elegant Data Solutions*. Sebastopol: O'Reilly.

Spence, Robert (2001) *Information Visualization*. London: Addison-Wesley.

Steele, Julie and Iliinsky, Noah (eds) (2010) *Beautiful Visualization: Looking at Data Through the Eyes of Experts*. Sebastopol: O'Reilly.

Steele, Julie and Iliinsky, Noah (2011) *Designing Data Visualizations*. Beijing: O'Reilly.

Tufte, Edward R. (1990) *Envisioning Information*. Connecticut: Graphics Press.

Tufte, Edward R. (1997) *Visual Explanations: Images and Quantities, Evidence and Narrative*. Connecticut: Graphics Press.

Tufte, Edward R. (2004) *The Visual Display of Quantitative Information*. Second Edition. Connecticut: Graphics Press.

Yau, Nathan (2011) *Visualize This: The Flowing Data Guide to Design, Visualization, and Statistics*. Hoboken, N.J.: Wiley.

9 Afterword: Image studies in the making . . .

In the 1990s, when visual culture was beginning to gain currency as a field of study, the art theory journal *October* published responses to a questionnaire on the subject. Many echoed the journal's provocative statement that visual studies was going 'to produce subjects for the next stage of globlized capital' (*October* No.77, 1996, p.25). The fear had been that up and coming generations would be prone to a diminished critical understanding of images, and worse would likely develop an ever-greater appetite for their *consumption*. It was an unfortunate perspective, and one that does not sit well with many in the field, who consider visual culture to be rooted in political and cultural critique. Yet, it reveals a persistent tension that exists *between* theoretical and practical pursuits of the image.

The underlying premise of this book is that to better understand images and visual culture we need to *bridge between* theory and practice; to think critically about images and image practices, but also – and at the same time – to make images, or engage with image-makers and image-making processes. As Jon Simons notes: 'When we become literate in a language, we learn to write as well as read. Competence in political imagery would thus demand the ability to make as well as interpret political images, just as science students learn to make as well as interpret images that represent data' (Simons, 2008, p.86). However, it is important to stress, learning about what it means to *make* as well as *read* images need not mean the same as learning to make (and/or consume) image 'products'. In this book, the bridging of theory and practice is intended as an experimental and reflective engagement with images and image-making – ultimately with the view to understanding images in context of their wide-ranging and complex ecologies.

The book has sought to establish outlining features of what we can call *image studies*. Three important, interconnecting considerations have been:

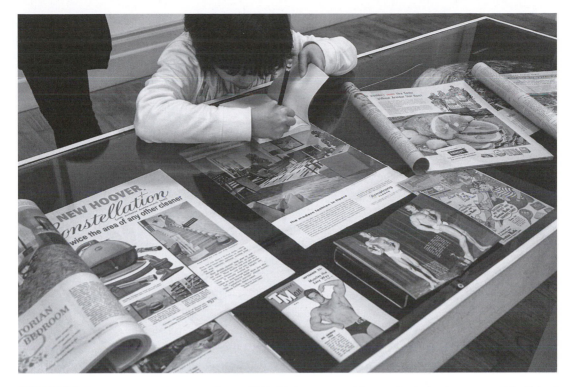

FIGURE 9.1 *This is Tomorrow,* Whitechapel Gallery, 2011. Display case containing sample of advertisements used for Richard Hamilton's *Just what is it that makes today's homes so different, so appealing?* 1956. Collection of John-Paul Stonard. Courtesy of Whitechapel Gallery.

■ *W.J.T. Mitchell's account of a 'pictorial turn' (covered in Chapter 3), and – by way of method – an expanded 'iconology',* or the study of images across media, domains and practices. 'Images, from an iconological standpoint', writes Mitchell, 'are both verbal and visual entities, both metaphors and graphic symbols. They are, at one and the same time, concepts, objects, pictures, and symbolic forms' (Mitchell, 2011, p.xvii).

■ *The need to explore a much wider set of image domains and ecologies of the image.* James Elkins' (1999; 2007) work is exemplary in thinking across domains, but also crucially with a desire to understand different domains in their own terms. This is a point raised explicitly in the chapter on scientific imaging. In order to bridge between theory and practice and across domains it is vital we understand different practices and perspectives at a deep level, before necessarily seeking out connections. It is also important to examine the full 'life' of an image – to understand how an image resonates within a complex set of contexts, processes and uses.

■ *The need, not just to be astute scholars of the image, but equally to be 'astute citizens'* (Simons, 2008, p.78). For Simons, this raises the more fundamental question of how we can teach politically in contemporary image society. 'Politics will have to come before pedagogy', he writes, 'or, rather, only a political pedagogy can bring the sort of university in which dream programs for visual literacy or image studies can flourish' (Simons, 2008, p.89).

There is no one single definition of image studies, and doubtless it will never be a distinct college program. In fact, it works against the aims of image studies to contain it as a single, bounded field of study. Nevertheless, we can hopefully look forward to a period of greater shared interest in the critical engagement with the image across *all* domains.

In lieu of a conclusion, we might usefully consider image studies to be still *in the making*. Firstly, *in the making* in that its true prospects lie in the bridging between theory and practice. We need to *make* images, as much as think about them, to gain insight into what images are and what they yield. But equally, image studies is *in the making* because arguably we have yet to fully harness the insights gained from a wide range of contemporary scholarship and interdisciplinary dialogue. Each of the chapters in this book have sought to bring to the fore theoretical exchanges and a diverse set of image domains and practices. Throughout, various connections and points of tension have been brought into focus, but it is not possible, nor necessarily desirable, to present in one book alone a fully comprehensive account of the image. Hopefully, this book can prompt (and aid) you to go further and develop your *own* approach to image studies. If so, it will have achieved its aim.

References

NB. *Where references appear in* **bold**, *a relevant extract is available in Manghani et al. (eds)* Images: A Reader *(Sage, 2006). The bibliographic details of the extract are provided in square brackets immediately following the entry of the original source.*

Ades, Dawn (1986) *Photomontage*. London: Thames and Hudson.

Agee, James and Evans, Walker (2006) *Let Us Now Praise Famous Men*. London: Penguin.

Allen, Graham (2003) *Roland Barthes*. London: Routledge.

Alloula, Malek (1986) *The Colonial Harem*. Minneapolis: University of Minnesota Press.

Alpers, Svetlana (1983) 'Interpretation without Representation, or, the Viewing of *Las Meninas*'. *Representations*, Vol.1, No.1, pp.30–42. [Extract available: Manghani *et al.* (eds) *Images: A Reader* (Sage, 2006), pp.94–98.]

Alphen, Ernst van (2008) 'Looking at Drawing: Theoretical Distinctions and their Usefulness' in Garner, Steve (ed.) *Writing on Drawing: Essays on Drawing Practice and Research*. Bristol: Intellect, pp.59–70.

Aristotle (1965) 'The Origins and Development of Poetry' from *On the Art of Poetry*, in *Classical Literary Criticism*, trans. T.S. Dorsch. London: Penguin Books, p.35. [Extract available: Manghani *et al.* (eds) *Images: A Reader* (Sage, 2006), pp.31–32.]

Armstrong, Carol (1996) 'Response to Visual Culture Questionnaire'. *October*, 77 (Summer), pp.27–28.

Bal, Mieke (1991) *Reading 'Rembrandt': Beyond the Word-Image Opposition*. Cambridge: Cambridge University Press. [Extract available: Manghani *et al.* (eds) *Images: A Reader* (Sage, 2006), pp.115–119.]

Bal, Mieke (1996) 'Semiotic Elements in Academic Practices'. *Critical Inquiry,* Vol.22, No.3, pp.573–589.

Bal, Mieke (2003) 'Visual essentialism and the Object of Visual Culture'. *Journal of Visual Culture*, Vol.2, No.5, pp.5–32.

Bal, Mieke and Bryson, Norman (1991) 'Semiotics and Art History'. *Art Bulletin*, Vol.73, pp.174–208.

Bann, Stephen (1970) *Experimental Painting: Construction, Abstraction, Destruction, Reduction*. London: Studio Vista.

Barthes, Roland (1977) *Image Music Text*, trans. by Stephen Heath. London: Fontana.

Barthes, Roland (1981) *Camera Lucida: Reflections on Photography*, trans. by Richard Howard. New York: Hall and Wang.

Barthes, Roland (1985a) *The Grain of the Voice: Interviews 1962–1980,* trans. by Linda Coverdale. London: Jonathan Cape.

Barthes, Roland (1985b) *The Responsibility of Forms: Critical Essays on Music, Art, and Representation*, trans. by Richard Howard. New York: Hill and Wang.

Barthes, Roland (1989) *The Rustle of Language*, trans. by Richard Howard. Berkeley: University of California Press.

Barthes, Roland (1994 [1975]) *Roland Barthes*, trans. by Richard Howard. Los Angeles: University of California Press.

Barthes, Roland (2000) 'Inaugural Lecture, Collège de France' in Susan Sontag (ed.) *A Barthes Reader*. London: Vintage, pp.457–478.

Barthes, Roland (2009) *Mythologies* (rev. ed., 2009), trans. by Annette Lavers. London: Vintage.

Baudrillard, Jean (1994) *Simulacra and Simulation*, trans. by Sheila Faria Glaser. Ann Arbor: The University of Michigan Press. [Extract available: Manghani *et al.* (eds) *Images: A Reader* (Sage, 2006), pp.70–74.]

Baudrillard, Jean (1995) *The Gulf War Did Not Take Place*. Bloomington: Indiana University Press.

Belting, Hans (2005) 'Image, Medium, Body: A New Approach to Iconology'. *Critical Inquiry*, Vol.31, pp.302–319.

Benjamin, Walter (1992) 'The Work of Art in the Age of Mechanical Reproduction' in *Illuminations,* trans. by Harry Zohn. London: Fontana Press, pp.211–244.

Benjamin, Walter (1997) 'A Small History of Photography' in *One Way Street*, trans. by Edmund Jephcott and Kingsley Shorter. London: Verso, pp.240–257.

Benjamin, Walter (2004a) 'Painting, or Signs and Marks' in *Selected Writings, Volume 1, 1913–1926*, ed. by Marcus Bullock and Michael W. Jennings. Cambridge, Mass.: Harvard University Press, p.83–86.

Benjamin, Walter (2004b) 'Painting and the Graphic Arts' in *Selected Writings, Volume 1, 1913–1926*, ed. by Marcus Bullock and Michael W. Jennings. Cambridge, Mass.: Harvard University Press, p.82.

Benson, Keith R. (2000) 'The Emergence of Ecology From Natural History'. *Endeavour*, Vol.24, No.2, pp.59–62.

Berger, John (1972) *Ways of Seeing*. London: Penguin Books.

Berger, John (1997) 'Ways of Remembering' in Jessica Evans (ed.) *The Camerawork Essays: Context and Meaning in Photography*. London: Rivers Oram Press, pp.41–51. [Extract available: Manghani *et al.* (eds) *Images: A Reader* (Sage, 2006), pp.214–216.]

Berger, John (2005) *Berger on Drawing*, ed. by Jim Savage. Cork: Occasional Press.

Berger, John (2011) *Bento's Sketchbook*. London: Verso.

Berger, John and Mohr, Jean (2010) *A Seventh Man*. London: Verso.

Boehm, Gottfried and Mitchell, W.J.T. (2010) 'Pictorial versus Iconic Turn: Two Letters', in Neal Curtis (ed.) *The Pictorial Turn*. London: Routledge, pp.8–26.

Bohm-Duchen, Monica (2001) *The Private Life of a Masterpiece*. London: BBC.

Boltanski, L. and E. Chiapello (2005) *The New Spirit of Capitalism*, trans. by Gregory Elliott. London and New York: Verso.

Bolter, Jay David and Grusin, Richard (2000) *Remediation: Understanding New Media*. Cambridge, Mass.: MIT Press.

Bordo, Susan (1997) *Twillight Zones: The Hidden Life of Cultural Images from Plato to O.J.* Berkeley: University of California Press. [Extract available: Manghani *et al.* (eds) *Images: A Reader* (Sage, 2006), pp.78–81.]

Bredekamp, Horst (2005) *Darwins Korallen: Frühe Evolutionsmodelle und die Tradition der Naturgeschichte*. Berlin: Klaus Wagenbach Verlag.

Buck-Morss, Susan (1996) 'Response to Visual Culture Questionnaire'. *October*, 77 (Summer), pp.29–31. [Extract available: Manghani *et al.* (eds) *Images: A Reader* (Sage, 2006), pp.99–100.]

Buck-Morss, Susan (2000) *Dreamworld and Catastrophe: The Passing of Mass Utopia in East and West*. Cambridge, Mass.: MIT Press.

Byrne, David and Doyle, Aidan (2004) 'The Visual and the Verbal: The Interaction of Images and Discussion in Exploring Cultural Change' in Caroline Knowles and Paul Sweetman (eds) *Picturing the Social Landscape: Visual Methods and the Sociological Imagination*. London: Routledge, pp.166–177.

Calvet, Louis-Jean (1994) *Roland Barthes: A Biography*, trans. by Sarah Wykes. Cambridge: Polity Press.

Chaplin, Elizabeth (2004) 'My Visual Diary' in Caroline Knowles and Paul Sweetman (eds) *Picturing the Social Landscape: Visual Methods and the Sociological Imagination*. London: Routledge, pp.35–48.

Çiçekoglu, Feride (2003) 'A Pedagogy of Two Ways of Seeing: A Confrontation of "Word and Image" in *My Name Is Red*'. *Journal of Aesthetic Education*, Vol.37, No.3, pp.1–20.

Clark-Ibáñez, M. (2007) 'Inner-City Children in Sharper Focus: Sociology of Childhood and Photo Elicitation Interviews' in G.C. Stanczak (ed.) *Visual Research Methods: Image, Society, and Representation*. Los Angeles: Sage, pp.197–224.

Cohen, I. Bernard (1984) 'Florence Nightingale'. *Scientific American*, Vol.250, No.3, pp.128–137.

Crary, Jonathan (1988) 'Modernizing Vision' in Hal Foster (ed.) *Vision and Visuality*. Seattle: Bay Press, pp.29–44. [Extract available: Manghani *et al.* (eds) *Images: A Reader* (Sage, 2006), pp.270–274.]

Davis, Whitney (2011) *A General Theory of Visual Culture*. Princeton: Princeton University Press.

Debray, Régis (1996) *Media Manifestos: On the Technological Transmission of Cultural Forms,* trans. by Eric Rauth. London: Verso. [Extract available: Manghani *et al.* (eds) *Images: A Reader* (Sage, 2006), p.308.]

Derrida, Jacques (1993) *Memoirs of the Blind: The Self-Portrait and Other Ruins*, trans. by Pascale-Anne Brault and Michael Naas. Chicago: University of Chicago Press.

Didi-Huberman, Georges (2005) *Confronting Images: Questioning the Ends of a Certain History of Art*, trans. by John Goodman. Pennsylvania: Pennsylvania State University Press.

DiFrancesco, Darryn Anne and Young, Nathan (2011) 'Seeing Climate Change: The Visual Construction of Global Warming in Canadian National Print Media'. *Cultural Geographies*, Vol.18, No.4, pp.517–536.

Edgerton, Samuel Y. (2009) *The Mirror, the Window, and the Telescope: How Renaissance Linear Perspective Changed Our Vision of the Universe*. Ithaca: Cornell University Press.

Elkins, James (1995) 'Marks, Traces, *Traits*, Contours, *Orli*, and *Splendores*: Nonsemiotic Elements in Pictures'. *Critical Inquiry,* Vol.21, No.4, pp.822–860.

Elkins, James (1996) 'What Do We Want Pictures to Be? Reply to Mieke Bal'. *Critical Inquiry,* Vol.22, No.3, pp.590–602.

Elkins, James (1998) *On Pictures and the Words That Fail Them.* Cambridge: Cambridge University Press.

Elkins, James (1999) *The Domain of Images.* **Ithaca: Cornell University Press**. [Extract available: Manghani *et al.* (eds) *Images: A Reader* (Sage, 2006), pp.300–303.]

Elkins, James (2000a) *How to Use Your Eyes.* New York: Routledge.

Elkins, James (2000b) *What Painting Is: How to Think Abut Oil Painting, Using the Language of Alchemy.* New York: Routledge.

Elkins, James (2003) *Visual Studies: A Skeptical Introduction.* New York: Routledge.

Elkins, James (ed.) (2007) *Visual Practices Across the University.* München: Wilhelm Fink Verlag.

Elkins, James (2008) *Six Stories from the End of Representation: Images in Painting, Photography, Astronomy, Microscopy, Particle Physics, and Quantum Mechanics, 1980–2000.* Stanford: Stanford University Press.

Elkins, James (2011) *What Photography Is.* New York: Routledge.

Evans, Harold (1997) 'Introduction: The Enduring Vitality of the Still Photograph' in *Pictures on a Page: Photojournalism, Graphics and Picture Editing.* London: Pimlico [no page numbers].

Evans, Jessica (ed.) (1997) *The Camerawork Essays: Context and Meaning in Photography.* London: Rivers Oram Press.

Ford, Brian (1992) *Images of Science: A History of Scientific Illustration.* London: The British Library.

Foster, Hal (ed.) (1988) *Vision and Visuality.* Seattle: Bay Press.

Foster, Hal (2010) 'Citizen Hamilton' in Hal Foster and Alex Bacon (eds) *Richard Hamilton.* Cambridge, Mass.: MIT Press, pp.145–159.

Foucault, Michel (1974) *The Order of Things: An Archaeology of the Human Sciences.* London: Tavistock Publications.

Foucault, Michel (1977) *Discipline and Punish: The Birth of the Prison*, trans. by Alan Sheridan. London: Allen Lane.

Foucault, Michel (1983) *This is Not a Pipe*, **trans. by James Harkness. Los Angeles: University of California Press**. [Extract available: Mangani *et al.* (eds) *Images: A Reader* (Sage, 2006), pp.179–183.]

Frankel, Felice (2002) *Envisioning Science: The Design and Craft of the Science Image.* Cambridge, Mass.: MIT Press.

Frankel, Felice (2007) *On the Surface of Things: Images of the Extraordinary in Science.* Second Edition. Cambridge, Mass.: Harvard University Press.

Freedberg, David (1989) *The Power Of Images: Studies In The History And Theory Of Response.* Chicago: Chicago University Press.

Fry, Ben (2008) *Visualizing Data.* Sebastopol: O'Reilly.

Galison, Peter (1997) *Image and Logic: A Material Culture of Microphysics.* Chicago: University of Chicago Press.

Galison, Peter (2002) 'Images Scatter into Data, Data Gather into Images' in Bruno Latour and Peter Weibel (eds) *Iconoclash: Beyond the Image Wars in Science, Religion and Art.* **Cambridge, Mass.: MIT Press, pp.300–323**. [Extract available: Manghani *et al.* (eds) *Images: A Reader* (Sage, 2006), pp.236–241.]

Gilroy, Paul (2002) *There Ain't No Black in the Union Jack: The Cultural Politics of Race and Nation.* **London: Routledge**. [Extract available: Manghani *et al.* (eds) *Images: A Reader* (Sage, 2006), pp.76–78.]

Gombrich (2000 [1960]) *Art and Illusion: A Study in the Psychology of Pictorial Representation.* **Princeton: Princeton University Press**. [Extract available: Manghani *et al.* (eds) *Images: A Reader* (Sage, 2006), pp.91–94.]

Goodman, Nelson (1968) *Languages of Art: An Approach to a Theory of Symbols.* London: Oxford University Press.

Greenough, Sarah (2009) *Looking in: Robert Frank's The Americans.* Washington, D.C.: National Gallery of Art.

Hansen, Stine Kleis (n/d) 'Vivek Vilasni', HEART Herning Museum of Contemporary Art. www.heartmus.com/Vivek-Vilasini-3401.aspx (accessed 26 September 2011).

Hariman, Robert and Lucaites, John Louis (2007) *No Caption Needed: Iconic Photographs, Public Culture, and Liberal Democracy.* Chicago: Chicago University Press.

Hockney, David (2001) *Secret Knowledge: Rediscovering the Lost Techniques of the Old Masters.* **London: Thames and Hudson**. [Extract available: Manghani *et al.* (eds) *Images: A Reader* (Sage, 2006), pp.233–236.]

Hoffman, Donald D. (1998) *Visual Intelligence: How We Create What We See.* New York: W.W. Norton and Company.

Hoffmann, Roald (1995) *The Same and Not the Same.* New York: Columbia University Press.

Holliday, R. (2007) 'Performances, Confessions, and Identities: Using Video Diaries to Research Sexualities' in G.C. Stanczak (ed.) *Visual Research Methods: Image, Society, and Representation.* Los Angeles: Sage, pp.255–279.

Howells, Richard and Matson, Robert W. (eds) (2009) *Using Visual Evidence.* Maidenhead, Berks.: Open University Press/McGraw-Hill Education.

Hunt, J.D., Lomas, D., and Corris, M. (2010) *Art, Word and Image: Two Thousand Years of Visual/Textual Interaction.* London: Reaktion Books.

Ihde, Don (1998) *Expanding Hermeneutics, Visualism in Science.* **Evanston, Ill.: Northwestern University Press**. [Extract available: Manghani *et al.* (eds) *Images: A Reader* (Sage, 2006), pp.141–144.]

Iliinsky, Noah (2010) 'On Beauty' in Julie Steele and Noah Iliinsky (eds) *Beautiful Visualization: Looking at Data Through the Eyes of Experts.* Sebastopol: O'Reilly Media, pp.1–13.

Iversen, Margaret (1986) 'Saussure v. Pierce: Models for a Semiotics of Visual Art', in A.L. Rees and F. Borzello (eds), *The New Art History.* London: Camden Press, pp.82–94.

Jay, Martin (1988) 'Scopic Regimes of Modernity' in Hal Foster (ed.) (1988) *Vision and Visuality.* Seattle: Bay Press, pp.3–23.

Jay, Martin (1994) *Downcast Eyes: The Denigration of Vision in Twentieth-Century French Thought.* Berkeley: University of California Press.

Jay, Martin (2002) 'Cultural Relativism and the Visual Turn'. *Journal of Visual Culture,* **Vol. 1, No.3, pp.267–278**. [Extract available: Manghani *et al.* (eds) *Images: A Reader* (Sage, 2006), pp.284–287.]

Kemp, Martin (2006) *Seen/Unseen: Art, Science, and Intuition from Leonardo to the Hubble Telescope.* Oxford: Oxford University Press.

Klee, Paul (1953 [1925]) *Pedagogical Sketchbook,* **trans. by Sibyl Moholy-Nagy. London: Faber and Faber**. [Extract available: Manghani *et al.* (eds) *Images: A Reader* (Sage, 2006), pp.221–223.]

Knight, Carolyn and Glaser, Jessica (2009) *Diagrams: Innovative Solutions for Graphic Designers*. Mies: RotorVision.

Knight, Diana (1997) 'Roland Barthes, or The Woman Without a Shadow' in Jean-Michel Rabaté (ed.) (1997) *Writing the Image After Roland Barthes*. Philadelphia: University of Pennsylvania Press, pp.132–143.

Knowles, Caroline and Sweetman, Paul (eds) (2004) *Picturing the Social Landscape: Visual Methods and the Sociological Imagination*. London: Routledge.

Krauss, Rosalind (1994) 'Cy's Up'. *Artforum*, September, Vol. XXXIII, No.1, pp.70–75, 118.

Kress, Gunther (2010) *Multimodality: A Social Semiotic Approach to Contemporary Communication*. London: Routledge.

Kress, Gunther and van Leeuwen, Theo (2006a) 'The Semiotic Landscape' in Sunil Manghani, Arthur Piper and Jon Simons (eds) *Images: A Reader*. London: Sage, pp.119–123.

Kress, Gunther and van Leeuwen, Theo (2006b) ***Reading Images: The Grammar of Visual Design***. **Second Edition. London: Routledge**. [Extract available: Manghani *et al*. (eds) *Images: A Reader* (Sage, 2006), pp.119–123.]

Lacan, Jacques (1977) *Écrits: A Selection*, trans. by Alan Sheridan. New York: W.W.Norton.

Lanham, Richard (1993) *The Electronic Word: Democracy, Technology, and the Arts*. Chicago: University of Chicago Press.

Latham, Alan (2004) 'Researching and Writing Everyday Accounts of the City: An Introduction to the Diary-Photo Diary-Interview Method' in Caroline Knowles and Paul Sweetman (eds) *Picturing the Social Landscape: Visual Methods and the Sociological Imagination*. London: Routledge, pp.117–131.

Latour, Bruno and Woolgar, Steve (1986) *Laboratory Life: The Construction of Scientific Facts*. Princeton: Princeton University Press.

Latour, Bruno and Weibel, Peter (eds) (2002) *Iconoclash: Beyond the Image Wars in Science, Religion, and Art*. Cambridge, Mass.: MIT Press.

Lemke, Jay (1998) 'Multiplying Meaning: Visual and Verbal Semiotics in Scientific Text' in J.R. Martin and Robert Veel (eds) *Reading Science: Critical and Functional Perspectives on Discourses of Science*. London: Routledge, pp.87–113.

Loran, Erle (1947) *Cézanne's Composition: Analysis of His Form with Diagrams and Photographs of His Motifs*. Second Edition. Berkeley: University of California Press.

Lowy, A. and Hood, P. (2004) *The Power of the 2 x 2 Matrix: Using 2 x 2 Thinking to Solve Business Problems and Make Better Decisions*. San Francisco, CA: Jossey-Bass.

Lury, Celia (2000) 'The United Colors of Diversity: Essential and Inessential Culture' in Sarah Franklin, Celia Lury and Jackie Stacey (eds) ***Global Nature, Global Culture***. **London: Sage, pp.146–287**. [Extract available: Manghani *et al*. (eds) *Images: A Reader* (Sage, 2006), pp.261–265.]

Lynch, Kevin (1960) ***The Image of the City***. **Cambridge, Mass.: MIT Press**. [Extract available: Manghani *et al*. (eds) *Images: A Reader* (Sage, 2006), pp.247–249.]

Lynch, Michael (1985) *Art and Artifact in Laboratory Science*. London: Routledge.

Lynch, Michael (2006) 'The Production of Scientific Images: Vision and Re-Vision in the History, Philosophy, and Sociology of Science', in Luc Pauwels (ed.) *Visual Cultures of Science: Rethinking Representational Practices in Knowledge Building and Science Communication*. Hanover, NH: Dartmouth College Press, pp.26–40.

McCandless, David (2009) *Information is Beautiful*. London: Collins.

McCloud, Scott (1994) *Understanding Comics: The Invisible Art*. New York: HarperPerennial.

McLuhan, Marshall (1997) *Understanding Media: the Extensions of Man.* London: Routledge. [Extract available: Manghani *et al.* (eds) *Images: A Reader* (Sage, 2006), pp.246–247.]

Maderspacher, Florian (2006) 'The Captivating Coral – the Origins of Early Evolutionary Imagery'. *Current Biology*, Vol.16, Issue 13, pp.R476–R478.

Maharaj, Sarat (1992) '"A Liquid, Elemental Scattering": Marcel Duchamp and Richard Hamilton' in *Richard Hamilton*. London: Tate Gallery, pp.40–48.

Manghani, Sunil (2003) 'Adventures in Subsemiotics: Towards a New "Object" and Writing of Visual Culture'. *Culture, Theory and Critique*, Vol.44, No.1, pp.23–36.

Manghani, Sunil (2008) *Image Critique and the Fall of the Berlin Wall.* Bristol: Intellect Books.

Manghani, Sunil (2011) 'Images: An Imaginary Problem?' in James Elkins and Maja Naef (eds) *What is an Image?* University Park, Pa.: Pennsylvania State University Press, pp.226–228.

Manghani, Sunil, Piper, Arthur and Simons, Jon (eds) (2006) *Images: A Reader*. London: Sage.

Marien, Mary Warner (2006) 'The Family of Man' in *Photography: A Cultural History*. London: Laurence King, pp.308–310.

Mauad, A.M. and Rouverol, A.J. (2004) 'Telling the Story of Linda Lord Through Photographs' in Caroline Knowles and Paul Sweetman (eds) *Picturing the Social Landscape: Visual Methods and the Sociological Imagination*. London: Routledge, pp.178–192.

Millar, Bruce (2004) 'The Eyes Have It'. *FT Magazine*, No. 57, 29 May 2004, pp.16–21.

Mirzoeff, Nicholas (ed.) (1998) *Visual Culture Reader*. London: Routledge.

Mirzoeff, Nicholas (1999) *An Introduction to Visual Culture*. First Edition. London: Routledge.

Mirzoeff, Nicholas (2009) *An Introduction to Visual Culture*. Second Edition. London: Routledge.

Mirzoeff, Nicholas (ed.) (2002) *The Visual Culture Reader*. Second Edition. London: Routledge.

Mirzoeff, Nicholas (2005) *Watching Babylon: The War in Iraq and Global Visual Culture*. New York: Routledge.

Mitchell, W.J.T. (1987) *Iconology: Image, Text, Ideology.* Chicago: University of Chicago Press. [Extract available: Manghani *et al.* (eds) *Images: A Reader* (Sage, 2006), pp.296–299.]

Mitchell, W.J.T. (1994) *Picture Theory: Essays on Verbal and Visual Representation*. Chicago: University of Chicago Press.

Mitchell, W.J.T. (1995) 'Interdisciplinarity and Visual Culture'. *Art Bulletin*, LXXVII (4), pp.540–543.

Mitchell, W.J.T. (2005) *What Do Pictures Want? The Lives and Loves of Images*. Chicago: University of Chicago Press.

Mitchell, W.J.T. (2011) *Cloning Terror: The War Of Images, 9/11 To The Present*. Chicago: University of Chicago Press.

Mitchell, William J. (1994b) *The Reconfigured Eye: Visual Truth in the Post-Photographic Era.* Cambridge, Mass.: MIT Press. [Extract available: Manghani *et al.* (eds) *Images: A Reader* (Sage, 2006), pp.227–232.]

Molyneux, John (1998) 'State of the Art: A Review of the "Sensation" Exhibition at the Royal Academy of Arts, September–December 1997'. *International Socialism*, Issue 79 (Summer): http://pubs.socialistreviewindex.org.uk/isj79/molyneux.htm (accessed 11 October 2011).

Morphet, Richard (1992) 'Richard Hamilton: The Longer View' in *Richard Hamilton*. London: Tate Gallery, pp.11–26.

Morrison, Phylis (2002) 'Images in Science: A Gallery of the Past' in Felice Frankel, *Envisioning Science: The Design and Craft of the Science Image*. Cambridge, Mass.: MIT Press, p.12–23.

Mulvey, Laura (1989) 'Visual Pleasure and Narrative Cinema' in *Visual and Other Pleasures*. London: Macmillan, pp.14–26. [Extract available: Manghani *et al.* (eds) *Images: A Reader* (Sage, 2006), pp.156–159.]

Murray, Susan (2008) 'Digital Images, Photo-sharing, and Our Shifting Notions of Everyday Aesthetics'. *Journal of Visual Culture*, Vol.7, No.2, pp.147–163.

Pamuk, Orhan (2001) *My Name is Red*, trans. by Erda M. Göknar. London: Faber and Faber.

Parr, Martin and Badger, Gerry (2004) *The Photobook: A History (Volume 1)*. London: Phaidon Press.

Pasveer, Bernike (2006) 'Representing or Mediating: A History and Philosophy of X-ray Images in Medicine' in Pauwels, Luc (ed.) *Visual Cultures of Science: Rethinking Representational Practices in Knowledge Building and Science Communication*. Hanover, NH: Dartmouth College Press, pp.41–62.

Pater, Walter (1986) *The Renaissance: Studies in Art and Poetry*, ed. by Adam Phillips. Oxford: Oxford University.

Pauwels, Luc (ed.) (2006) *Visual Cultures of Science: Rethinking Representational Practices in Knowledge Building and Science Communication*. Hanover, NH: Dartmouth College Press.

Peirce, Charles Sanders (1932) *The Collected Papers of Charles Sanders Peirce: Vol. II: Elements of Logic*, ed. by Charles Hartshorne and Paul Weiss. Cambridge, Mass.: Harvard University Press. [Extract available: Manghani *et al.* (eds) *Images: A Reader* (Sage, 2006), pp.107–109.]

Pink, Daniel (2006) *A Whole New Mind: Why Right-Brainers Will Rule the Future*. New York: Riverhead Books.

Plato (1955) *The Republic*, trans. by H.D.P. Lee. London: Penguin Classics. [Extracts available: Manghani *et al.* (eds) *Images: A Reader* (Sage, 2006), pp.26–29, 29–31.]

Porter, M.E. (1979) 'How Competitive Forces Shape Strategy'. *Harvard Business Review*, 1979 (March–April), pp.137–145.

Porter, M.E. (1980) *Competitive Strategy: Techniques for Analyzing Industries and Competitors*. New York: The Free Press.

Priest, S.H. (1998) 'Public Opinion, Expert Opinion, and the Illusion of Consensus: Gleaning Points of View Electronically', in D.L. Borden and K. Harvey (eds) *The Electronic Grapevine: Rumor, Reputation, and Reporting in the New On-line Environment*. Mahwah: Lawrence Erlbaum Associates.

Prosser, Jon (ed.) (1998) *Image-Based Research: A Sourcebook for Qualitative Researchers*. Philadelphia: Falmer Press.

Proust, Marcel (2002) *In Search of Lost Time: Volume I: The Way By Swann's*, trans. by Lydia Davis. London: Allen Lane, Penguin. [Extract available: Manghani *et al.* (eds) *Images: A Reader* (Sage, 2006), pp.202–204.]

Putman, R.J. and Wratten, S.D. (1984) *Principles of Ecology*. London: Croom Helm.

Rancière, Jacques (2004) *The Politics of Aesthetics: The Distribution of the Sensible*, trans. by Gabriel Rockhill. London: Continuum.

Rasmussen, Nicolas (1997) *Picture Control: The Electron Microscope and the Transformation of Biology in America, 1940–1960*. Stanford: Stanford University Press.

Reynolds, G. (2008) *Presentation Zen: Simple Ideas on Presentation Design and Delivery*. Berkeley, CA: New Riders.

Riis, Jacob (1998) *How the Other Half Lives: Studies Among the Tenements of New York*. London: Penguin.

Roberts, John (1998) *The Art of Interruption: Realism, Photography and the Everyday*. Manchester: Manchester University Press.

Rogers, Simon (2011) 'Data journalism at the Guardian: what is it and how do we do it?', *Guardian Datablog*, 28 July 2011: www.guardian.co.uk/news/datablog/2011/jul/28/data-journalism (accessed 19 November 2011).

Rogoff, Irit (2002), 'Studying Visual Culture' in Nicholas Mirzoeff (ed.) *The Visual Culture Reader*. Second Edition. London: Routledge, pp.24–36.

Rorty, Richard (1979) *Philosophy and the Mirror of Nature*. Princeton: Princeton University Press.

Rosand, David (2002) *Drawing Acts: Studies in Graphic Expression*. Cambridge: Cambridge University Press.

Rose, Gillian (2012) *Visual Methodologies: An Introduction to the Interpretation of Visual Materials*. Third Edition. London: Sage.

Roth, Wolff-Michael, Bowen, G. Michael, and Masciotra, Domenico (2002) 'From Thing to Sign and "Natural Object": Toward a Genetic Phenomenology of Graph Interpretation'. *Science Technology and Human Values*, Vol.27, No.3, pp.327–356.

Samuels, J. (2007) 'When Words Are Not Enough: Eliciting Children's Experiences of Buddhist Monastic Life' in G.C. Stanczak (ed.) *Visual Research Methods: Image, Society, and Representation*. Los Angeles: Sage, pp.167–196.

Saussure, Ferdinand de (1983 [1966]) *Course in General Linguistics*, trans. by Roy Harris. New York: McGraw Hill. [Extract available: Manghani *et al.* (eds) *Images: A Reader* (Sage, 2006), pp.105–107.]

Schefer, Jean Louis (1995) *The Enigmatic Body: Essays on the Arts*, trans. by Paul Smith. Cambridge: Cambridge University Press.

Scott, Clive (1999) *The Spoken Image: Photography and Language*. London: Reaktion Books.

Scott, Clive (2007) *Street Photography: From Atget to Cartier-Bresson*. London: I. B. Tauris.

Segaran, Toby and Hammerbacher, Jeff (eds) (2009) *Beautiful Data: The Stories Behind Elegant Data Solutions*. Sebastopol: O'Reilly.

Seuss, Dr (1955) *On Beyond Zebra*. New York: Random House.

Shapiro, Matthias (2010) 'Once Upon a Stacked Time Series: The Importance of Storytelling in Informational Visualization' in Julie Steele and Noah Iliinsky (eds) *Beautiful Visualization: Looking at Data Through the Eyes of Experts*. Sebastopol: O'Reilly Media, pp.15–36.

Sherwin, Richard K. (2008) 'Visual Literacy in Action: "Law in the Age of Images"' in James Elkins (ed.) *Visual Literacy*. New York: Routledge, pp.179–194.

Simons, Jon (2008) 'From Visual Literacy to Image Competence' in James Elkins (ed.) *Visual Literacy*. New York: Routledge, pp.77–90.

Snow, C.P. (1998) *The Two Cultures*. Cambridge: Cambridge University Press.

Sontag, Susan (1979) *On Photography*. London: Penguin Books. [Extract available: Manghani *et al.* (eds) *Images: A Reader* (Sage, 2006), pp.249–253.]

Sontag, Susan (2003) *Regarding the Pain of Others*. New York: Farrar, Straus and Giroux.

Stafford, Andy (1998) *Roland Barthes, Phenomenon and Myth: An Intellectual Biography*. Edinburgh: Edinburgh University Press.

Stafford, Barbara Maria (2008) 'The Remaining 10 Percent: The Role of Sensory Knowledge in the Age of the Self-Organizing Brain' in James Elkins (ed.) *Visual Literacy*. New York: Routledge, pp.31–57.

Stafford, Barbara Maria (2009) 'Thoughts Not Our Own: Whatever Happened to Selective Attention'. *Theory, Culture and Society*, Vol.26, No.2–3, pp.275–293.

Stanczak, G.C. (ed.) (2007) *Visual Research Methods: Image, Society, and Representation*. Los Angeles: Sage.

Steichen, Edward (1955) *The Family of Man: Photographic Exhibition*. New York: Museum of Modern Art.

Sturken, Marita and Cartwright, Lisa (2009) *Practices of Looking: An Introduction to Visual Culture*. Second Edition. Oxford: Oxford University Press.

Sundt, Christine, L. (2002) 'The Image User and the Search for Images' in Murtha Baca (ed.) *Introduction to Art Image Access: Issues, Tools, Standards, Strategies*. Los Angeles: Getty Research Institute.

Thrift, N. (2005) *Knowing Capitalism*. London: Sage Publications.

Trumbo, Jean (2006) 'Making Science Visible: Visual Literacy in Science Communication' in Luc Pauwels (ed.) *Visual Cultures of Science: Rethinking Representational Practices in Knowledge Building and Science Communication*. Hanover, NH: Dartmouth College Press, pp.266–283.

Tufte, Edward R. (1990) *Envisioning Information*. Connecticut: Graphics Press.

Tufte, Edward R. (2004) *The Visual Display of Quantitative Information*. Second Edition. Connecticut: Graphics Press.

Wilde, Judith and Wilde, Richard (1991) *Visual Literacy: A Conceptual Approach to Graphic Problem Solving*. New York: Watson-Guptill Publications.

Wittgenstein, Ludwig (1958) *The Blue and Brown Books*. New York: Harper.

Wong, Mou-Lan (2009) 'Generations of Re-generation: Re-creating Wonderland though Text, Illustrations, and the Reader's Hands' in Cristopher Hollingsworth (ed.) *Alice Beyond Wonderland: Essays for the Twenty-first Century*. Iowa City: University of Iowa Press, pp.135–151.

Zeki, Semir (1999) *Inner Vision.* **Oxford: Oxford University Press**. [Extract available: Manghani *et al.* (eds) *Images: A Reader* (Sage, 2006), pp.287–291.]

Index